PENGUIN  CLASSICS

THE PENGUIN BOOK OF CULTS

JOSEPH P. LAYCOCK is an associate professor of religious studies at Texas State University; coeditor of *Nova Religio*, the premier journal for the study of new religious movements; the author of several books about new religious movements, possession and exorcism, and moral panic; and the editor of *The Penguin Book of Exorcisms*.

The Penguin Book
of Cults

Edited by
JOSEPH P. LAYCOCK

PENGUIN BOOKS

PENGUIN BOOKS

An imprint of Penguin Random House LLC
1745 Broadway, New York, NY 10019
penguinrandomhouse.com

Set in Sabon LT Pro

LIBRARY OF CONGRESS CONTROL NUMBER: 2025005096
ISBN 9780143138693 (paperback)
ISBN 9780593512821 (ebook)

Printed in the United States of America
1st Printing

The authorized representative in the EU for product safety and compliance is Penguin Random House Ireland, Morrison Chambers, 32 Nassau Street, Dublin D02 YH68, Ireland, https://eu-contact.penguin.ie.

Contents

THE TWENTIETH CENTURY

Introduction

Ritualistic frenzy. Insane leaders wielding godlike authority over their flocks. Minds enslaved by isolation and relentless propaganda. Absurd doctrines and doomsday prophecies. Sexual perversion. Mass suicide.

These are some of the ideas conjured by the word "cult." It is a powerful word. Probably for as long as human beings have had religion, they have had a potent fear of the wrong kind of religion. This book explores both the history of religious experimentation and our ancient fear of the religious other.

Humans are constantly developing new forms of religion, some of which have been strange and fantastic. As historian of religion Robert Orsi observes, "There is no end to human religious creativity (a comment that has nothing to do with whether this is a positive thing or not). One would have to look to the staggering varieties and complexities of what humans have made of sexuality to find another site of such explosive and inventive activity."[1] Examples in this book alone include accounts of drinking the blood of sacrificed cats, theories that we are living inside a hollow Earth, and reports that space brothers from Venus are coming to redeem us from the threat of nuclear war. At their best, new and alternative religious movements can function like laboratories that explore new solutions to human problems. At their worst, they can foster patterns of abuse that last for generations or end in violence. Humans have adapted to keep a lookout for potential threats, and when viewing other people's religion, we have a tendency to focus on the bad and the bizarre while filtering out that which is harmless or even praiseworthy. There have been many cases in which fear of some newly discovered religious group creates far more danger than the group itself ever could.

Socially, religion functions to provide a sense of communal identity along with beliefs and rituals that orient people toward the world. To the degree that people value their religion and their community, it is understandable that they might fear the idea of a community that is bound together even more closely than their own but that fosters the wrong beliefs and rituals. In some cases, the world of the cultists is imagined as a nightmarish mirror of society where normal values are inverted: Demons are worshipped instead of exorcized, incest is encouraged rather than banned, and babies are sacrificed instead of protected. This is disturbing enough if the cult is believed to exist in some far-off or barbaric land. But cults are often said to live among us, hiding in plain sight. Worst of all, they are imagined as spreading parasitically, using all manner of nefarious practices to corrupt otherwise good citizens into becoming agents of the cult. Women and adolescents are often thought to be the most vulnerable to cult indoctrination. When fears like this are stoked high enough, the results have included moral panic, the passage of draconian laws, mob violence, and the burning of heretics.

In many countries, cults are regarded as a symptom of modernity. In the United States, cults are often described as a social problem that began in the 1960s. According to this story, Americans lost faith in their religious, political, and economic institutions, and this made them vulnerable to self-proclaimed gurus and prophets who exploited their anxieties and sold them false hope. By the 1970s, the fear of cults had become so great that parents whose adult offspring had joined alternative religions could hire "deprogrammers" who would abduct the wayward son or daughter and sequester them—often in basements or cheap hotel rooms—until they renounced their new religion. According to the deprogrammers, the abductees had never truly converted to a new faith but were "brainwashed" by deceptive cult-recruitment tactics. The deprogrammers were simply using "good" brainwashing to reverse the programming of the cult. Some of these deprogrammers were found guilty of kidnapping and false imprisonment but were usually given token sentences. In the field of new religions studies, this period is sometimes referred to as "the cult wars."

But there were "cults" long before the 1960s. Sociologists have noted that certain conditions—such as rapid social change—tend to correlate with the emergence of new religions. But even in relatively stable times, religious innovation has been a constant throughout human history. As the selections in this book show, people were both frightened and fascinated by the idea of weird or coercive religions long before the 1970s. In fact, Western civilization was preoccupied with the idea of "evil" religions even before the advent of Christianity.

WHAT IS A CULT?

The word "cult" comes from the Latin *cultus*, meaning "worship," with the verb form meaning to cultivate, attend to, or respect. Cicero used the expression "*cultus deorum*," meaning "the honoring of the gods." In this original sense, "cult" referred to any form of organized worship. But in modern times, "cult" has come to mean something very different. As a label, it is pejorative and stigmatizing. But aside from this, it is not clear what exactly constitutes a cult. The definition shifts from person to person and from case to case. When asked to name the characteristics of a cult, people might list an infallible leader who can never be questioned, social isolation in a compound, or deceptive recruitment tactics. But groups can still be branded as cults without possessing any of these features.

When I examine this problem with my students, we watch a news clip from the 2012 US election cycle in which Mitt Romney, a member of the Church of Jesus Christ of Latter-day Saints (also known as the LDS Church or the Mormon Church), sought the Republican nomination for president. At the conservative Value Voters Summit, Pastor Robert Jeffress, a Southern Baptist, urged Republicans to nominate someone else, stating, "Mitt Romney's a good, moral person. But he's not a Christian. Mormonism is not Christianity. It has always been considered a cult by the mainstream of Christianity." On the cable news show *Hardball*, host Chris Matthews asked Jeffress what he meant when he stated that Mormonism is a cult. Jeffress answered: "I wasn't talking about a sociological cult like David Koresh or Jim Jones. I'm talking about a theological cult. I mean it's a fact: Mormonism came 1,800 years after Jesus Christ and the founding of the Church." But Matthews continued to press: "People hear the word cult, they hear Charles Manson, they hear Jonestown." Jeffress clarified that he did not mean "that kind of cult" but that he preferred a president who is a Christian. (Followers of the LDS Church would argue that they are Christians, just as much as Jeffress is.) Matthews answered that in this case, Jeffress's use of the label was actually just "a prejudice" and that his position was "no different than some Rastafarian saying I'm only going to vote for Rastafarians for president."[2]

Michael Barkun is a political scientist who has consulted with federal agencies following the FBI's disastrous standoff with the Branch Davidian group in 1993. He writes that "the term 'cult' is virtually meaningless. It tells us far more about those who use it than about those to whom it is applied. It has become little more than a label slapped on religious groups regarded as too exotic, marginal or dangerous. As soon as a group achieves respectability by numbers or longevity, the label drops away."[3] In other words, the label often has less to do with the group itself and more with how the majority regards it. Christianity was itself once seen as a dangerous cult. The LDS Church experienced extreme persecution during the so-called Mormon Wars of the nineteenth century but has far more acceptance today. In the future, the cult label will likely drop away from this group entirely.

But when Jeffress deployed the cult label to attack Romney's political aspirations, he was not just being imprecise. As Matthews pointed out, this label calls to mind dangerous figures like Charles Manson, Jim Jones, and David Koresh. The word "cult" connotes all manner of negative claims and associations without ever saying them out loud. This makes it an extremely effective political tool. As sociologist James T. Richardson notes, "If those opposing certain groups can successfully attach the label 'cult' to a group, then they virtually automatically get to heap the negative baggage of the popular definition on that group. In short, the term has become a 'social weapon' to use against groups which are not viewed with favor."[4]

The political usefulness of this term is probably why all manner of things—not just religious groups—are now described as cults. The cult label has been applied to political ideologies, exploitative multilevel marketing groups, unusually intense fitness programs, and fan communities surrounding pop stars like Taylor Swift. On the political left, Donald Trump's supporters have been identified as a cult. On the right, acceptance of transgenderism is framed as a cult. New religious movement scholar James R. Lewis wrote that "the labeling and persecution of minorities is really more of a response to doubts and anxieties about norms and values within the dominant culture than a response to tangible threats from minority groups."[5] In our current, politically divided landscape, everything is a cult and nothing is a cult, depending on whom you ask.

A CULT BY ANY OTHER NAME

In France and Belgium, the word "*secte*" serves the same function that "cult" does in English. Several European countries maintain official lists of religions that are deemed *sectes*. In Belgium the Quakers and the YWCA are listed as *sectes*, and the Methodist Church appears on a similar list in Greece. In France and Belgium, religions that are declared *sectes* have been subjected to government restrictions and surveillance. In May 2001 France passed a law that prohibited *sectes* from operating near "sensitive places" such as schools and hospitals, and had provisions for disbanding groups whose leaders had been convicted of a crime.[6]

In Japan cults are called *karuto*. In 1995 a religious group called Aum Shinrikyo released sarin nerve gas on the Tokyo subway, killing twelve people and injuring thousands. Much as the massacre at Jonestown shaped US stereotypes about cults, after 1995 many alternative religions in Japan fell under suspicion as potentially being "the next Aum."[7]

In China only five religions are legally recognized: Buddhism, Daoism, Catholicism, Protestantism, and Islam. Some religions are not only unrecognized but are also declared *xie jiao*: Even participating in them is a criminal offense punishable by three to seven years of imprisonment. Government documents translate *xie jiao* into English as "evil cults," but a more direct translation might be "heterodox teachings." Lists of known *xie jiao* have been kept since the Ming Dynasty.[8]

One of the most notorious examples of a *xie jiao* is Falun Gong. This group, founded in 1992, practices a form of *qigong*, exercises meant to cultivate one's *qi* (life force). In 1999 thousands of Falun Gong practitioners assembled near the residences of top party leaders in Beijing to demand recognition from the government. This backfired horribly. The government outlawed Falun Gong, arrested practitioners, and began an extensive propaganda campaign to vilify the movement. Falun Gong now operates in many countries and has launched its own propaganda campaign against the Chinese government. Falun Gong's Shen Yun performing-arts company is one part of the group's campaign and stages spectacular dance performances in cities around the world.

Anticult activists sometimes refer to "high-demand groups" or "high-control groups." These terms are meant to signal that their quarrel is not with the group's theology but with the way it is structured. In practice, though, "high-demand group" is just a synonym for "cult." How much demand constitutes "high demand" is subjective. At worst, these terms are used to conceal prejudice and imply a degree of sociological training and expertise that the person using them does not actually possess.[9]

New religions scholar Massimo Introvigne has proposed the category of "criminal religious movements" to describe groups like Al Qaeda and Aum Shinrikyo that use their religious beliefs to justify terrorism or other crimes.[10] One advantage of this approach is that the criteria are objective: A religious group has either been found guilty of criminal activity or it has not. This approach also acknowledges that religions are not always nice and that when groups do evil things, they do not cease to be religions. However, this term has not caught on, partly because it is not as politically useful as the word "cult."

CULTS AND MIND CONTROL

One of the most common claims about cults is that the people who participate in them are not being their authentic selves but are unknowingly victims of some form of mind control. In the Middle Ages, heresy was sometimes explained as a result of black magic that enchants people so that they can no longer see the truth of Christianity. Explanations like this gave way to pseudoscientific theories that framed religious difference in medicalized terms. In the nineteenth century, women who became interested in alternative religions might be diagnosed as "hysterical." During the Cold War the CIA introduced the term "brainwashing" to the US public, making it possible to interpret any idea or opinion in medicalized terms as the product of a corrupted mind.

During the cult wars of the 1970s, brainwashing provided a counterargument to claims that alternative religions have a right to religious freedom. Anticult activists argued that although religion is protected by the Constitution, a disease is not. For example, anticult journalists Flo Conway and Jim Siegelman claimed that cults were actually an "information disease" or a "disorder of awareness caused not by germs, drugs, or physical abuse but by the manipulation of information feeding every sensory channel of the nervous system."[11]

"Brainwashing" has been dismissed by the American Psychological Association as an unscientific concept. But it remains incredibly popular because it allows us to explain away other people's choices. If your child goes to college and adopts a lifestyle you find bizarre, or your uncle ruins Thanksgiving by spouting racist political talking points, it is tempting to believe that this behavior does not reflect who your family member really is and instead indicates that someone else is *making* them act like this. Brainwashing is also a useful narrative for those who have left controversial groups and may have done embarrassing or even illegal things: If they were brainwashed, then they cannot be held responsible for anything they said or did; in fact, they are victims.

This is not to say that so-called cult groups do not have sophisticated methods of controlling their members' behavior. Many of them do, as do mainstream religions, governments, and corporate marketing campaigns. But claims of brainwashing only distract from the actual methods of control being used, which are usually not very mysterious. New religions scholar Rebecca Moore had two sisters who helped plan the mass deaths that occurred in Jonestown, Guyana, on November 18, 1978. She has argued that her sisters were not brainwashed and that to claim so denies their agency. Instead, she suggests that the concept of brainwashing be replaced with the concepts of conversion, conditioning, and coercion.[12]

Conversion is common: People do genuinely convert to new religions and worldviews, and we cannot claim that their conversion does not reflect their true self simply because we believe they have made bad choices. Conditioning refers to the psychological process of learning to respond to new stimuli. If someone has learned that they will be rewarded or punished—and even disappointing someone can be a form of punishment—this may affect their behavior, especially within a group situation where they are being observed by their peers. Finally, much of what is attributed to "brainwashing" is simply coercion. During the poisoning in Guyana, Jim Jones told his followers that government forces were about to kill them and torture their children. He also posted armed guards to prevent people from leaving. Keith Raniere's group NXIVM, which was nominally a self-improvement course but engaged in human trafficking and sexual slavery, collected blackmail material on members to ensure that they obeyed orders. Tactics like these do not constitute mind control but are simple lies and threats.

It should also be noted that people who have become disillusioned with a stigmatized group may not have many good options if they leave: The group may have a policy of shunning or "disfellowshipping" ex-members, the member may have disassociated from their family or never cultivated friends outside the group, or they may have no savings and no work experience. People in this situation may reluctantly decide to stay. This is not brainwashing; it is actually exerting one's free will to choose within a range of bad options.

THE BIG SIX (SEVEN)

Of course, dangerous religious groups really do exist. But it is important to have a balanced perspective about the threat attributed to "cults." The overwhelming majority of new religious movements are basically harmless, and they form and die out in obscurity. It is only when groups engage in shocking or violent behavior that they gain serious attention from the media. This can lead to a fallacy called the availability heuristic, in which we misjudge a situation based on the information that comes readily to mind. If asked to name a cult, people often think of the Peoples Temple, the Branch Davidians, or other groups that ended with spectacular mass-casualty events because these are the ones most discussed in the media. This can create the impression that *most* new or alternative religions are prone to extreme violence. In reality, these episodes are extraordinarily rare.

James R. Lewis listed what he called "the big six."[13] The first of these is the Peoples Temple. In 1978 more than 900 people died drinking Flavor Aid (it was not Kool-Aid) laced with cyanide in what was essentially a massive murder-suicide. The second is the Branch Davidians. After a botched raid on their home by the Bureau of Alcohol, Tobacco, and Firearms, the Davidians engaged in a 51-day siege with the FBI, culminating in a catastrophic fire in which 76 people died, including many children. The third is an esoteric group called the Order of the Solar Temple. In 1994, 5 members died by suicide in Quebec and 48 more in Switzerland, with additional suicides in 1995 and 1997. The fourth is Aum Shinrikyo, which attacked the Tokyo subway in 1995. The fifth is the Heaven's Gate group. In 1997, 39 members of this group died by suicide in an event that was timed to coincide with the passing of the Hale-Bopp comet. The sixth is an apocalyptic group in Uganda called the Movement for the Restoration of Ten Commandments of God. On March 17, 2000, an estimated 338 people were found dead in a burned church near the town of Kanungu. Days later, an additional 153 were discovered in mass graves near the town. Yet more bodies were found buried in the yard of one of the leaders and beneath a concrete floor in his home. Demonstrating the problem of the availability heuristic, with the exception of the Peoples Temple none of the big six were ever mentioned in *The New York Times* or *The Washington Post* prior to the violence.

In 2023 the big six became the big seven. Police in Kenya investigated a farm used by Good News International Ministries. They discovered emaciated people and shallow graves containing more than 100 bodies. The group's leader, Paul Nthenge Mackenzie, had told his followers that they could meet Jesus by cutting off contact with the outside world and starving themselves to death. The total body count from what is being called the "Shakahola Forest Incident" is currently at more than 400 people, with another 600 missing. The total number of deaths may never be known. Mackenzie based his prophecy on the teaching of American Pentecostal missionary William M. Branham and is on trial for manslaughter at the time of this writing.

Some may be surprised that the Manson family is not counted among the big seven. Career criminal Charles Manson gathered a group of young people who had become caught up in the hippie movement of the 1960s. This group was known as "the family." In 1969, at Manson's direction, the Manson family committed at least nine murders, including the gruesome stabbing of actress Sharon Tate, who was pregnant at the time. For many, the Manson murders marked the death of the progressive spirit of the 1960s. To conservative Americans, the Manson family seemed to prove their suspicion that the hippie counterculture was evil. But although Manson is commonly referred to as a "cult leader," most religion scholars do not regard the Manson family as a religious group, but rather a criminal gang of drug dealers and sex workers.

It is true that Manson used many forms of manipulation to maintain control over his followers, including grooming them sexually, giving them LSD, and playing on the fact that his long hair and beard made him resemble popular American images of Jesus. But the Manson family does not appear to have had a coherent belief system or ideology. It was prosecutor Vincent Bugliosi who claimed that the Manson murders were part of a plot called "Helter Skelter." This was also the title of Bugliosi's 1974 book, which became the bestselling true-crime book of all time. According to Bugliosi, the murders were intended to foment an apocalyptic race war that would destroy US civilization, allowing the Manson family to rule over the ashes.

But several members of the Manson family made confessions after their arrest and never mentioned "Helter Skelter." Skeptics have suggested that Bugliosi invented this theory because he was seeking the death penalty for all members of the Manson family. Because Charles Manson was not physically present at the murders, Bugliosi needed to show there was a special context and that Manson was directly responsible. An alternative theory is that the murders were simply an attempt to secure the loyalty of his followers: Manson had already killed several people in the course of selling drugs and other criminal endeavors, and any member of the family could have turned him in, but by making the family also commit murders, Manson made them complicit in his crimes. A third possibility is that there was no coherent motive: rather, a group of unstable criminals using large amounts of LSD and taking orders from a man who suffered from disordered thinking may have made a more or less spontaneous decision to murder a celebrity. It may feel more satisfying to assert that the Manson murders happened "because of a cult," but this claim is far from certain.

There are some common factors across the big seven: Most had (1) a leader whose authority came from their "charisma" as a prophet or enlightened figure rather than some position within a church organization, (2) a group of people closed off from society, (3) a tendency to see the world strictly in terms of good and evil, and (4) "millennialism," the belief in a coming collective salvation. But the circumstance that ultimately led to the tragedies associated with each of these groups is unique. No religious group forms with the intention of engaging in this sort of violence. This is why new religions scholars continue to examine documents from these cases to discover what went wrong. It is also both unhelpful and disrespectful to the victims to stereotype these groups with tasteless jokes about "drinking the Kool-Aid."

This book offers primary sources from four of the big seven cases: the Peoples Temple, the Branch Davidians, Aum Shinrikyo, and Heaven's Gate. The remaining three have not been included either because they are less well-known in the English-speaking world or because researchers are still trying to determine what exactly happened. My hope is that the reader will see both how different these four cases are and that a series of mistakes led up to each of them. This book also includes examples going back thousands of years in which new religious groups came into conflict with mainstream society and the result was not mass violence. (Spelling and punctuation have been altered for consistency across all selections.) In several cases, these groups went on to become mainstream themselves. Being thoughtful about these cases does not exonerate figures who chose violence, but it does respect the humanity of the victims, and—in a small way—it may help to prevent similar events in the future.

JOSEPH P. LAYCOCK

NOTES

1. Robert Orsi, *Between Heaven and Earth: The Religious Worlds People Make and the Scholars Who Study Them* (Princeton University Press, 2004), 191.
2. *Hardball,* aired October 10, 2011, on MSNBC.

3. Michael Barkun, "Reflections After Waco: Millennialists and the State," *Christian Century* 110 (June 2–9, 1993): 597.

4. James T. Richardson, "Definitions of Cult from Sociological-Technical to Popular-Negative," *Review of Religious Research* 34 (1993): 348–56, esp. 352.

5. James R. Lewis, *Legitimating New Religions* (Rutgers University Press, 2003), 168.

6. Daniéle Hervieu-Léger, "France's Obsession with the 'Sectarian Threat,'" in *New Religious Movements in the Twenty-First Century*, ed. Philip Charles Lucas and Thomas Robbins (Routledge, 2004), 57.

7. Ian Reader, "Consensus Shattered: Japanese Paradigm Shift and Moral Panic in the Post-Aum Era," in *New Religious Movements in the Twenty-First Century*, ed. Lucas and Robbins, 196–97.

8. Massimo Introvigne, "Xie Jiao as 'Criminal Religious Movements': A New Look at Cult Controversies in China and Around the World," *Journal of CESNUR* 2, no. 1 (2018): 13–32, esp. 13.

9. Joseph P. Laycock, "Perspective Essay: A Cult by Any Other Name: Is 'High Demand Group' a Useful Category?," *Nova Religio* 28, no. 1 (2024): 90–104.

10. Introvigne, "Xie Jiao as 'Criminal Religious Movements,'" 13.

11. Flo Conway and Jim Siegelman, "Information Disease: Have Cults Created a New Mental Illness?" *Science Digest*, January 1982, 86–92, esp. 88.

12. Rebecca Moore, "The Brainwashing Myth," *The Conversation*, July 18, 2018, https://theconversation.com/the-brainwashing-myth-99272.

13. James R. Lewis, "Violence," in *The Bloomsbury Companion to New Religious Movements*, ed. George D. Chryssides and Benjamin E. Zeller (Bloomsbury, 2014), 149–62.

Suggestions for Further Reading

Barker, Eileen. *The Making of a Moonie: Choice or Brainwashing?* Basil Blackwell, 1984.

Chryssides, George D., and Benjamin E. Zeller, eds. *The Bloomsbury Companion to New Religious Movements.* Bloomsbury Academic, 2014.

Festinger, Leon, Henry W. Riecken, and Stanley Schachter. *When Prophecy Fails: A Social and Psychological Study of a Modern Group That Predicted the Destruction of the World.* University of Minnesota Press, 1956.

Goodwin, Megan. *Abusing Religion: Literary Persecution, Sex Scandals, and American Minority Religions.* Rutgers University Press, 2020.

Laycock, Joseph P. *New Religious Movements: The Basics.* Routledge, 2022.

Lewis, James R., ed. *Violence and New Religious Movements.* Oxford University Press, 2011.

Lifton, Robert Jay. *Thought Reform and the Psychology of Totalism.* W. W. Norton, 1961.

Moore, Rebecca. *Beyond Brainwashing: Perspectives on Cult Violence.* Cambridge University Press, 2018.

Wessinger, Catherine. *How the Millennium Comes Violently: From Jonestown to Heaven's Gate.* Seven Bridges Press, 2000.

Zablocki, Benjamin, and Thomas Robbins, eds. *Misunderstanding Cults: Searching for Objectivity in a Controversial Field.* University of Toronto Press, 2001.

The Penguin Book
of Cults

THE
PREMODERN ERA

THE BACCHANALIAN AFFAIR

186 BCE

Titus Livius, known in English as Livy, was a Roman historian who lived from 59 BCE to 17 CE. His life's work was the History of Rome, *which details the nation's founding in 753 BCE through the death of military commander Drusus the Elder in 9 BCE. The work originally consisted of 142 books, of which 35 have survived. Livy was a patriotic Roman, and his accuracy as a historian was sometimes questionable.*

In Book 39 of his history, Livy describes an event that occurred in 186 BCE, in which the senate passed a decree that severely restricted—but did not ban outright—the Bacchanalia. This was a cult that revolved around Bacchus, the god of wine. Little is known about the beliefs or rituals of this cult, although they likely involved the use of dance, music, and intoxicants to achieve a state of religious ecstasy. The Bacchanalia was also privately organized and funded, which made it the object of suspicion in Rome, where religious rituals were closely linked to the authority of the state.

Livy describes the Bacchanalia in nightmarish terms. As he tells it, a patriotic young Roman named Publius Aebutius discovered the cult's true nature and reported it to the consul Postumius. (During the Roman Republic, consul was the highest political office to which one could be elected. Each year, two consuls were elected who shared power.) Publius's mother and stepfather had persuaded him to be initiated into the cult as part of a plot to steal his inheritance. But Publius's lover—a courtesan named Hispala Faecina—told him that the cult was evil. Hispala was a former slave to a Roman woman who had brought her to the Bacchanalia. She warned, "As each person was brought in, he was handed over to the priests like a victim and taken into a place which resounded with yells and songs, and the jangling of cymbals and drums, so that no cry from those who were suffering violation could be heard."[1] When Publius refused initiation, he was cast out of his home. He consulted his aunt, who urged him to inform the consul. The consuls began collecting testimony, first from Hispala and then from others. They were horrified by the size that the cult had reached in secret, its corrupting influence, and the many crimes it had committed. It was not just a cult but also a conspiracy that threatened to overthrow the Republic. With the senate's approval, up to seven thousand cult members from throughout Italy were arrested and interrogated, and many were publicly executed.

Most historians assume that the senate was already familiar with the Bacchanalia by 186 BCE and that it was not a hideous discovery as described by Livy. The cult was not really committing mass murder or otherwise threatening the Republic. Instead, the Bacchanalian Affair was political. The senate sought to establish itself as the arbiter over which of Rome's many cults were legitimate and which were not, and that its power to do so extended throughout all of Italy. Furthermore, as Rome became the dominant power in the Mediterranean, it had an interest in curbing the influence of "foreign" cults. As classics scholar Sarolta A. Takács concludes, "The high number of executions leaves me with the feeling, though, that in 186 B.C.E., as it happens too often in human history, religion served as a smokescreen. That those who were singled out for undermining the ruling authority, Rome, were executed not for their participation in a cult but so that a political order could prevail."[2]

A striking feature of Livy's account is how much it resembles contemporary conspiracy theories about cults engaged in evil rituals. Livy paints a picture of a conspiracy that acquires power by corrupting people with sensual *pleasures. It calls to mind scenes from Stanley Kubrick's movie* Eyes Wide Shut *(1999), which conspiracy theorists claim reveals actual Illuminati rites. Incredibly, Livy records that the cult had locked away in caves a population of prisoners that was almost equal to the population of Rome. This image of a secret population trapped underground resembles the wildest contemporary conspiracy theories about the government experimenting on people in secret underground bases.*

Another feature that Livy's account shares with contemporary fears about cults is that Livy seems preoccupied with the corruption of the youth, particularly young men. He writes that the Bacchanalia did not initiate anyone over the age of twenty and that men corrupted by its influence would be unfit for military service. Cults are still imagined today as essentially parasitical entities that spread by seducing the innocent. There is also more than a little misogyny in Livy's account. In Rome, boys became full citizens as teenagers and were given the toga virilis *("toga of manhood") in front of their oldest male relative. After this, they began military service. For young men to be initiated by women wielding foreign rites was an inversion of this tradition.*

Ultimately, the Bacchanalia in Livy's account is nothing less than an evil reflection of the Republic. The consul warns, "This Assembly legally convened by a consul in the daylight will be confronted by another assembly gathered together in the darkness of the night." In this, Livy gave Western civilization a prototype for a conspiracy of evil that would be replicated throughout the next two millennia. Much like the Bacchanalia, it was claimed that witches, Satanists, the Illuminati, and other subversives were all around us, hiding in plain sight and holding secret meetings where they engaged in orgies, human sacrifices, and the corruption of the innocent. As with the Bacchanalian Affair, the moral panics, arrests, and executions that resulted from these claims served a variety of political interests.

THE BACCHANALS IN ROME AND ITALY[3]

During the following year the consuls Sp. Postumius Albinus and Q. Marcius Philippus had their attention diverted from the army and the wars, and the administration of provinces, by the necessity of putting down a domestic conspiracy. The provinces were allotted to the praetors as follows: the civic jurisdiction to T. Maenius, the alien to M. Licinius Lucullus, Sardinia to C. Aurelius Scaurus, Sicily to P. Cornelius Sulla, Hither Spain to L. Q. Crispinus, and Further Spain to C. Calpurnius Piso. Both the consuls were charged with the investigation into the secret conspiracies.

A low-born Greek went into Etruria first of all, but did not bring with him any of the numerous arts which that most accomplished of all nations has introduced among us for the cultivation of mind and body. He was a hedge-priest and wizard, not one of those who imbue men's minds with error by professing to teach their superstitions openly for money, but a hierophant of secret nocturnal mysteries. At first these were divulged to only a few; then they began to spread among both men and women, and the attractions of wine and feasting increased the number of his followers. When they were heated with wine and the nightly commingling of men and women, those of tender age with their seniors, had extinguished all sense of modesty, debaucheries of every kind commenced; each had pleasures at hand to satisfy the lust he was most prone to. Nor was the mischief confined to the promiscuous intercourse of men and women; false witness, the forging of seals and testaments, and false informations, all proceeded from the same source, as also poisonings and murders of families where the bodies could not even be found for burial. Many crimes were committed by treachery; most by violence, which was kept secret, because the cries of those who were being violated or murdered could not be heard owing to the noise of drums and cymbals.

This pestilential evil penetrated from Etruria to Rome like a contagious disease. At first, the size and extent of the City allowing more scope and impunity for such mischiefs, served to conceal them, but information at length reached the consul, mainly through the following channel.

Then Hispala gave an account [to the consul] of the origin of these rites.

At first they were confined to women; no male was admitted, and they had three stated days in the year on which persons were initiated during the daytime, and matrons were chosen to act as priestesses. Paculla Annia, a Campanian, when she was priestess, made a complete change, as though by divine monition, for she was the first to admit men, and she initiated her own sons, Minius Cerinnius and Herennius Cerinnius. At the same time she made the rite a nocturnal one, and instead of three days in the year celebrated it five times a month. When once the mysteries had assumed this promiscuous character, and men were mingled with women with all the license of nocturnal orgies, there was no crime, no deed of shame, wanting. More uncleanness was wrought by men with men than with women. Whoever would not submit to defilement, or shrank from violating others, was sacrificed as a victim. To regard nothing as impious or criminal was the very sum of their religion. The men, as though seized with madness and with frenzied distortions of their bodies, shrieked out prophecies; the matrons, dressed as Bacchae, their hair disheveled, rushed down to the Tiber with burning torches, plunged them into the water, and drew them out again, the flame undiminished, as they were made of sulfur mixed with lime. Men were fastened to a machine and hurried off to hidden caves, and they were said to have been rapt away by the gods; these were the men who refused to join their conspiracy or take a part in their crimes or submit to pollution. They formed an immense multitude, almost equal to the population of Rome; among them were members of noble families, both men and women. It had been made a rule for the last two years that no one more than twenty years old should be initiated; they captured those to be deceived and polluted.

When she had finished giving her evidence, she fell on her

knees and again begged the consul to send her abroad. He
asked his mother-in-law to set apart some portion of her house
where she could take up her abode. An upper room was assigned to her which was approached by a flight of steps from
the street; these were blocked up and an entrance made from
inside the house. All [Hispala] Fecenia's effects were at once
transferred, and her household slaves brought in, and [Publius]
Aebutius was ordered to take up his quarters with a client of
the consul's. As both his informants were now in his hands,
Postumius reported the affair to the senate. Everything was
explained as it occurred, the information which he had first
received, and then that which he had obtained in answer to
his questions. The senate were greatly alarmed for the public
safety; these secret conspiracies and nocturnal gatherings were
a danger to the State; and they were alarmed for themselves,
lest their own relations and friends might be involved. They
passed a vote of thanks to the consul for having conducted his
investigations so carefully and without creating any public disturbance. Then, arming the consuls with extraordinary powers, they placed in their hands the inquiry into the proceedings
at the Bacchanalia and the nocturnal rites. They were to take
care that Aebutius and Fecenia suffered no injury for the information they had given, and they were to offer rewards to induce other informers to come forward. Those who presided
over these mysteries were to be sought out not only in Rome,
but everywhere where people were in the habit of assembling,
so that they might be delivered up to the consuls. Edicts were
published in Rome and throughout Italy forbidding any who
had been initiated from meeting together to celebrate their
mysteries or performing any rites of a similar character, and
above all, strict inquiry was to be made in the case of those
who attended gatherings in which crime and debauchery had
occurred.

These were the measures which the senate decreed. The consuls sent orders to the curule aediles[4] to search out all the
priests of those rites and, when they were arrested, to keep
them in such custody as they thought best until their trial. The
plebeian aediles were to see that no rites were performed in

open day; the police commissioners were instructed to post watches throughout the City and take care that no nocturnal gatherings took place; and as a precaution against fires, five men were appointed to assist the commissioners and take charge of the buildings assigned to them on this side [of] the Tiber.

When the various officials had been told off to their duties, the consuls convened the Assembly and mounted the Rostra. After the usual prayers with which proceedings are opened before the magistrates address the people, the consul began thus: "In no meeting of the Assembly has this solemn appeal to the gods been so appropriate and, I would add, so necessary. For it reminds you that it is these gods whom your ancestors ordained that we should worship, reverence, and pray to; not those who have driven the minds of people enslaved by foul and foreign superstitions, as though by goading furies, into every form of crime and every kind of lust. I am at a loss to know how far I ought to keep silence, and how far I ought to go, in what I have to say. I fear, if you remain in ignorance of anything, that I may leave an opening for neglect, while, if I disclose everything, I may create too much alarm. Whatever I say, you may be certain that it does not come up to the enormity and horror of the thing. We shall make it our business to say enough to put you on your guard.

"That the Bacchanalia have for some time been going on throughout Italy and are now practised in many parts of the City you have, I am sure, learned not only by report, but also by the nightly noises and yells which resound all over the City; but I do not think you know what it all means. Some of you fancy that it is a particular form of worship; others think that it is some permissible kind of sport and dalliance; its real nature is understood by few. As to their numbers, you would inevitably be very much alarmed if I were to say that there are many thousands of them, unless I went on to explain who and what sort of people they are.

"In the first place, then, women form the great majority, and this was the source of all the mischief. Then there are the males, the very counterparts of the women, committing and submitting to the foulest uncleanness, frantic and frenzied, driven out of their senses by sleepless nights, by wine, by nocturnal shouting and uproar. The conspiracy does not so far possess any strength, but its numbers are rapidly increasing day by day, and its strength is growing. Your ancestors would not have even your Assembly meet in an irregular and haphazard way, but only when the standard was hoisted on the citadel and the centuries in their array marched out, or when the tribunes had given notice of a meeting of the plebs, or the Assembly had been duly convened by one of the magistrates. Whenever the people met together there was bound to be a lawful authority to preside over it. Have you any idea what these nocturnal gatherings, these promiscuous associations of men and women are? If you knew at what age those of the male sex are initiated, you would feel not only compassion for them, but shame as well. Do you consider, Quirites,[5] that young men who have taken this un-hallowed oath are to be made into soldiers? That after the training they have received in that shrine of obscenity they are to be entrusted with arms? Shall these men, reeking with their impurity and that of those round them, wield their swords in defense of the chastity of your wives and children?

"The mischief would not be serious, if they had only lost their manhood through their debauchery—the disgrace would fall mainly upon themselves—and had kept from open outrage and secret treason. Never has there been such a gigantic evil in the commonwealth, or one which has affected greater numbers or caused more numerous crimes. Whatever instances of lust, treachery, or crime have occurred during these last years, have originated, you may be perfectly certain, in that shrine of un-hallowed rites. They have not yet disclosed all the criminal objects of their conspiracy. So far, their impious association confines itself to individual crimes; it has not yet strength enough to destroy the commonwealth. But the evil is creeping stealthily on, and growing day by day; it is already too great to limit its action to individual citizens; it looks to be supreme in the State. Unless, Quirites, you take precautions, this Assem-

bly legally convened by a consul in the daylight will be confronted by another assembly gathered together in the darkness
of the night. Now they, disunited, fear you, a united Assembly,
but when you are dispersed to your homes and your farms they
will hold their assembly and plot their own safety and your
ruin. It will then be your turn, scattered as you will be, to fear
them in their united strength.

"You ought, therefore, every one of you, to pray that your
friends may have preserved their good sense. If unbridled and
maddening lust has swept any one away into that whirlpool,
you must judge him as belonging not to you but to those whom
he has joined as fellow-conspirators in every kind of wickedness. I do not feel sure that even some of you may not have
been misled. For there is nothing which wears a more deceptive appearance than a depraved superstition. Where crimes
are sheltered under the name of religion, there is fear lest in
punishing the hypocrisy of men we are doing violence to something holy which is mixed up with it. From these scruples you
are delivered by numberless decisions of the pontiffs, resolutions of the senate and responses of the augurs. How often in
the times of your fathers and grandfathers has the task been
assigned to the magistrates of forbidding all foreign rites and
ceremonies, prohibiting hedge-priests and diviners from entering either the Forum, the Circus, or the City, seeking out and
burning all books of pretended prophecies, and abolishing
every sacrificial ritual except what was accordant with Roman
usage! Those men were masters of all human and divine love,
and they believed that nothing tended so much to destroy religion as the performance of sacrificial rites, not after the manner of our fathers, but in fashions imported from abroad. I
thought I ought to tell you this beforehand, so that none of you
may be distressed by fears on the score of religion when you
see us demolishing the seats of the Bacchanalia and dispersing
their impious gatherings. All that we shall do will be done
with the sanction of the gods and in obedience to their will. To
show their displeasure at the insult offered to their majesty by
these lusts and crimes they have dragged them out of their

dark hiding-places into the light of day, and they have willed that they shall be exposed not to enjoy impunity, but to be punished and put an end to.

"The senate has entrusted my colleague and myself with extraordinary powers for conducting an inquiry into this matter. We shall make an energetic use of them, and we have charged the subordinate magistrates with the care of the night-watches throughout the City. It is only right that you should show equal energy in doing your duty in whatever position you may be placed and whatever orders you receive, and also in making it your business to see that no danger or disturbance arise through the secret plots of the criminals."

They then ordered the resolutions of the senate to be read, and offered a reward for any one who should bring a guilty person before the consuls, or give in his name if he were not forthcoming. In the case of any one who had been denounced and then taken to flight, they would fix a day for him to answer the charge, and if he failed to appear, he would be condemned in his absence; for any one who was abroad at the time they would extend the date should he wish to make his defense. They then published an edict forbidding any one to sell or buy anything for the purpose of flight, or to receive, harbor, or in any way assist those who fled.

After the Assembly had broken up, the whole of the City was thoroughly alarmed. Nor was the alarm confined within the walls of the City or the frontiers of Rome; there was uneasiness and consternation throughout the whole of Italy when letters began to arrive announcing the resolutions of the senate, the proceedings in the Assembly and the edict of the consuls. During the night following the disclosure of the affair in the Assembly, guards were posted at all the gates, and many who tried to escape were arrested by the police commissioners and brought back. Many names were handed in, and some of these, both men and women, committed suicide. It was asserted that more than 7000 of both sexes were implicated in the conspiracy. The ring-leaders were, it appears, the two Atinii, Marcus and Caius, both members of the Roman plebs; L. Opiternius of

Falerium, and Minius Cerrinius, a Campanian. They were the authors of all the crime and outrage, the high priests and founders of the cult. Care was taken that they should be arrested as soon as possible, and when brought before the consuls they at once made a complete confession.

So great, however, was the number of those who fled from the City that law-suits and rights of property were in numerous cases lost by default, and the praetors were compelled through the intervention of the senate to adjourn their courts for a month, to allow the consuls to complete their investigations. Owing to the fact that those whose names were on the list did not answer to the summons, and were not to be found in Rome, the consuls had to visit the country towns and conduct their inquiries and try the cases there. Those who had simply been initiated, who, that is, had repeated after the priest the prescribed form of imprecation which pledged them to every form of wickedness and impurity, but had not been either active or passive participants in any of the proceedings to which their oath bound them, were detained in prison. Those who had polluted themselves by outrage and murder, those who had stained themselves by giving false evidence, forging seals and wills and by other fraudulent practices, were sentenced to death. The number of those executed exceeded the number of those sentenced to imprisonment; there was an enormous number of men as well as women in both classes. The women who had been found guilty were handed over to their relatives or guardians to be dealt with privately; if there was no one capable of inflicting punishment, they were executed publicly.

The next task awaiting the consuls was the destruction of all the Bacchanalian shrines, beginning with Rome, and then throughout the length and breadth of Italy; those only excepted where there was an ancient altar or a sacred image. The senate decreed that for the future there should be no Bacchanalian rites in Rome or in Italy. If any one considered that this form of worship was a necessary obligation and that he could not dispense with it without incurring the guilt of irreligion, he was to make a declaration before the City praetor and the praetor was to consult the senate. If the senate gave permission, not less than one hundred senators being present, he might observe those rites on condition that not more than five persons took part in the service, that they had no common fund, and that there was no priest or conductor of the ceremonies.

LEGENDS OF
THE WICKER MAN
58 BCE–18 CE

The cult film The Wicker Man *(1973) is one of the most significant depictions of a murderous cult in a horror movie. It tells the tale of police sergeant Neil Howie, who visits the mysterious Scottish island of Summerisle in search of a missing girl. Howie discovers that the people of Summerisle practice a form of Celtic Paganism. Their crops are failing, and they are preparing to offer a human sacrifice to restore the island's abundance. The victim must willingly enter an enormous wicker statue that is subsequently set on fire. Howie enters the wicker man hoping to rescue the victim, only to discover too late that he is the intended sacrifice. Written by Anthony Schaffer and directed by Robin Hardy, this film almost single-handedly defined the genre of folk horror. It inspired a lackluster 2006 remake and influenced celebrated films such as* Midsommar *(2019). But the idea of cultists burning people in a wicker man did not originate in Schaffer's imagination. It is a legend with a history dating back two millennia.*

To create the customs and beliefs practiced by the Pagans of Summerisle, including the wicker man, Schaffer and Hardy turned to the book The Golden Bough, *by anthropologist James Frazer (1854–1941). Frazer was an armchair anthropologist who theorized that most ancient religions were fertility cults that engaged in the periodic sacrifice of a sacred king to renew the land. He scoured ancient sources for accounts of human sacrifice and stories of Celtic druids burning people alive within wicker effigies.*

A report of druids using a wicker man first appears in Julius Caesar's *Commentaries on the Gallic War, published between 58 and 49 BCE. It appears next in* Geography, *written by the Greek geographer Strabo sometime between 7 BCE and 18 CE. Caesar waged a nine-year war to subjugate the people of Gaul—a region of Western Europe encompassing modern-day France and surrounding territories that was inhabited by Celtic tribes. But he never actually saw a wicker man. Instead, both Caesar and Strabo are drawing on reports from an older source—a wandering Greek geographer named Posidonius (or Poseidonius), who lived from 135 to 51 BCE. Posidonius's writings have been lost to history, so there is no way to know whether he actually saw druids sacrificing people in a wicker man, if he too was drawing on hearsay, or if he simply invented the story.*

Because of the lack of eyewitness accounts or corroborating archaeological evidence, there is a strong possibility the wicker man is just a legend. However, it is still an interesting case study in how claims about the wrong sort of religion are deployed. Caesar's political ambitions required the support of the plebeians (commoners), and one goal of his book was to win their favor. By presenting the Gauls as a monstrous people, Caesar emphasized his own role as a courageous hero.

Strabo, a Roman citizen, also characterizes the Gauls as backward and superstitious. His account seems designed to excite the reader with lurid stories of the barbaric religion of the other. His account of the wicker man is followed by another of Posidonius's stories about the women of the Samnitae, who were supposedly worshippers of Dionysus and murdered one of their own every year while rethatching their temple. Some have speculated that this is actually a reference to the Namnitae or Namnetes, a Gaulish tribe. This account could be based on actual practices such as rethatching temples every year. But regardless of how true it is, it demonstrates an ongoing Greco-Roman fascination and horror with the idea of women driven to frenzy by the cult of Dionysus.

FROM *CAESAR'S COMMENTARIES ON THE GALLIC WAR*[1]

The nation of all the Gauls is extremely devoted to superstitious rites; and on that account they who are troubled with unusually severe diseases and they who are engaged in battles and dangers, either sacrifice men as victims, or vow that they will sacrifice them, and employ the Druids as the performers of those sacrifices; because they think that unless the life of a man be offered for the life of a man, the mind of the immortal gods cannot be rendered propitious, and they have sacrifices of that kind ordained for national purposes. Others have figures of vast size, the limbs of which formed of osiers [willow twigs] they fill with living men, which being set on fire, the men perish enveloped in the flames. They consider that the oblation of such as have been taken in theft, or in robbery, or any other offense, is more acceptable to the immortal gods; but when a supply of that class is wanting, they have recourse to the oblation of even the innocent.

FROM *THE GEOGRAPHY OF STRABO*[2]

Among all the Gallic peoples, generally speaking, there are three sets of men who are held in exceptional honor; the Bards, the Vates, and the Druids. The Bards are singers and poets; the Vates, diviners and natural philosophers; while the Druids, in addition to natural philosophy, study also moral philosophy. The Druids are considered the most just of men, and on this account they are entrusted with the decision, not only of the private disputes, but of the public disputes as well; so that, in former times, they even arbitrated cases of war and made the opponents stop when they were about to line up for battle, and the murder cases, in particular, had been turned over to them for decision. Further, when there is a big yield from these cases, there is forthcoming a big yield from the land too, as they think. However, not only the Druids, but others as well, say that men's souls, and also the universe, are indestructible, although both fire and water will at some time or other prevail over them.

In addition to their trait of simplicity and high-spiritedness, that of witlessness and boastfulness is much in evidence, and also that of fondness for ornaments; for they not only wear golden ornaments—both chains round their necks and bracelets round their arms and wrists—but their dignitaries wear garments that are dyed in colors and sprinkled with gold. And by reason of this levity of character they not only look insufferable when victorious, but also scared out of their wits when worsted. Again, in addition to their witlessness, there is also that custom, barbarous and exotic, which attends most of the northern tribes—I mean the fact that when they depart from the battle they hang the heads of their enemies from the necks of their horses, and, when they have brought them home, nail the spectacle to the entrances of their homes. At any rate, Poseidonius says that he himself saw this spectacle in many places, and that, although at first he loathed it, afterward, through his familiarity with it, he could bear it calmly. The heads of enemies of high repute, however, they used to embalm in cedar oil and exhibit to strangers, and they would not deign to give them back even for a ransom of an equal weight of gold. But the Romans put a stop to these customs, as well as to all those connected with the sacrifices and divinations that are opposed to our usages. They used to strike a human being, whom they had devoted to death, in the back with a saber, and then divine from his death-struggle. But they would not sacrifice without the Druids. We are told of still other kinds of human sacrifices; for example, they would shoot victims to death with arrows, or impale them in the temples, or, having devised a colossus of straw and wood, throw into the colossus cattle and wild animals of all sorts and human beings, and then make a burnt-offering of the whole thing.

In the ocean, he [Poseidonius] says, there is a small island, not very far out to sea, situated off the outlet of the Liger River; and the island is inhabited by the women of the Samnitae, and they are possessed by Dionysus and make this god propitious by appeasing him with mystic initiations as well as other sacred performances; and no man sets foot on the island, although the women themselves, sailing from it, have intercourse with the men and then return again. And, he says, it is a custom of theirs once a year to unroof the temple and roof it again on the same day before sunset, each woman bringing her load to add to the roof; but the woman whose load falls out of her arms is rent to pieces by the rest, and they carry the pieces round the temple with the cry of "Ev-ah" [a cry associated with the worship of Dionysus], and do not cease until their frenzy ceases; and it is always the case, he says, that some one jostles the woman who is to suffer this fate.

THE ORGIES OF THE CHRISTIANS

SECOND CENTURY CE

As demonstrated in the previous entries, the Romans were fascinated by tales of dark conspiracies and barbaric people engaging in frenzied orgies and human sacrifices. By the end of the second century, it was rumored that the new religion of Christianity engaged in such practices. Christians were said to murder and eat babies as part of their initiation rituals so that new Christians could be blackmailed into obedience. It was also claimed that Christian feasts would be lit by a candle that was tied to a dog; when scraps were thrown to the dog, it would knock over the candle, and in the ensuing darkness, an orgy would begin where no one could see the face of their lover or avoid incest.

The descriptions of nocturnal Christian orgies resemble older stories about the Bacchanalia. But they also resemble accusations that Christians would make against others once they were no longer a minority. European Christians claimed that Satanists and witches held secret orgies where they engaged in these same practices: sexual deviance, the murder of babies, and the consumption of blood. In 2016, twenty-eight-year-old Edgar Maddison Welch fired a rifle inside a pizza parlor in Washington, DC, and demanded to be taken to the basement. Welch believed in an internet conspiracy theory called "Pizzagate," which claimed that Hillary Clinton and other Democrats held orgies beneath the pizza parlor, where they sexually abused children and drank their blood—more or less the same charges leveled against second-century Christians. Welch surrendered to authorities when he learned that the pizza parlor had no basement. (In 2025, Welch was shot and killed by police after he pulled out a handgun during a traffic stop.)

We know about these Roman accusations against Christians primarily through the work of Christian apologists who protested their absurdity. Marcus Minucius Felix lived sometime in the late second and third centuries CE. He was a lawyer, but beyond this, little is known about his life. His only surviving work, Octavius, *takes the form of a debate between his two friends: a skeptic Pagan named Caecilius Natilus and a Christian named Octavius Januarius. In the passage below, Caecilius lists the various rumors he has heard about Christians. Some of the allegations appear to be distortions of known Christian practices such as the Eucharist, while others seem totally imaginary.*

Curiously, Caecilius is not alone in claiming that Christians worship a god with the head of an ass. In 1857 an etching was discovered carved into the plaster on a wall near the Palentine Hill in Rome. It depicts a young man worshipping a crucified entity with the head of a donkey. An inscription reads, "Alexamenos worships [his] god." Known as the "Alexamenos graffito," it likely dates to about 200 CE. Pagans also accused Jews of worshipping a god with the head of an ass. Caecilius concedes that some of these stories may be false but is firm that Christians should be condemned for disrespecting the gods.

The apologist Tertullian addresses many of these same rumors in his work To the Nations. *It is unclear whether Tertullian read* Octavius *or if the influence was in the opposite direction. He begins by pointing out that there is no evidence for such claims and no reliable source for them. He then adopts a sarcastic tone, asking what would-be Christians are to do if they have no female relatives to fornicate with at their initiation. He also asks the reader whether they would perform these horrible rituals if they believed doing so would grant them immortality. He asks whether Christians are fantastic humanoids like the Cynopae—people with heads of dogs said to live in the mountains of India—or the Sciapodes—"shadow feet" people said to live in either Ethiopia or India who have one enormous foot that they can use to shade themselves from*

the sun. Tertullian suggests that the reader should consider
our shared humanity when evaluating these rumors. He
writes, "For even a Christian is a man; and whatever else
you are yourself, he is also."

Although Christianity is now the largest religion in the
world, our tendency to imagine the religious other as mon-
sters has changed little. The reason that accusations of eat-
ing babies and incest have been raised again and again
across millennia is because all cultures and religions share
an abhorrence of these practices. Although it is true that
some people have done monstrous things in the name of
their religion, people have also done monstrous things
when they label their neighbors as "cultists" or use simi-
larly dehumanizing terms.

FROM *OCTAVIUS*[1]

If the Athenians not only banished Protagoras of Abdera[2] from
their territories, but also in public assembly burned his writings, because, even circumspectly and without avowed pro-
faneness, he questioned the existence of the divinity; shall
wretches—for you must allow me with all freedom to enforce
that plea which I have undertaken to argue—shall wretches, I
say, of an abandoned, interdicted, and desperate society assault the gods? And is not this to be deeply lamented? These
are they who, having collected the more ignorant part of the
dregs of the people, together with women credulous and,
through the facility of their sex, unstable, form a rout of impious conspirators, leagued by their nocturnal assemblies and
solemn fasts and inhuman banquets, not in holy rites, but in
execrable flagitiousness; a lurking party, studious to avoid the
light; in public silent, but talkative in corners: temples they despise as charnel-houses; they vilify the gods, they mock at religious ceremonies; pitiable themselves, they pretend to pity our
priests; and, although half-naked, they scornfully look down
on secular honors and the purple of magistracy. With strange
and even incredible foolhardiness, they make light of present

tortures, while they dread those which are uncertain and future, and afraid to perish after their death, they in the meantime are not afraid to die; and thus does the delusive consolation of a fancied revival mitigate their terrors; and already, as the worst weeds spring up rankest, evil customs are creeping on daily; and throughout the whole world the pestilent assemblies of this impious confederacy have attained to their full growth: it is a confederacy meriting indeed to be subverted and laid under a curse.

Those men distinguish one another by secret tokens and signs; and even while hardly acquainted they love one another. Among them there is a species of religion in promiscuous lusts; and they call themselves brothers and sisters, that impurities not unusual may, by the intervention of those hallowed names, become as incest; and after this manner their capricious and frantic superstition glories in crime.

Neither would inquisitive fame relate many important circumstances concerning them, which are so enormous as not to be mentioned without an apology, were it not from some foundation in truth. I hear that, on account of I know not what frivolous conceit, they consecrate and worship the head of that vilest of all animals, an ass; a fit religion for such men, and congenial with their character! Others also say, that the Christians worship the secret parts of their priest as of a common father. Perhaps these reports are untrue; but surely their nocturnal and hidden rites are liable to suspicion; and he who relates that the religious ceremonies of the Christians have for their objects a man capitally punished as a delinquent, and the funereal and ominous wood of a cross, assigns proper objects of adoration for such profligates, and supposes them to venerate that which they deserve.

And as to the story of their manner of initiating novices, it is equally well known and abominable. An infant, covered over with paste, is served up to the novice; who, ignorant of the disguise and without suspicion, is excited to prick holes in the paste; and thus by unperceived wounds is the infant murdered: then the persons present eagerly lap his blood and tear his limbs asunder. By this sacrifice they are covenanted together, and by such conscious wickedness do they pledge themselves to mutual secrecy. Religious rites these more foul than any kind of sacrilege.

Then as to their banquet, it is a subject of common conversation; and the harangue of our own Fronto of Cita bears testimony to it.[3] On a day of general solemnity, men and women of every age, with all their children, sisters, and mothers, assemble at a feast; and after they have eaten and drunk largely, the entertainment waxes riotous, and the heat of wine inflames incestuous desires: a dog is fixed by a cord to that lamp which gives light to the room, and a morsel is placed just without his range; he is incited to leap at the morsel, and by his springing forward the lamp is overthrown and extinguished; and then, in the midst of impudent darkness, all present are involved, as chance leads them, in the gratification of appetites not to be named; and thus the whole company becomes incestuous, in purpose at least, if not in deed; for whatever may happen to any of them is intended by all.

FROM *THE APOLOGY OF TERTULLIAN FOR THE CHRISTIANS*[4]

We are daily beset, daily betrayed, we are unexpectedly seized, and oftenest in our actual assemblies and meetings. Yet who even thus ever chanced on a squalling infant? Who ever kept us for the judge with our mouths bloody as he found them, like Cyclops and Sirens? Who ever detected in their wives any traces of unchastity? Who ever first found out and then concealed such crimes, or sold his information with the culprits in his grasp? If we are always escaping detection, when was our guilt made known? nay, by whom could it be divulged? Certainly not by the criminals themselves, since the duty of secrecy is imperatively demanded in all mysteries. The Samothracian and Eleusinian mysteries are kept secret; how much more, then, such as, if disclosed, would at once provoke human punishment and for which Divine wrath would be reserved? If then they are not themselves their own betrayers, it follows that outsiders must have furnished the information. And whence have outsiders derived their acquaintance with the facts? when from religious initiations the profane are always excluded, and precautions are taken against witnesses—unless indeed the impious know less of fear!

Now in order that I may appeal to the trustworthy testimony of Nature herself against those who assume the credibility of such crimes, lo, we place before you the reward of these atrocities; Eternal Life is promised in return. Believe it for the time being, for argument's sake. And then I ask you this; whether, although you believe it, you think it worth while to attain it at such a cost to your conscience. Come, plunge your knife into an infant, harmless, innocent, and helpless; or if this be the duty of another, do you at least stand by while this human being dies before it has really lived; wait for the flight of the newly-entered soul; catch the immature blood; soak your bread in it; feed freely upon it. Meantime reclining at the feast, note the positions of your mother and sister; observe them diligently, so that when the darkness has been ushered in by the dogs, you may make no mistake. For you will contract pollution unless you commit incest. Thus initiated and sealed, you will live for ever. I want you to say whether Eternity is worth all this; and if it is not, in that case it ought not to be believed to be so. Even if you did believe it, I say that you would not do it; and even if you wished to do it, I say that you could not. Why, then, should others be capable of doing what you cannot? why should not you be able to do it if others can? We, I suppose, are of another nature—monstrosities like the Cynopæ or Sciapodes! with different rows of teeth, and other nerves for incestuous lust! You who can believe these things of a human being can also do them. You, too, are a man yourself, and so is also a Christian. You who cannot do it ought not to believe it. For even a Christian is a man; and whatever else you are yourself, he is also.

But you may say that deceit and imposition are practised upon the ignorant neophytes. For they might be unaware of any such assertions about the Christians as ought at any rate to have been inquired into and investigated with all carefulness. And yet it occurs to me that it is customary for those who are desirous of being initiated to go first to the director of the sacred ritual and to take down the requisite preparations. He of course would say: "An infant is indispensable, one quite young, and ignorant of the meaning of death, who will smile under your knife; bread likewise, in which to soak up the juicy blood; candlesticks, too, and lights, and some dogs and bits of offal to make them strain forward and overturn the lights; above all, you must bring your mother and sister with you." What if they will not come; or if you have none? What, in fine, are solitary candidates without relatives to do? He will not be a valid Christian, I suppose, who is not a brother or a son. Grant, if you like, that all these preliminaries have been prepared for neophytes without their knowledge; at least they learn them afterward, and bear up under the shock, and condone it. They fear, you say, lest they should be punished; whereas if they were to proclaim the infamy they would deserve every protection, and they would prefer even voluntary death to life with such a consciousness of guilt. But granting that they are afraid; why do they still continue Christians? For it follows that you no longer wish to be that which you never would have become, had you known beforehand.

THE *NARRATIONS* OF PSEUDO-NILUS

FOURTH TO SIXTH CENTURY CE[1]

Narrations *is a Greek text composed sometime between the late fourth and late sixth centuries CE. The narrator is an unnamed monk who has a son, Theodulus, from before he began his monastic life. On January 14, as father and son are visiting Mount Sinai in the Sinai Peninsula a week after Epiphany, a mysterious tribe of barbarians attacks. They kill many of the monks and abduct Theodulus, whom they plan to sacrifice to their god, the Morning Star, at dawn. The narrator escapes and makes it to a community called Pharan. A member of the Pharanite council, Magadōn, has a servant who describes being captured and escaping from the barbarians. Meanwhile, Theodulus escapes being sacrificed when the barbarians oversleep, missing their opportunity to make a sacrifice at dawn. Instead, the barbarians sell Theodulus into slavery. He is purchased by the bishop of Elusa. The narrator eventually finds his son and obtains his release. Both return home to live lives of asceticism.*

The earliest Greek manuscripts attribute the text to "Nilus the Desert Monk." This has led some to assume that the author was Nilus of Ancryra, a fifth-century saint. But most scholars reject this attribution. Because the narrator remains anonymous, modern scholars refer to the author as the "Pseudo-Nilus." Scholars originally accepted Narrations *as a more or less factual account that describes the violent religion of Bedouin tribes living in the Sinai Peninsula. However, more recent scholars regard* Narrations *as a work of fiction. Among other things, it strongly resembles fictional romance stories of the period. However, there remains a historical kernel to the narrative. During the period* when this text was written, Christian ascetics were increasingly venturing into the deserts of the Sinai Peninsula, where they interacted with nomadic tribes. These encounters sometimes turned hostile, but the depiction of the barbarians in this text cannot be considered reliable or accurate. Rather, it is part of a genre of writings about barbaric peoples at the edge of the Roman Empire who were driven by cannibalism and bizarre religions. Theodulus's account is a classic captivity narrative, in which a vulnerable person (often a woman) describes being captured by the racial or religious other. The function of captivity narratives is generally to present another culture or religion as subhuman, thereby frightening and exciting the reader.

Only a few details ascribed to the barbarian religion are likely to have much basis in fact. The sacrifice of camels was performed by Arab peoples prior to the rise of Islam. The worship of the morning star as a god or goddess may be historically accurate. Some historians speculate that the morning star was in fact Al-'Uzza, a pre-Islamic goddess worshipped throughout Arabia. But the description of the barbarians descending on the camel in a "blood orgy," devouring even the bones, can be regarded as a fantasy.

Still, it is a fantasy with historical significance because for nearly a century it was regarded as a literal account and it informed theories of religious violence. Historian of religion David Frankfurter points out that this account of barbarians sacrificing humans and camels to the Morning Star was taken literally by Robertson Smith in his book Religion of the Semites (1899). Sigmund Freud drew on Smith's account in Totem and Taboo (1913), and Freud was cited by René Girard in Violence and the Sacred (1972).[2] This book, in turn, has been cited by contemporary alarmists, who claim that Girard's theories explain why Satanic cults are driven to murder. As one such author writes, "Occult groups that practice ritual murder have an authentic understanding of the sacred nature of violence. You do not have to convince Vampyres or Satanists that humans are violent by nature; as living examples of Girardian theory, they *fundamentally comprehend this."*[3] *Groups of Satanists do exist, as do senseless murders, but this image of a subculture driven to kill by its Girardian commitment to "sacred violence" has as much to do with actual Satanism as Pseudo-Nilus's barbarians have to do with actual Bedouin tribes. Thus, a text that appears to be a fantasy of nightmarish cannibals oppressing early Christians continues to fuel fantasies of cults performing evil rituals a millennium and a half later.*

[NARRATIVE III: ETHNOGRAPHIC EXCURSUS ON BARBARIANS AND MONKS]

"The aforesaid nation [of Barbarians] inhabits the desert extending from Arabia to Egypt's Red Sea and the River Jordan. They practise no craft, trade, or agriculture at all, but use the dagger alone as their means of subsistence. They live by hunting desert animals and devouring their flesh, or else get what they need by robbing people on roads that they watch in ambush. If neither is possible and their provisions run out, then they consume pack animals—they use camels called dromedaries—for food. Theirs is a bestial and bloodthirsty way of life. Killing one camel per clan or cluster of tents, they soften its flesh with heat from a fire only insofar as it makes it yield to their teeth without having to be too forcefully torn. In a word, they eat like dogs.

"They know no god abstractly conceived or materially handcrafted, but bow down instead to the Morning Star. When it appears on the horizon they offer to it the best of their spoils, if anything suitable for sacrifice falls into their hands from their bandit raids.

"They especially like to offer children distinguished by beauty and the bloom of youth. These they sacrifice on piles of stones at dawn. What troubles and worries me so, my friends, is that my boy's comeliness might be appetizing to the lawless ones for their accustomed impieties, seeming serviceable for their purpose. I fear lest his pure soul's body be offered up as a sacrificial victim to abominable demons on behalf of unclean people, to be, as they believe, their atonement and cleansing. Habituated as they are to performing human sacrifice without reservation, they feel no pity for the children whom they slaughter, even if the suppliants sing their laments as seductively as Sirens.

"But if no children are available, they make a camel that is white and free from blemishes bend down on its knees. Then they circle around it three times in a procession that is drawn out by the multitude of participants involved. The person who leads in the procession and in singing a hymn they compose for the star is either one of their kings or one of their priests distinguished by old age. After the third circuit, but before the throng has finished its hymn, while the last refrain is still carrying on their tongues, this man draws a sword and vigorously strikes at the victim's sinews. Eagerly, he is the first to have a taste of the blood. Then the rest run up with daggers drawn. Some cut off just a small patch of hide and hair, others seize whatever flesh they see and hack away, while others go straight for the innards and entrails. No part of the sacrifice is left unconsumed, so that nothing remains to be seen when the sun appears. They do not even refrain from eating bone and marrow, gradually overcoming its hardness and toughness through perseverance."

———

[NARRATIVE IV: BARBARIAN RAID AND SLAUGHTER OF MONKS]

"It was against men of such character and so attentive to the divine that the phalanx of Barbarians fell so suddenly and unexpectedly, like a squall out of nowhere. The lawless ones attacked at break of dawn, just when the reverent ones had finished their sacred hymns. I happened to be there too with my boy, having come down from the Holy Mountain to visit the holy ones in [the church of] 'the Bush,' as long had been my habit. They ran at us howling like mad dogs, shouting incomprehensibly as they plundered. They seized the food that had been gathered for the winter—for [the monks] set aside to dry whatever fruit can be preserved for that purpose—making us collect it and carry it ourselves. Then they led us out of the church. After stripping off our ragged cloaks, they ordered the oldest among us to line up, naked, for execution.

"Next, some Barbarians nearby drew their swords, utterly enraged, eyes ablaze and glancing from side to side. They ordered the celebrant of the holy place to stretch out his neck first. The two men [standing] beside him did not strike at once, but took turns hacking away at his upper back from either side. The victim did not cry in pain, twist his face, or show any sign of anguish. All he said, as he sealed himself, was 'Blessed be the Lord,' with a whisper from his mouth. The first blow cut from his upper back to his jaw and ear; the second came down from his shoulder to his chest. After gently swaying, the blessed one fell with decorous poise: neither in being slain nor in being naked did he present any unsightliness, since his body glowed with a certain grace that covered the unseemliness of his nakedness.

"Indeed, the holy one had nearly prophesied all this the previous evening both in word and deed. For he greeted with more than his usual welcome those who had gathered at dinner, saying, 'Who knows if we shall all meet together again at one hearth and table before we die?'

"Next they slew the man who lived with that elder. He was also quite old, and had worn himself down by rather excessive labors of ascetic training. Then they killed the boy who attended them in the following way.

"One of the Barbarians ordered him to pick up some fruit that had spilled to the ground. To please the one who had given this command, the boy quickly bent down and stretched out his hands to gather the scattered fruits as ordered. He showed the same eagerness to please as he always did in his ministrations, believing that he might be able to gain his life by appearing to be eager. But he gained nothing. He failed to soften their barbaric cruelty or coax them to be kinder—something far from likely. Another Barbarian standing behind him secretly pulled his sword from its sheath. Either sensing that a sword had been drawn or expecting his slaughter, the boy turned back his head in terror as if startled by a sound. While the one standing over him filled him with fright through his twisted look and barbaric cry, the other, leaning down upon [the boy's] collar bone, thrust his sword most forcefully straight up, from [the boy's] diaphragm to his chest. The boy rolled over dead before it was even pulled out. Either he died ahead of time through fright or died at the moment of the blow: either way, he was not aware that death would soon oust his soul from his corporeal cavities, instantly releasing it from the bonds that had so firmly constrained it in its mesh.

"The rest of us they let go, though I do not know why. They ordered us to flee with a gesture of their hands, which were still clenching bloody swords. The others [i.e., the monks] ran through the ravines in a hurry to reach the mountain—for they [i.e., the Barbarians] do not approach it, in the belief that God once stood upon it and uttered commandments to His people—but I remained where I was, completely still and transfixed, with my mouth open, unable to do anything. I could not leave my lad; his very vitals bound me to him. Held as I was by nature's bonds, I felt no urge to save myself, till the child signaled me to leave, gesturing with his eyes, gradually persuading me to go.

"And so my feet moved forward, and somehow my whole body was borne and followed them. But my heart refused to budge: it constantly kept me turning to face the boy. I could not keep my eyes to myself; instead of looking straight forward where my feet were going, they kept piteously turning back. Finally, following those who had gone ahead, I proceeded toward the mountain.

"As I looked down I could see the poor boy being led away. Although he was not free to look around, he shot a glance toward me with his eyes without his captors knowing. And so it is with nature's bond: physical separation cannot sever it, but only make it stronger. For if a soul cannot be near its object of longing, it becomes vexed and distracted in the extreme, devoting all of its memory to what it wants, having no other means at hand to fulfill its desire."

"As we approached the gate, they called [Theodulus], saying I had come, and led him out to meet me. But when we saw each other, he and I, neither of us showed signs of pleasure. Instead we began to sob and lament, drenching our faces and tunics with tears. He ran toward me, not entirely recognizing me—for how could I be easily recognized, my clothes being filthy, as was the hair on my head?—nonetheless, he evidently put more trust in the report of my arrival than in the sight before his eyes, for he approached me with open arms, eager to wrap them around me. As for me, I recognized him instantly, despite the crowd surrounding him: for his face still had those same features that were etched so deeply in my memory.

"No longer could I suppress my joy. All muscles in my body suddenly went limp; I fell to the ground and lay dumbstruck, so that most everyone thought I had died.

"Indeed, my long period of grief had made me no different from a corpse, [albeit] one capable of breath and sight. But by wrapping me in his embrace, [Theodulus] gradually helped me revive from my swoon, making me realize who I was, where I was, and who it was that my eyes were now seeing. So I offered my arms to meet his, returning his embrace with my own, savoring this satisfaction of a desire that I had felt for so long.

"Then I began to speak. I tried to apologize and persuade him that I was to blame for all of the evils that he had experienced. I was the one who took him from his homeland and made him dwell in a land that was constantly being ravaged: for truly it was as I've stated. While he dwelt in the country in which he was born and bred, when did he ever experience anything one might pray to avoid? There it was everywhere peaceful, and nowhere was there fear of such treachery. But let those, who think the Fates cannot be escaped, be gone! Away with those, who assert that some Necessity leads its victims to their Destinies!

"Finally I asked him to describe what he had endured among the Barbarians, since his trials were over and no longer would be painful to recount. For as health after illness or healing after trauma brings cheer instead of despair, so too is it pleasant to describe sad affairs once they are over; their narration may even bring as much pleasure as the original experience brought pain."

[NARRATIVE VII: THEODULUS'S STORY]

"[Theodulus] sighed deeply as he began to speak, his eyes brimming full of tears. 'What profit is there, father, in recalling our sorrows? Memory is wont to scratch a sufferer's sores. When told for love of storytelling, its narration may charm the listener's ears, since hearing about another person's suffering can bring delight to someone else; but it does not release the one who endured it from the pain that befalls him through the retelling. For not much is needed to stir up sensations similar to those that were suffered in the past, just as pain from a wound can easily be caused by touching a scar that has not yet fully healed.

"'But I know that you will continue to press me until you have heard what you want to learn. For I know you intend to make my incredible salvation the theme of your doxology, as it is your habit to sing God's hymns for every benefaction that He grants you. So hear me with a manly frame of mind, and let paternal sentiments not make you cry out in sympathy at the dreadful misfortunes that befell me. Do not interrupt me with sad laments. Your sobbing would hinder the telling of my story, and my words would likely be smothered by your wailing.

"'Magadōn's servant has already told you most of what happened before he escaped. To go back over those things would prolong my narrative and perhaps be tiresome to hear, eager as you are for the essentials. For hearing something over and over again is not only tedious but irksome to listeners. But since you insist, I will tell what happened after his escape.

"'The Barbarians had decided upon our sacrifice, as no

doubt he told you. Everything had been made ready for the ritual since dusk: altar, dagger, libation, receptacle, incense. It was avowed that death would come just before dawn—unless God intended to deter it. Then Magadōn's servant revealed his plan and made his escape. It seemed unlikely that he would be caught, considering the difficulty of a distant pursuit. For not only did the time from dusk to dawn suffice to escape under darkness, but it was also unclear what route he had taken, making it anyone's guess which direction to pursue. Who could follow a trail in that desert expanse, where it is impossible to find any trace of a path? What tracker is so clever, what seer so expert in detecting invisible signs? For everywhere the desert's terrain is rough and riven with ravines, hiding any tracks left upon it.

"'Meanwhile I lay prone on the ground. While keeping my head down, I lifted my mind aloft on the wings of affliction. Secretly I began to address God, focusing my thoughts so completely on prayer that I was in no way distracted by impending death.

"'For the mind, if free from fear, tends to disperse itself on frivolous affairs like trading, sailing, building, planting; betrothals, nuptials, the begetting of children; military service and procuring provisions; lawsuits, law courts, tribunal benches, high seats of state, bailiffs, magistrates; warding off enemies, convivial companies and feasting with friends; becoming tribune, governor, or procurator, and imagining this to be a royal rank. But catastrophe makes it concentrate through fear of danger, dispelling all that distracted it when free and secure. Entirely consumed by the cause of its grief, it supplicates God as the only one who, with an effortless nod of assent, might effect its release from its hapless straits. And so I began:

"'"Master and Maker of all creation known to sight and mind, You Who hold the hearts of Your creatures in Your hand; Who can turn senseless rage into acts of mercy, and can save those being sentenced to death by authority's decree whenever Your blessed judgment wishes; Who can tame the ferocity of fierce wild beasts that feed on human bodies for their food; Who can repel the surging rage of fire, or freeze flames at full blaze with a mere nod; Who keep safe and unharmed men condemned to destruction, and show with ineffable and incredible power that hair and skin have more force than fire.

"""Save one who has no hope for succor from anywhere else, who has not yet lost life by his enemy's decision, since he is already as good as dead. Don't let my blood become a libation for demons. Don't let sinister spirits feast on the fatty smell of my flesh.

"""They are ready to make me a sacrifice to a star that takes its appellation from the passion of lust. Do not let my body, kept chaste to this day, become a sacrificial offering to the demon called wantonness. No, change these savages' bestial hearts to kindness, just as You changed the wrath of Ahasuerus, King of the Medes, when it burned against Esther, and turned his rough anger to compassion and mercy.

"""Save a soul that seeks to become Your slave, and restore to my elderly father, who also adores You, an innocent son who is ready to revere You, God, as he has proposed. Not out of fear of danger do I now make this vow, so that my promise might be thought the price of salvation; but on the basis of my freedom to reason I have already anticipated the necessity of a struggle.

"""Demonstrate that faith attains salvation more swiftly than flight, and that it is safer to take hope in You than in flight by our feet. For he who was to be made an offering tomorrow together with me has evaded that death and secured his salvation by running away, while I remained here, awaiting Your judgment, in my enemy's hands, trusting in Your aid. I am trusting in Your power as he did in his feet. May the expectations I placed in divinity prove more auspicious than the hope he put in his body. He was saved because he used full cover of darkness to make his escape, and well was he saved. Behold, daylight has caught me! May You now save me by Your sagacity—You, Who gave this light to the living so that they could fulfill Your commands!"

"'This was how the sunrise found me—sleepless, praying, and shedding bitter tears. Lifting up my head I could see the Dawn-bearer glimmering on the horizon. I sat up, put my

hands on my knees and pressed my tearful face upon them.
Once more I cried with my heart to the Power that could whisk
me away with the mighty force of its breath, saying,

""Master, You Who have authority over life and death,
make Your mercy toward me a thing of wonder, as You won-
drously have done for holy ones who have been rescued from
tribulation after falling under compulsion. Do this, that we
might confidently call on You, encouraged that we too will be
delivered from whatever disasters befall us, pondering them as
a paradigm of the succor that is Yours.""

"'While I was occupied with these words, [the Barbarians]
sprang up with great alarm because the moment for sacrifice
had come and gone—the sun already shining down upon the
earth. Unable to find the other victim, they asked me what had
happened. When they learned that, since I had been with them,
I could offer no intelligence about his disappearance, they fell
silent, without threatening me or giving indication of an-
noyance.

"'At that point my spirit settled and I blessed God for not
ignoring a humble one's prayers. From then on I was filled with
confidence and courage—surely because God had granted me
this grace. When they bid me to eat forbidden food, I refused;
when they ordered me to dally with their women, I declined.

"'Finally we approached the inhabited world. Then, without
me knowing what they had planned, they entered a village
called Subaïta, and announced my sale to the people who lived
there. Many times they went there and returned without selling me, since no one was willing to give more than two pieces
of gold. Finally they led me out and stood me in front of the
village naked, as was their custom. Then they put a sword to
my throat and told everyone that they would cut off my head
unless someone immediately bought me. And so, spreading my
arms outward like a suppliant before those who had gathered
for the sale, I pleaded with them to give as much as was asked
and not to haggle over the price of human blood. I said that
I would soon repay whatever price they paid, would eagerly

serve the buyer as a slave if he wanted, and would acknowledge as my master whoever bought my life even after I had redeemed my price.

"'And so, since I was tearfully importuning them in this way, someone eventually took pity and bought me. To sum it up briefly: I was then sold from there to here, as you have found.'"

THE ORLÉANS HERESY

1022 CE[1]

The Orléans heresy of 1022 is one of the earliest instances of heresy in Europe. A small sect led by two canons, Stephen and Lisois, practiced a variant form of Christianity. They were probably "dualists" who saw matter and spirit as opposing forces. As such, they rejected the sacraments, which incorporate food and other material substances, and denied that Christ had a material nature that could be born, suffer, or die.[2] They were tried and condemned by the Council of Orléans, and the entire sect—save two members who recanted—were burned alive. This is the earliest recorded incident of burning heretics in medieval Europe.

Much of what historians know about this event comes from Paul of St. Père-de-Chartres, who wrote about six decades after 1022. In Paul's account, a noble named Arefast infiltrated the sect to learn their beliefs and practices. He then sent word to the king, who convened a council to try Stephen and Lisois. According to Paul, they confessed not only to denying Catholic doctrine but also to engaging in nocturnal orgies at which literal demons were present. These details are clearly an embellishment.

Two features of Paul's account are significant for understanding the fear of cults across history. First, it is striking that the orgiastic activities of the heretics—extinguishing the lights and then copulating with the nearest partner in the dark with no regard for incest, as well as murdering children—are exactly the same accusations that Roman Pagans leveled against Christians in the second century CE. Only this time, there is an added element of demon worship and opposition to "true" Christianity. Thus, we can trace a direct line from Roman claims about early Christians to medieval Christian claims about heretics, and then on to the "Satanic panic" of the 1980s and the contemporary conspiracy theories like the QAnon movement.

Second, Paul's description of heresy anticipates future ideas of cult mind control. He does not describe heresy in terms of beliefs or ideas but in medicalized terms of contamination: They are "inebriated" with heresy, their religion is a "plague," their ideas are "vomited out," etc. For Paul, heresy is not a different religion but an infectious disease of the mind. Furthermore, Paul describes the heretics as manufacturing magical ashes from sacrificed children that can be fed to victims, forcing them to accept heretical beliefs. Prior to Paul's account, an earlier French monk named Adémar de Chabannes had described the religion of Manichaeism gaining converts by tricking people into eating a powder made from the bones of dead boys.[3] As will be seen in subsequent entries, people have always attempted to explain away other people's decision to affiliate with "cults." Paul's account of forcing conversion through black magic was replaced by ideas of "tilted wombs" and other dubious medical theories in the nineteenth century, and finally by notions of "brainwashing" and "undo influence" in the twentieth century. Although we no longer burn people alive, the hunt for heretics has never truly ended.

I thought it worthy, for the sake of future generations, to tell of how a man named Aréfast, with divine aid and his own innate praiseworthy shrewdness, not only detected but also utterly destroyed a perverse heresy in the city of Orléans which was secretly spreading deadly poison throughout the provinces of Gaul.

Aréfast was truly of the lineage of the counts of Normandy: polished in speech, prudent in judgment, and formed in noble behavior. For these reasons he became the most highly regarded emissary in service to the king of the Franks and among the other nobles. On his estate he had a cleric named Herbert who had decided to go study in the city of Orléans. However, while he bustled about seeking teachers of truth, his journey took a dark turn and he stumbled into the abyss of heresy. In the city, two clerics, Stephan and Lisois, were held among all to be famous for their wisdom, distinguished in sanctity, and generous with alms. Herbert sought them out, and shortly the impressionable student, inebriated by a deadly draft of wickedness hidden by the sweetness of the divine word, succumbed to madness and became entangled in a devilish error. He believed himself to have scaled the fortress of wisdom without any divine help.

Returning home, he longed to draw his lord, whom he loved deeply, to the way of his error. He coaxed him with subtle words, saying that Orléans glimmered with the light of wisdom and the lamp of sanctity. Aréfast rebuked him. He understood by Herbert's words that he had wandered from the upright path. He quickly notified Count Richard and asked that he write to King Robert about the plague lurking in his kingdom before the gates could be thrown open and the disease spread. He should also ask that the king grant Aréfast the aid he needed to drive it out. And so, stunned by this news, the king commanded Aréfast to go quickly to Orléans with his cleric, promising him help of every sort in the venture.

When, at the king's bidding, he set off, Aréfast went first to Chartres to consult the venerable bishop Fulbert concerning the heresy. But, as luck would have it, he was away, having traveled to Rome for the sake of prayer. He then told a wise cleric and sacristan of the church of Chartres named Everard the reason for his journey. He also asked for his counsel on where he should stand in the battle line, and with which weapons he should arm himself against the numerous arts of devilish deceit. Everard wisely advised him to seek the power of the almighty every day. First thing in the morning he should go to church devoted to prayer and strengthen himself with the holy communion of the body and blood of Christ. Then, protected by the sign of the holy cross, he would be able to listen to the depraved heretics without fear. He should not contradict anything he might hear, but rather he should feign the demeanor of a disciple, gathering their secrets in the abode of his heart.

Aréfast did as he had been instructed. When he arrived at Orléans he fortified himself daily with holy communion and by kneeling in prayer. Then he sat inside the heretics' house to hear their teaching as if he was the simplest disciple. At first, they instructed him with examples from divine books and similar sources, but when they noticed his attentive ear—just like that of a perfect student—they presented him with the image of a tree in the woods, among other analogies. "We must treat you," they explained, "like a tree in a forest, which is transferred to a garden and frequently watered until it takes root in the soil. Then, having been shorn of thorns and excess debris, the tree is pruned down to the ground with a hoe, and a better small branch is grafted on which will later be fertile with sweet fruit. In a similar way you have been transferred from the hostile world into our sacred company. You will be bathed in the waters of wisdom until you have matured, and with the sword of the word of God you will be able to hew away the thorns of vice. Foolish doctrine will be blocked from your heart, and you will be able to receive our teaching, which is handed down by the Holy Spirit, with a pure mind."

Aréfast reported on every word they said, always with thanks to God, until they thought he had converted to their errors. Now at ease, they laid bare the cesspool of their wickedness which they had previously clothed with the words of divine books. They said, "Christ was not born of the Virgin Mary, neither did he suffer for humankind, nor was he actually buried in the tomb, nor did he rise from the dead." They added, "There is no cleansing of evil deeds in baptism, nor in the priest's consecration of the sacrament of the body and blood of Christ, and praying to the holy martyrs and confessors is worthless."

When these depraved and wretched men had finished vomiting out these and other detestable ideas from their foul bellies, Aréfast responded: "If the salvation of humankind is not in what you have enumerated, as they hope, I beg you to show me what will offer hope, lest my soul—which you have thrust into doubt—soon fall into the ruin of despair."

"Without a doubt, brother," they replied, "thus far you have languished with the ignorant in the Charybdis[4] of false ideas. Now you have been elevated to the peak of all truth. With a sound mind you have understood and may now open your eyes to the light of true faith. We will open the doorway of salvation to you who will enter by the laying on of our hands. You will be cleansed from every stain of sin and replenished with the gift of the Holy Spirit, who will teach you the depth of the entirety of the scriptures and true worth without doubt. Then, having fed on heavenly food and revived by inner satiety, you will often see angelic visions with us. Bolstered by those comforting experiences, you will be able to go anywhere you wish without hindrance or difficulty. You will lack nothing, because your ally, the God of all things in whom the treasures of wisdom and riches are found, will never fail you."

In the meantime, the king and Queen Constance came to the city of Orléans with a group of bishops, just as Aréfast had asked. The following day, at Aréfast's suggestion, royal officials dragged everyone in that wickedest congregation from the house where they gathered. They then brought them before the king and the group of bishops and clerics at the church of Sainte-Croix.

But before we come to the trial, I must take the trouble to explain the meal which they called heavenly and the particular art by which they prepared it to those who do not know about it. They gathered on certain nights in the aforementioned house. With everyone holding lamps, they called out the names of demons, in the same manner as a litany, until suddenly they saw a demon descend among them in the form of some little beast. When that vision appeared, they extinguished all the lights, and at once each one pulled close any woman who came to hand and seized her for misuse without thought for sin. Whether he held a mother, or sister, or nun, they reckoned this sex to be a holy and religious observance.

On the eighth day, having kindled a large fire in the middle of them, a child begotten of that foulest copulation was tested by flame per the custom of the ancient pagans, and thus consumed in the fire. The cold ashes of the child were then collected and guarded with great veneration—like the Christian religion is accustomed to guard the body of Christ—to later be given as a sacrament to the sick about to depart from this world. Truly that ash contained an immense power of diabolical delusion so that whoever had been initiated into the heresy and tasted only the smallest bit of that ash, afterward hardly had the power to steer their mind away from that heresy and back toward the way of truth.

It suffices to say only enough about this affair so that Christians may guard themselves against this nefarious artifice and not desire to follow it and imitate it. But I digress, with that finished, I will return to the original story with the barbarity of these adulterers hastily passed over, lest a lengthier discussion of this controversy might disgust a delicate reader.

THE LONG
NINETEENTH
CENTURY

WILLIAM DORRELL, THE INVINCIBLE VEGETARIAN MESSIAH

1798[1]

The strange story of William Dorrell (1752–1846) and his followers, the Dorrellites, has been preserved by a series of local historians in Massachusetts and Vermont. Dorrell, an illiterate British soldier turned Massachusetts farmer, declared himself a messiah and began preaching a doctrine of vegetarianism and free love. His movement ended shortly after he claimed that nothing could harm him, which prompted one Captain Ezekiel Foster to test this proposition by assaulting him in front of his congregation. The story has been recorded as a morality tale, depicting Dorrell as an intemperate, lecherous con artist while emphasizing Foster's heroic physique. Reading between the lines, there are several interesting insights here into how the discourse of "cult leaders" was evolving at the dawn of the nineteenth century.

The Dorrellites reached their height in 1798. This was the beginning of a period of religious revival known as the Second Great Awakening, when church attendance soared. Following the American Revolution, there was a desire to discover a "pure" or primitive form of Christianity that— somewhat paradoxically—led to the rise of many new religious movements, including the Church of Jesus Christ of Latter-day Saints, often called the Mormons. Throughout the nineteenth century, new religious movements continued to form all over the United States. Many created their own communities, and like the Dorrellites, some experimented with vegetarianism and free love.

Not everyone approved of these religious innovations.

Although the word "cult" did not yet have its current meaning, terms like "sect" and "fanaticism" were used to describe the wrong kind of religion. (In fact, the Roman Bacchanalia is referenced in the excerpt below.) Opponents of these groups assumed that their followers did not choose to join them but were somehow manipulated into doing so. An 1846 tract by a Presbyterian minister accused revival preachers of the Second Great Awakening of using an emotional preaching style to override the free will of the audience: "Great violence is done to ordinary habits of thinking and feeling . . . in short, their minds must be entirely dislodged from accustomed positions, and from all former ground, however good and proper it may have been, and they must be compelled, in a moment of the greatest possible excitement, to yield themselves entirely, their intellect, their reason, their imagination, their belief, their feelings, their passions, their whole souls—to a single and new position, that is prescribed to them. . . . The mind, reduced to such a bondage, can never afterward be free."[2] This is another early version of the "brainwashing" theory that would emerge in the 1950s.

The entry below describes Dorrell's followers as "victims" who were taken in by his "power"—a quality of persuasiveness that emerged from his physical stature, his keen memory, his "pleasing address," and his "good native talent." His spell over his followers is instantly broken after he is beaten by Foster. Scholars of new religious movements might say this assessment is not entirely wrong: Sociologists describe prophets like Dorrell as having a characteristic they call "charisma." But charisma is not simply the product of one's appearance and personality: Ultimately, charisma describes the relationship between a leader and their followers. It is less the case that leaders have followers because they are charismatic and more that we call them charismatic because they have followers. This means that charisma is fragile. As with Dorrell, anything that causes a leader to appear as another ordinary person can potentially destroy their charisma. Charismatic leaders such as David Koresh and Jim Jones made seemingly irrational decisions, not because they had total control over their followers but because their leadership was fragile: They feared an outcome that might cause them to lose face and inspire their followers to abandon them.

The counterpart to the myth of the "all-powerful leader" is that of the brainwashed follower. This text describes a blacksmith named Amos Burrows, who, as a Dorrellite, was not supposed to use leather in his bellows. Other accounts describe Dorrellite blacksmiths who used bellows made of painted cloth instead of leather. But here the author reports that underneath Burrows's cloth was leather and that he was merely pretending to comply with Dorrell's edict. Burrows's obedience to the leader was performative, not absolute. Sociologists know that this sort of nominal compliance is common in new religious movements. In the 1970s, sociologist Robert Balch observed the Heaven's Gate group. One member was an ex–piano tuner who seemed to be among the most dedicated to the group's teachings and awaited an apocalyptic event called the "Demonstration." But Balch noticed that he still kept an expensive set of piano tools in the trunk of his car, just in case the Demonstration never happened.[3] Balch concluded that people in new religious movements typically have doubts even if they are reluctant to share them.

This account of William Dorrell's career seems rather contradictory. After receiving a beating in 1798, Dorrell appears to admit to being a charlatan who "led the people [on] a wild goose chase." But in 1834, he is described as still believing that the Bible is "all wrong" and saying that some of his followers still believe in his teachings. So was Dorrell lying in 1798 or lying in 1834? An even greater contradiction concerns the depiction of Ezekiel Foster, who is praised as a hero in every account of the Dorrellites. Although Dorrell's teachings may have been dishonest or annoying, they were within the confines of the law. Foster, on the other hand, committed assault and battery in a church because he was offended by his neighbor exercising his religious freedom.

In various parts of the country one frequently reads accounts of and wonders at the strange so-called religious zeal manifested. Fanaticism seems oftentimes a more appropriate term. While we see and wonder, how many of the younger generation, surely, realize that about the year 1794, there sprang up here in our midst, a sect whose teachings were just as fanatical and just as foreign to all civilized Christian practises as was possible for them to be. From the name of the founder of this order, William Dorrell, came the name of these strange believers, "The Dorrellites." In 1882 F. M. Thompson, Esq., read a most excellent paper upon this subject before the P.V.M.A.,[4] and free reference has been made to his production for much of the following, supplemented by notes of the conversations held by Gov. Cushman with both Mr. Dorrell and some of his followers.

On Monday, January 27, 1834, in company with Geo. T. Davis Esq., of Greenfield, Gov. Cushman writes that he visited "William Dorrell—alias—the famous imposter, Dorrell." He was the son of an English farmer, born in Yorkshire, Eng., March 15, 1752. He became in early life a soldier, serving through three campaigns in Ireland; after this he emigrated to America and served through two campaigns here, being under Burgoyne at his surrender in 1777.

Upon his resumption of civil life, he settled at Petersham, Mass. Here he married Polly Chase, a woman ten years his junior. At the expiration of two years he moved to Warwick; his home for some succeeding years was in Northfield, in 1784 going thence to Leyden.

In appearance he was described as being large of stature, six feet or more in height, his forehead full and sloping, eyes quick, "and having the phrenological development of firmness very full indeed." He was in many respects a most remarkable man, although a most ignorant and intemperate one. Intoxicated to the worst degree, or perfectly sober, he was never known to make an engagement which he did not fulfill to the letter. Uneducated, not even able to read or write, he nevertheless possessed an unusually retentive memory, being able to repeat a large portion of the Bible from hearing it read by his wife. He was possessed of a pleasing address, which, combined with good native talent, must have constituted an important factor of his power.

His home at the time of Gov. Cushman's visit, was in the north-west corner of Leyden, in a poor old smoky house, situated away from the traveled road and remote from any residence of human beings. The furniture consisted of a table, loom, bed, crockery shelves and two or three chairs. There at the age of 82 or 83 he lived alone, possessed of remarkably good health. Although he then had no followers, he still clung to his belief, saying that the Bible was "all wrong, all wrong!" He thought that some of the old Dorrellites still clung to the religion, even though they might not publicly acknowledge it. Even at that age he took a pride in telling his callers that he would persist in getting drunk occasionally.

With his beliefs and the teachings he sought to instill into the minds of his followers, it seems unparalleled that so many prominent men of the time should class themselves as among his adherents. As a rule the Dorrellites were respectable, churchgoing men, several of them town officials, and numbered some 20 or 30 families. Among them we find the names of Hezekiah Newcomb, Samuel and John Connable, Ezra Shattuck, Charles Packer, Messrs. Dewey and Eddy, Zenas, Reuben and Michael Frizzell, Capt. Parmenter, Joshua Wells, Abner Evans, Mr. Paige, Amos Burrows, Reuben Sheldon, James and Pitts Phillips, Charles Stearns, David Potter, Jedediah Fuller and John Dixon. Probably the greater part of these were residents of Leyden.

The first revelation which led to the founding of the faith came to Dorrell while he was "chopping." He did not seem to be able to recall it exactly, but in his conversation gave it as "Render yourself an agreeable sacrifice," or something similar. There were many subsequent ones pertaining, no doubt, to the practises to be put in execution. "His first success as a preacher

was about 1794, and gaining a few followers the strange doctrines soon spread from neighborhood to neighborhood and
quite a number of respectable people were attracted by them
and cast in their lot with their humanitarian leader, for the
doctrine as first declared was founded upon the principle that
man should not eat of flesh, and should not cause the death of
any living creature. The doctrine was carried to that extent
that no member might wear shoes or use harnesses made of
leather, or use the skins of animals for any domestic purpose.
The majority of his followers wore wooden shoes made by one
of their number, Ezra Shattuck. To this rule Mr. Amos Burrows was an exception, and from the fact that his blacksmith
bellows were first covered in the usual manner with leather,
and a covering of painted cloth put on outside so that he nominally conformed to the custom merely, we may conclude that
he was not as enthusiastic a member of the fold as some. The
harnesses were made of rope, and much of the cloth used for
domestic purposes was a coarse tow cloth.

With his success in obtaining followers, his inspiration increased and he was led to preach that every generation of men
had its Messiah: that *He* was the Messiah of *his* generation;
that no arm of flesh could hurt him; that there was no resurrection from the dead; that when "resurrection" was spoken of in
the Bible its meaning was a resurrection from a state of sin to
spiritual life; that Jesus Christ was a spirit; that he took a body;
that he died, but that he never was raised from the dead; that all
who are raised from a state of sin to this spiritual life become
perfect; that they can then do no sin, and are no more responsible to the civil law, and are beyond all "principalities and
powers." There was no future judgment, no knowledge after
death of what passed in this world; that God had no power over
man to control his actions, therefore there was no need of
prayer. He had no hope for the future, but he had an abundance
of assurance that all was well. He was perfect, his body being
in perfect obedience to the spirit, and his followers were com-
paratively perfect, as the members of the body are perfect when
compared with the head; that all covenants made by God with
men were ended, and he was the head of a new covenant; that

neither Moses nor Christ wrought miracles, and that he stood precisely the same as Jesus Christ, and that while no person might worship his human body yet he might be worshiped as Christ was worshipped, as God united to human flesh.

This is the substance of a "confession of faith," if it might be so called, obtained from the lips of Dorrell by the Rev. John Taylor of Deerfield in 1798, the interview being had for that purpose. As the freedom of sin arrived at by the followers of this new seer led them into the commission of acts condemned by the majority of people as grossly immoral, Dorrell was very cautious, the Rev. Mr. Taylor says, about committing himself on those subjects, but upon the subject of marriage he declared that when a husband or wife became perfect, by being raised to the spiritual life, the other party was not holden by the old covenant or the civil law; and if both were raised, still the parties were not holden to each other and had perfect right to promiscuous intercourse.

The sect had no meetings for worship, as they considered all days alike, one day as holy as another, and according to report their later meetings were scenes of most outrageous and beastly conduct, interspersed with the singing of "bacchanalian songs and lascivious addresses." At one time seven Dorrellites were complained of for raising a building on Sunday. Securing Richard F. Newcomb of Greenfield as their attorney, all were cleared but one.

The sect had a common treasury, and the office was filled by a shrewd business man, and it is a common report that the Dorrellite treasury was the foundation of the fortune of one of the wealthiest and most influential families in this portion of the county, but whether there is more truth in the story than the fact that the founder of one of our most highly respected families was the treasurer of the sect, I know not.

The sect was at the height of its prosperity about 1798, but Dorrell having become addicted to habits of intemperance, his influence with the more respectable portion of his followers began to wane, while he more vigorously proclaimed his possession of superior powers and his immunity from all bodily weaknesses and harm, to the disgust of the better portion of the community, who believed that he was the representative of the evil spirit rather than the good. The final meeting of the sect is described by Thompson, in his gazetteer of Vermont, in the following language: "At length, at one of their meetings, a goodly number having assembled, Dorrell opened with music, and began to deliver a discourse. Among the spectators was one, Capt. Ezekiel Foster, a man of good sense, of a giant frame, having a countenance which bespoke authority. When Dorrell, in the course of his remarks, uttered the words 'No arm of flesh can harm me,' Foster arose, indignant at the blasphemy and boasting of Dorrell, and stretching forth his brawny arm, knocked him down with his fist. Affrighted and almost senseless, Dorrell attempted to rise, when he received a second blow, at which he cried for mercy. Foster promised to forebear on condition that he would renounce his doctrine, yet continued to beat him. A short parley ensued, when Dorrell yielded and renounced his doctrines in the hearing of all his astonished followers." They, ashamed of having been the victims of such duplicity, quickly departed, and it is a remarkable fact that none of them were afterward known to form any connection with any religious society. Dorrell himself was made to promise that his own life should pay the penalty of any future impositions.

In the practices of his religion he claimed the assistance of his black fiddler, Jack, who was, he said, possessed of plenty of both ignorance and cunning. When asked why he had set up a religion of his own, his reply was "To see what fools I can make of people." He admitted himself to be an ignorant old countryman, and that he had led the people [on] a wild goose chase long enough.

Dorrell spent the remainder of his life in Leyden, nearly 50 years, but for many years prior to his death he was maintained as a town charge. He died Aug. 28, 1846, aged 94 years, 5 months, 13 days. He had literally starved himself to death by refusing any food, saying that he had lived long enough, and that if he continued to eat he never should die. He has descendants living in and near the territory which witnessed the scenes brought about by Dorrellism, who are numbered as being among our intelligent, respected citizens.

THE AWFUL DISCLOSURES
OF MARIA MONK
1836[1]

In 1834 a Protestant mob burned down an Ursuline convent in Charlestown, Massachusetts. Cities on the East Coast were just beginning to experience large-scale Catholic immigration, and the Nativist backlash was preoccupied with convents. Nativists believed that secret immoral activities took place within the walls of convents and that the Catholic Church used promises of education to seduce Protestant women into becoming nuns. In Charlestown, the riot was preceded by the story of one Rebecca Reed, an Episcopalian charity scholar at the convent. In 1832 she joined the convent as a novice but left after six months. Reed's story became conflated with newspaper articles alleging that a "mysterious woman" was being held captive inside the convent. On August 11 a group of angry Protestants arrived at the convent and demanded that the mysterious woman be released. The mother superior bid the mob to leave, allegedly warning, "The Bishop has twenty thousand of the vilest Irishmen at his command, and you may read your riot act till your throats are sore, but you'll not quell them."[2] Rioters looted the convent, set it on fire, and even desecrated a tomb where several sisters were interred. Some of the corpses' teeth were reportedly stolen, presumably because they contained gold. In 1835 Reed published her memoir Six Months in a Convent, describing the convent as a prison where anyone who refused to convert to Catholicism was severely punished. It sold two hundred thousand copies in one month.

The following year, a far more salacious account was published about the secret lives of nuns. In The Awful Disclosures of Maria Monk, Maria Monk described her experience *joining the convent of the Hotel Dieu, a Catholic hospital in Montreal, Canada. Monk's initiation involved lying in her own coffin. Afterward, she was instructed that all nuns were to have sex with priests whenever ordered to do so. When such unions resulted in pregnancy, the babies were baptized and then strangled. Lime pits beneath the convent contained the corpses of countless such babies. Nuns who disobeyed were thrown into cells, and frequently bound and gagged as well. Monk witnessed one nun, Saint Frances, who questioned the practice of infanticide and was executed for it by order of the bishop. Nuns were taught that it was their religious duty to lie to the public about all these practices. When Monk became pregnant by a priest, she could not bear the thought of murdering her baby, and so she escaped the Hotel Dieu and made it to New York, where she published her story.* The Awful Disclosures of Maria Monk *sold three hundred thousand copies prior to the Civil War. It was one of the most widely read books in the United States before the publication of* Uncle Tom's Cabin.

Unlike Rebecca Reed, Monk never set foot inside a convent: Her story is a complete hoax, promoted by anti-Catholic groups. Most of what is known about what really happened comes from a lawsuit over the book's copyright. Court records indicate that one Reverend William Hoyt, a prominent anti-Catholic, brought Monk to New York. There, he recruited Reverend J. J. Slocum to write the book. Slocum admitted to writing the text but insisted that his account was dictated by Monk. The book was originally titled The Hotel Dieu Nunnery Unveiled, Illustrating the Character and Conduct of Priests at Montreal. *Stereotype plates of the book were cut, but they were confiscated because of lack of payment. Harper Brothers acquired the plates and copyrighted the book under another name. Hoyt sued, but a judge found for Harper Brothers. The judge invited Monk to sue for damages, adding that he would love for a jury to assess the truth of her story. But Monk and her colleagues sought no further action in court.*[3]

Monk's mother, a Protestant living near Montreal, testified that her daughter had stabbed herself in the head with a slate pencil as a child and that she had acted irrationally ever since. Monk had grown up a "wild child" who was constantly in trouble. She had never been to the Hotel Dieu, but her parents had committed her to the Catholic Magdalen Asylum for "fallen women." But while there, she had apparently gotten pregnant and escaped with her lover. This lover, not a Catholic priest, was the actual father of her child born in New York.

The plot thickened in September 1836, when a second nun appeared in New York and also reported having escaped the Hotel Dieu. This woman claimed to be Saint Frances Patrick (even though in Monk's book this character is murdered and her body dissolved with chemicals). Historian Ray Allen Billington suggests that Saint Frances emerged as a result of jealousy among rival Nativist groups. The cabal that sponsored Maria Monk also backed an Anti-Catholic paper called The American Protestant Vindicator. Their success upset Samuel B. Smith, editor of The Downfall of Babylon: Smith's rival had access to new stories about Monk's abuse, and he did not. So he simply found a fugitive nun of his own and began publishing pamphlets with new tales of abuse in the Hotel Dieu. Monk and Frances were brought together in a public meeting, where they embraced each other and wept.

There were multiple investigations of the Hotel Dieu to see if there was any evidence to support Monk's claims. An investigation by the bishop of Montreal did nothing to dissuade Protestant critics. In October of 1836, a Protestant newspaper editor named William Stone inspected the Hotel Dieu, armed with a copy of Monk's book. Stone even opened jars in the basement and smelled for chemicals that might have been used to dispose of baby corpses. He concluded there was no evidence that Monk "had ever been within the walls of the cloister."[4]

Meanwhile, Monk was cheated out of most of the profits from her story. In 1838 she again gave birth to a fatherless *child.* The American Protestant Vindicator *claimed she had been impregnated through a Jesuit plot to discredit her, but most of her Nativist supporters abandoned her. She was briefly married but then descended into alcoholism and prostitution. In 1849 she was arrested for pickpocketing and died in a New York prison at the age of thirty-three.*

Nineteenth-century Nativist claims about Catholicism as a superstitious tradition that enslaves women became a prototype for hostility toward other religions being imported by immigrants, including Hinduism and Islam. Like the anti-Semitic hoax The Protocols of the Elders of Zion *(1903),* The Awful Disclosures *refuses to die. It is still promoted by anti-Catholic groups today. Troublingly, in the Library of Congress cataloging system, it is listed in the BX 4200s, a designation for books about religious orders of women.*

Many of the themes in The Awful Disclosures *have echoes in accounts of Roman cults and of the Satanic panic of the 1980s. All of these stories involve tales of secret passages and other underground settings where cultists engage in sexual perversions and infanticide.* The Awful Disclosures *is also a classic captivity narrative and the model for many subsequent narratives of women "escaping" dangerous religions.*

For all this, we know that sexual abuse has been an enduring problem in the Catholic Church and in convents. Scholar Karen Hanrahan interviewed former nuns in Ireland for her dissertation. Some ex-nuns used words like "abuse" and "brainwashing" to describe their experiences. One reported being sexually assaulted by a priest when she was a fifteen-year-old nun.[5] On the other hand, historian Philip Jenkins has suggested that sensationalist stories like The Awful Disclosures *ironically contributed to this sort of abuse going undetected for so long.[6] Like Aesop's fable of "the boy who cried wolf," decades of jokes about lecherous Catholic priests may have conditioned the public and the media to take actual reports of abuse less seriously.*

CHAPTER VI

I was introduced into the Superior's room on the evening preceding the day on which I was to take the veil, to have an interview with the Bishop. The Superior was present, and the
interview lasted about half an hour. The Bishop on this, as on
other occasions, appeared to be habitually rough in his manner. His address was by no means prepossessing.

Before I took the veil, I was ornamented for the ceremony,
and was clothed in a dress belonging to the convent, which was
used on such occasions; and placed not far from the altar in
the chapel in the view of a number of spectators who had assembled, in number perhaps about forty. Taking the veil is an
affair which occurs so frequently in Montreal, that it has long
ceased to be regarded as a novelty; and although notice had
been given in the French parish church as usual, only a small
audience assembled, as I have mentioned.

Being well prepared with a long training and frequent rehearsals for what I was to perform, I stood waiting in my large
flowing dress for the appearance of the Bishop. He soon presented himself, entering by a door behind the altar; I then
threw myself at his feet, and asked him to confer upon me the
veil. He expressed his consent; and then turning to the Superior, I threw myself prostrate at her feet, according to my instructions, repeating what I had before done at rehearsals, and
made a movement as if to kiss her feet. This she prevented, or
appeared to prevent, catching me by a sudden motion of her
hand, and granted my request. I then kneeled before the Holy
Sacrament, that is, a large round wafer held by the Bishop between his forefinger and thumb, and made my vows.

This wafer I had been taught to regard with the utmost veneration as the real body of Jesus Christ, the presence of which
made the vows that were uttered before it binding in the most
solemn manner. After taking the vows I proceeded to a small
apartment behind the altar, accompanied by four nuns, where
there was a coffin prepared with my nun's name engraved
upon it:

"SAINT EUSTACE."

My companions lifted it by four handles attached to it, while I threw off my dress and put on that of a nun of Soeur Bourgeoise; and then we all returned to the chapel. I proceeded first, and was followed by four nuns, the Bishop naming a number of worldly pleasures in rapid succession, in reply to which I as rapidly repeated, "*Je renounce, je renounce, je renounce*—I renounce, I renounce, I renounce."

The coffin was then placed in front of the altar, and I advanced to place myself in it. This coffin was to be deposited, after the ceremony, in an outhouse, to be preserved until my death, when it was to receive my corpse. There were reflections which I naturally made at that time, but I stepped in, extended myself, and lay still. A pillow had been placed at the head of the coffin to support my head in a comfortable position. A large thick black cloth was then spread over me, and the chanting of Latin hymns immediately commenced. My thoughts were not the most pleasing during the time I lay in that situation. The pall, or *Drap Mortel*, as the cloth is called, had a strong smell of incense, which was always disagreeable to me, and then proved almost suffocating. I recollected the story of the novice, who, in taking the veil, lay down in her coffin like me and was covered in the same manner, but on the removal of the covering was found dead.

When I was uncovered, I rose, stepped out of my coffin and kneeled. Other ceremonies then followed of no particular interest; after which the music commenced, and here the whole was finished. I then proceeded from the chapel, and returned to the Superior's room, followed by the other nuns, who walked two by two, in their customary manner, with their hands folded on their breasts and their eyes cast down upon the floor. The nun who was to be my companion in future then walked at the end of the procession. On reaching the Superior's door they all left me, and I entered alone, and found her with the Bishop and two priests.

The Superior now informed me that having taken the black veil, it only remained that I should swear the three oaths customary on becoming a nun; and that some explanation would be necessary from her. I was now, she told me, to have access to every part of the edifice, even to the cellar, where two of the sisters were imprisoned for causes which she did not mention. I must be informed that one of my great duties was to obey the priests in all things; and this I soon learned, to my utter astonishment and horror, was to live in the practice of criminal intercourse with them. I expressed some of the feelings which this announcement excited in me, which came upon me like a flash of lightning; but the only effect was to set her arguing with me, in favor of the crime, representing it as a virtue acceptable to God and honorable to me. The priests, she said, were not situated like other men, being forbidden to marry; while they lived secluded, laborious, and self-denying lives for our salvation. They might, indeed, be considered our saviors, as without their service we could not obtain pardon of sin, and must go to hell. Now, it was our solemn duty, on withdrawing from the world, to consecrate our lives to religion, to practice every species of self-denial. We could not be too humble, nor mortify our feelings too far; this was to be done by opposing them and acting contrary to them; and what she proposed was, therefore, pleasing in the sight of God. I now felt how foolish I had been to place myself in the power of such persons as were around me.

From what she said, I could draw no other conclusions but that I was required to act like the most abandoned of beings, and that all my future associates were habitually guilty of the most heinous and detestable crimes. When I repeated my expressions of surprise and horror, she told me that such feelings were very common at first, and that many other nuns had expressed themselves as I did, who had long since changed their minds. She even said that on her entrance into the nunnery she had felt like me.

Doubts, she declared, were among our greatest enemies. They would lead us to question every point of duty and induce us to waver at every step. They arose only from remaining imperfections, and were always evidences of sin. Our only way was to dismiss them immediately, repent, and confess them.

Priests, she insisted, could not sin. It was a thing impossible. Everything that they did and wished was of course right. She hoped I would see the reasonableness and duty of the oaths I was then to take, and be faithful to them.

She gave me another piece of information which excited other feelings in me scarcely less dreadful. Infants were sometimes born in the convent, but they were always baptized and immediately strangled. This secured their everlasting happiness; for the baptism purifies them from all sinfulness, and being sent out of the world before they had time to do anything wrong, they were at once admitted into heaven. "How happy," she exclaimed, "are those who secure immortal happiness to such little beings! Their souls would thank those who kill their bodies if they had it in their power."

Into what a place and among what society had I been admitted! How different did a convent now appear from what I had supposed it to be! The holy women I had always fancied the nuns to be, the venerable Lady Superior, what are they? And the priests of the seminary adjoining (some of whom, indeed, I had reason to think were base and profligate men), what were they all? I now learned that they were often admitted into the nunnery and allowed to indulge in the greatest crimes, which they and others call virtues.

After having listened for some time to the Superior alone, a number of the nuns were admitted and took a free part in the conversation. They concurred in everything which she told me, and repeated, without any signs of shame or compunction, things which criminated themselves. I must acknowledge the truth, and declare that all this had an effect upon my mind. I questioned whether I might not be in the wrong, and felt as if their reasoning might have some just foundation. I had been several years under the tuition of Catholics, and was unaccustomed to the society, example, and conversation of Protestants; but had been taught, both by precept and example, to receive as truth everything said by the priests. I had not heard their authority questioned, nor anything said of any other standard of faith but their declarations. I had long been familiar with the corrupt and licentious expressions which some of them use at confessions, and believed that other women were also. I had no standard of duty to refer to and no judgment of my own which I knew how to use or thought of using.

All around me insisted that my doubts proved only my own ignorance and sinfulness; that they knew by experience that they would soon give place to true knowledge and an advance in religion; and I felt something like indecision.

Nothing important occurred till late in the afternoon, when, as I was sitting in the community-room, Father Dufresne called me out, saying he wished to speak with me. I feared what was his intention, but I dared not disobey. In a private apartment he treated me in a brutal manner, and from two other priests I afterward received similar usage that evening. Father Dufresne afterward appeared again; and I was compelled to remain in company with him until morning.

I am assured that the conduct of priests in our convent had never been exposed, and it is not imagined by the people of the United States. This induces me to say what I do, notwithstanding the strong reasons I have to let it remain unknown. Still, I cannot force myself to speak on such subjects except in the most brief manner.

CHAPTER XI

But I must now come to one deed in which I had some part, and which I look back upon with greater horror and pain than any occurrences in the convent, in which I was not the principal sufferer. It is not necessary for me to attempt to excuse myself in this or any other case. Those who have any disposition to judge fairly will exercise their own judgment in making allowances for me, under the fear and force, the command and examples before me. I, therefore, shall confine myself, as usual, to the simple narration of facts. The time was about five months after I took the veil, the weather was cool, perhaps in September or October. One day the Superior sent for me and several other nuns, to receive her commands at a particular room. We found the Bishop and some priests with her; and speaking in an unusual tone of fierceness and authority, she said, "Go to the room for the Examination of Conscience; and drag St. Frances up stairs." Nothing more was necessary than this unusual command, with the tone and manner which accompanied it, to excite in me the most gloomy anticipations. It did not strike me as strange that St. Frances should be in the room to which the Superior directed us. It was an apartment to which we were often sent to prepare for the communion, and to which we voluntarily went, whenever we felt the compunctions which our ignorance of duty, and the misinstructions we received, inclined us to seek relief from self-reproach. Indeed I had seen her there a little before. What terrified me was, first, the Superior's angry manner; second, the expression she used, being a French term, whose peculiar use I had learnt in the convent, and whose meaning is rather softened when translated into "drag";[7] third, the place to which we were directed to take the interesting young nun, and the persons assembled there, as I supposed to condemn her. My fears were such concerning the fate that awaited her, and my horror at the idea that she was in some way to be sacrificed, that I would have given anything to be allowed to stay where I was. But I feared the consequences of disobeying the Superior, and proceeded with the rest toward the room for the examination of conscience.

The room to which we were to proceed from that was in the second story, and the place of many a scene of a shameful nature. It is sufficient to say, after what I have said in other parts of this book, that things had there occurred which made me regard the place with the greatest disgust. Saint Frances had appeared melancholy for some time. I well knew that she had cause, for she had been repeatedly subject to trials which I need not name—our common lot. When we reached the room where we had been bidden to seek her, I entered the door, my companions standing behind me, as the place was so small as hardly to hold five persons in a line. The young nun was standing alone near the middle of the room; she was probably about twenty, with light hair, blue eyes, and a very fair complexion. I spoke to her in a compassionate voice, but at the same time with such a decided manner, that she comprehended my meaning.

"Saint Frances, we are sent for you."

Several others spoke kindly to her, but two addressed her very harshly. The poor creature turned round with a look of meekness, and without expressing any unwillingness or fear, without even speaking a word, resigned herself to our hands. The tears came into my eyes. I had not a moment's doubt that she considered her fate as sealed, and was already beyond the fear of death. She was conducted, or rather hurried to the staircase, which was near by, and then seized by her limbs and clothes and in fact almost dragged up stairs, in the sense the Superior had intended. I laid my own hands upon her—I took hold of her, too, more gently indeed than some of the rest; yet I encouraged and assisted them in carrying her. I could not avoid it. My refusal would not have saved her, nor prevented her from being carried up; it would only have exposed me to some severe punishment, as I believe some of my companions would have seized the first opportunity to complain of me.

All the way up the staircase, Saint Frances spoke not a word nor made the slightest resistance. When we entered, with her, the room to which she was ordered, my heart sank within me. The Bishop, the Lady Superior, and five priests, namely, Bonin, Richards, Savage, and two others, I now ascertained, were assembled for trial, on some charge of great importance.

When we had brought our prisoner before them, Father Richards began to question her, and she made ready but calm replies. I cannot pretend to give a connected account of what ensued; my feelings were wrought up to such a pitch that I knew not what I did, or what to do. I was under a terrible apprehension that if I betrayed the feelings which overcame me I should fall under the displeasure of the cold-blooded persecutors of my poor innocent sister; and this fear on the one hand, with the distress I felt for her on the other, rendered me almost frantic. As soon as I entered the room, I had stepped into a corner on the left of the entrance, where I might partially support myself by leaning against the wall between the door and the window. This support was all that prevented me from falling to the floor, for the confusion of my thoughts was so great that only a few of the words I heard spoken on either side made any lasting impression upon me. I felt as if struck by some insupportable blow; and death would not have been more frightful to me. I am inclined to think that Father Richards wished to shield the poor prisoner from the severity of her fate, by drawing from her expressions that might bear a favorable construction. He asked her, among other things, if she was not sorry for what she had been overheard to say (for she had been betrayed by one of the nuns), and if she would not prefer confinement in the cells to the punishment which was threatened. But the Bishop soon interrupted him, and it was easy to perceive that he considered her fate as sealed, and was determined she should not escape. In reply to some of the questions put to her, she was silent; to others I heard her voice reply that she did not repent of words she had uttered, though they had been reported by some of the nuns who had heard them; that she had firmly resolved to resist every attempt to compel her to the commission of crimes which she detested. She added that she would rather die than cause the murder of harmless babes.

"That is enough; finish her!" said the Bishop.

Two nuns instantly fell upon the woman, and in obedience to directions given by the Superior, prepared to execute her sentence. She still maintained all the calmness and submission of a lamb. Some of those who took part in this transaction, I believe, were as unwilling as myself; but of others I can safely say, I believe they delighted in it. Their conduct certainly exhibited a most blood-thirsty spirit. But above all others present, and above all human fiends I ever saw, I think Saint Hypolite was the most diabolical; she engaged in the horrid task with all alacrity, and assumed from choice the most revolting parts to be performed. She seized a gag, forced it into the mouth of the poor nun, and when it was fixed between her extended jaws, so as to keep them open at their greatest possible distance, took hold of the straps fastened at each end of the stick, crossed them behind the helpless head of the victim, and drew them tight through the loop prepared as a fastening.

The bed, which had always stood in one part of the room, still remained there; though the screen, which had usually been placed before it, and was made of thick muslin, with only a crevice through which a person might look out, had been folded up on its hinges in the form of a W., and placed in a corner. On the bed the prisoner was laid with her face upward, and then bound with cords so that she could not move. In an instant, another bed was thrown upon her. One of the priests, named Bonin, sprang like a fury first upon it, with all his force. He was speedily followed by the nuns, until there were as many upon the bed as could find room, and all did what they could, not only to smother, but to bruise her. Some stood up and jumped upon the poor girl with their feet, some with their knees: and others, in different ways, seemed to seek how they might best beat the breath out of her body and mangle it without coming in direct contact with it or seeing the effects of their violence. During this time my feelings were almost too strong to be endured. I felt stupefied, and was scarcely conscious of what I did. Still, fear for myself remained in a sufficient degree to induce me to some exertion; and I attempted to talk to those who stood next, partly that I might have an excuse for turning away from the dreadful scene.

After the lapse of fifteen or twenty minutes, and when it was presumed that the sufferer had been smothered and crushed to death, Father Bonin and the nuns ceased to trample upon her, and stepped from the bed. All was motionless and silent beneath it.

They then began to laugh at such inhuman thoughts as occurred to some of them, rallying each other in the most unfeeling manner, and ridiculing me for feelings which I in vain endeavored to conceal. They alluded to the resignation of our murdered companion; and one of them laughingly said, "She would have made a good Catholic martyr." After spending some moments in such conversation, one of them asked if the corpse should be removed. The Superior said it had better remain a little while. After waiting a short time longer, the feather-bed was taken off, the cords unloosed, and the body taken by the nuns and dragged down stairs. I was informed that it was taken into the cellar and thrown unceremoniously into the hole which I have already described, covered with a great quantity of lime, and afterward sprinkled with a liquid, of the properties and name of which I am ignorant. This liquid I have seen poured into the hole from large bottles, after the necks were broken off; and have heard that it is used in France to prevent the effluvia rising from cemeteries.

I did not soon recover from the shock caused by this scene; indeed, it still recurs to me with most gloomy impressions. The next day there was a melancholy aspect over everything, and recreation time passed in the dullest manner; scarcely anything was said above a whisper. I never heard much said afterward about Saint Frances.

I spoke with one of the nuns a few words one day, but we were all cautioned not to expose ourselves very far, and could not place much reliance in each other. The murdered nun had been brought to her shocking end through the treachery of one of our number in whom she confided. I never knew with certainty who had reported her remarks to the Superior, but suspicion fastened on one, and I never could regard her but with detestation.

I was more inclined to blame her than some of those employed in the execution; for there could have been no necessity for the betrayal of her feelings. We all knew how to avoid exposing each other.

I was often sent by the Superior to overhear what was said by novices and nuns, when they seemed to shun her; she would say, "Go and listen, they are speaking English"; and though I obeyed her, I never informed her against them. If I wished to clear my conscience, I would go to a priest and confess, knowing that he dared not communicate what I said to any person, and that he would not choose as heavy penances as the Superior.

We were always at liberty to choose another confessor when we had any sin to confess, which we were unwilling to tell one to whom we should otherwise have done.

Not long after the murder just related, a young woman came to the nunnery and asked for permission to see St. Frances. It was my former friend, with whom I had been an assistant teacher, Miss Louisa Bousquet, of St. Denis. From this, I supposed the murdered nun might have come from that town or its vicinity. The only answer was that St. Frances was dead.

Some time afterward some of St. Frances' friends called to inquire after her, and they were told that she had died a glorious death; and further told that she made some heavenly expressions, which were repeated in order to satisfy her friends.

"THE PATHOLOGY AND TREATMENT OF MEDIOMANIA"

1874[1]

Little is known about Frederic Rowland Marvin, the author of this lecture. He came from Portland, Oregon, and in 1874 he held the title of "professor of psychological medicine and medical jurisprudence" at the New York Free Medical College for Women. We have a collection of his sermons and essays on such topics as Christian compassion for animals and the importance given to women in the Bible. Several of his books are dedicated to his wife. However, his attitude toward women in "The Pathology and Treatment of Mediomania" is undeniably misogynistic.

Marvin is responding to Spiritualism, a religious movement that holds that certain people have the power to operate as "mediums" who can communicate with the dead. Although Spiritualism has several important precursors, its starting point is generally said to be in 1845, when two girls named Kate and Margaret Fox of Hydesdale, New York, reported that they had made contact with a spirit. The spirit appeared to give audible "raps" whenever the girls asked it questions, drawing the attention of scientists and the curious. The Fox sisters became celebrities, and soon many people—most of them women—also claimed to be mediums. In 1888 Margaret Fox confessed that the rapping had been a hoax but later recanted this confession. Interest in Spiritualism grew exponentially in the wake of the Civil War, and by 1897 there were as many as eight million Spiritualists in the United States and Europe.

Those interested in Spiritualism were often drawn to

*other alternative beliefs and lifestyles as well, including ab-
olition, temperance, prison reform, vegetarianism, socialism, and free love. Part of the appeal of Spiritualism was
that it appeared to be empirical and scientific. Spiritualists
often spoke in terms of electricity and magnetism. Gender
essentialism was also part of Spiritualist thought: Circles
holding séances would often sit with men and women al-
ternating, to balance their magnetic energies.*

*Sociologists have noted that established religious organi-
zations tend to exclude women from leadership: Either
female leadership is officially forbidden or women are mysteriously absent from higher leadership positions (a phenomenon sometimes called "the stained-glass ceiling").
But female leadership is relatively common in new religious
movements. Often this takes the form of "charismatic"
leadership. That is, female leaders in new religious movements have authority not because they have assumed some
respected office but because they are thought to have some
extraordinary ability. Female mediums in Spiritualist groups
are a prime example of charismatic leadership.*

*For Dr. Marvin, belief in mediums and having an expe-
rience of communicating with the dead are not religious
phenomena at all but rather a disease of the mind that he
dubs "mediomania." Furthermore, female mediums are
not extraordinary or charismatic; they are sick. Although
he concedes that men can suffer from mediomania, in his
diagnosis it is usually the result of a misaligned uterus. In
fact, Marvin diagnoses female participation in many of the
movements that emerged during the Second Great Awakening (Mormonism, Mesmerism, Fourierism, and Socialism) as evidence of "utromania."*

*Reading this lecture, one wonders about Dr. Marvin's
own mental health. He confesses to playing a cruel trick on
a patient grieving her dead child. He then describes infil-
trating a Spiritualist group discussing the "Harmonial Philosophy" for the purpose of diagnosing its female members
as mentally ill. (In the contemporary study of new religious*

movements, such tactics are called "covert research." Covert research is generally regarded as unethical, but it is also a flawed method of gathering data because the researcher's deceptive behavior tends to affect the behavior of the group.) After mocking a woman from the Harmonial Society, Dr. Marvin states that were he allowed to treat her insanity, his therapy might include administering strychnine and electrical shocks.

Dr. Marvin's views seem absurd today, but his theory of mediomania is part of a much larger pattern of discourse that sociologists call "the medicalization of deviance." Throughout modern history, there has been an impulse to diagnose anyone participating in alternative lifestyles or religions as mentally ill. The best-known example of the medicalization of deviance is the listing for homosexuality as a mental illness in the Diagnostic and Statistical Manual of Mental Disorders. *This listing remained until 1973, when homosexuality was no longer interpreted as a form of madness. During the "cult wars" of the 1970s, the medicalization of deviant religion returned. Instead of claiming that followers of alternative religions were suffering from tilted wombs, it was now claimed that cults act as an "information disease" that spreads through brainwashing. As in Dr. Marvin's day, this medicalizing discourse was an effective way of silencing anyone participating in alternative lifestyles. After all, what is the point of debating metaphysics or values with someone who is merely experiencing a bout of mental illness?*

Mediomania has its own peculiar phenomena, and the best way of bringing them before you is by reciting a case, with the history of which I am familiar:

Mrs. W., aged 23, of nervous temperament, and delicate habit, was seized with a sharp pain over the axis of the lumbar vertebra. This pain was repeated at irregular intervals and followed by syncope. The syncope alternated with a state of nervous exaltation known as ecstasis. During the ecstasis she was, to use her own words, "entranced with joy." The ecstasis would last from a few minutes to many hours. When I first saw the patient she was recovering from a prolonged attack of ecstasis and was suffering profound exhaustion. Her pulse was rapid, feeble, and irregular; her limbs were cold; pupils dilated; cheeks flushed; lips dry; tongue heavily coated and bordered with a broad red line running from base to apex and sharply defined; and the respiration was rapid, shallow and sighing. To such questions as I asked her she returned evasive answers and seemed to be endeavoring to conceal her thoughts and emotions. I saw her the second time while she was entranced and remained with her until she recovered normal consciousness. About this time visions were presented to her of which she spoke with great reserve. Her husband told me she had spoken to him of a communication which she had received from their dead child. Desiring to discover the patient's intellectual condition, I held with her a long and somewhat enthusiastic conversation concerning the immortality of the soul. At first I received nothing but a general consent to the doctrine, but suddenly, and without preparing her mind for the declaration, I confessed to her not only a belief in the doctrine of personal immortality, but possession of convincing proof of a life to come; I declared myself able to see a spirit child, and, having previously examined the husband on the subject and inspected the family photographs, I accurately described the little spirit of her child. This was more than she could endure. Turning her keen, luminous eyes toward the window, she said in a hoarse whisper, "It is my little Harry! where do you see him?" Following the direction of her eyes I took the hint and promptly replied, "In front of the window." Before the conversation ended the patient confessed that she was in daily communication with the spirit of her child and that her whole life was spent in the alternate excitement and depression which accompanied these spiritual communications. She was afflicted with obstinate amenorrhea, and physical examination revealed retroversion of the uterus. The case passed at my request into the hands of an obstetrician with whom I visited the patient. During the treatment of this case I had an opportunity of witnessing many of the most wonderful phenomena of Spiritualism.

A neurosis in no way essentially different from hysteria is what is known as utromania. Utromania frequently results in mediomania; indeed, at the present day the two are seldom entirely dissociated. Many women undergo perceptible mental disturbance at every menstrual epoch. The dangers of puberty are greater to girls than to boys, and more girls between the ages of twelve and eighteen become insane than boys. I dread to treat no form of insanity more than utromania, for of all derangements it is the most violent and persistent, and yet it is a very common disorder. The angle at which the womb is suspended in the pelvis frequently settles the whole question of sanity or insanity. Tilt the organ a little forward—introvert it, and immediately the patient forsakes her home, embraces some strange and ultra ism—Mormonism, Mesmerism, Fourierism, Socialism, oftener Spiritualism. She becomes possessed by the idea that she has some startling mission in the world. She forsakes her home, her children, and her duty, to mount the rostrum and proclaim the peculiar virtues of free-love, elective affinity, or the reincarnation of souls. Allow the disorder to advance and it becomes a chronic malady, and, alas! the once intelligent, cultivated, and pure woman sinks through a series of strange isms and remarkable affinities until she reaches the despicable level of the *demi monde*.

Utromaniacs imbibe very strange notions, and, what is remarkable, they reflect the spirit of the age with great accuracy. In the classic ages of Greece and Rome they were sibyls, priestesses, and vestal virgins; in the darker days of the Middle Ages they were witches, saints, and worshippers at sacred shrines; and in these times they are what the age makes them. They drift with neither rudder nor compass on the tide of human affairs, the sport of every wind that blows. They usually conceive the idea that they are reformers, though themselves wo[e]fully in need of reformation. They adopt strange modes of dress, and conduct themselves in so eccentric a manner as to attract attention. They entertain bitter and unnatural dislike for everything which has helped to make their lives happy, useful and pure. They trample upon the sacredness of their marriage relations and despise their religious obligations. They regard their husbands as tyrants bent on their enslavement, and they are likely to forsake their homes for positions of public trust for which they are unfitted.

Every one is acquainted with utromaniacs, for this is the age of utromania. They assemble in strange and eccentric meetings, which they advertise with sad audacity in every daily print.

It was my fortune to attend one of these singular meetings under the most favorable circumstances. In a dark, dingy room, with still more dingy furniture, in a narrow street, in a city many miles from this, I attended a meeting of these strange and pitiful creatures. The meeting was called for the purpose of discussing what they termed a "Harmonial Philosophy." Around a long and somewhat dilapidated table sat eight or ten of these unfortunate beings, with here and there a male enthusiast to keep them company. At the head of the table sat a lank, tall, angular woman whose ashy countenance made the scene, if possible, even more dismal. There was spread before her a map, which she said was a map of celestial circles, and on which she eagerly gazed. I requested a seat by her side. After several minutes of silence, raps on the table informed the party that I was not in "harmonic condition," and must endeavor to become "psycho-passive." After a little maneuvering and a great deal of diplomacy, I came to occupy a seat on the left of this woman—she would not permit me to sit upon her right. The poor woman was evidently suffering from some displacement of the womb and aggravated hysteria resulting therefrom— she had all the usual symptoms, not excepting the nervous twitches and tremors, *globus hystericus*, and sighing respiration. We were all requested to join hands, when I took the opportunity to examine the woman's pulse without her understanding the operation. The pulse was short, quick, nervous, and irregular. I could not time it without exciting suspicion. The skin was dry and cold and the secretions were suppressed. I afterward gathered from her conversation that she was a sufferer from constipation and sub-acute gastric symptoms. Being weary of examining the woman by strategy, I asked the bold question, What is the Harmonial Philosophy? The following paragraph in my note book is from her very lucid reply:

> The Harmonial Philosophy, which is our religion, is this: The grand ultimate of all thought to bring all to a higher ultimate; or, in simpler words, to establish static states of psychic condition on this mundane plane which shall correspond with the highest manifestations of conscious intelligence in the sphere of disembodied thought—that is, to make a spiritual way from the psychic terrestrial to the psychic plane of the celestial; hence we are all brothers and sisters, and hold all things in common, and are as the angels in heaven, pure.

Here you have the incoherence of ordinary insanity united with the peculiarly bombastic style which characterizes the average lunatic.

But how shall we treat such patients? I did not have an opportunity of practicing upon the weird sister whose communications I have presented; but had I been called to do so, I should have satisfied myself as to the condition of the pelvic organs and should have shaped my treatment accordingly. I should have endeavored to tone up the system with such tonics as strychnine, iron and quinine in connection with a liberal diet. I might have resorted to electricity, but as the patient entertained singular notions with regard to the electric current, perhaps the exhibition of a battery would have been injurious. I should have looked to the patient's habits, which I fear were not very moral. I should have recommended a moderate amount of exercise and should have secured to the patient plenty of refreshing sleep. I should also have removed her associates and given her healthier surroundings, and I should have recommended but one husband, for I am informed she had three.

A VAMPIRE CULT IN KANSAS CITY

1890[1]

On January 27, 1890, a story appeared in newspapers from New York to Honolulu describing a strange new sect in rural Missouri called the Samaritans. They drank human blood. Their founder, one Silas Wilcox, taught that blood could heal most diseases and that willingly giving one's blood to heal others was an act of Christian charity. One Samaritan suffering from tuberculosis began feeding extensively on his children, prompting a neighbor to report the matter to the police.

The story of Wilcox and his blood-drinking Samaritans was even referenced in The New York Times in an article on November 30, 1890, about the proliferation of "false Christs." But there is no evidence to corroborate this story. It appears to be an example of the "yellow journalism" that became common in the 1890s, especially as New York newspapers competed for readers. The story describes cultists drinking cow blood in slaughterhouses and was likely set in Kansas City, because in 1890 the city hosted numerous stockyards and was famous for its steak.

But even if a church of "human vampires" never existed near Kansas City, this episode still says a lot about our fascination with and horror of cults. This was a story that editors across the country knew that people wanted to read. Even when dealing with actual new religious movements (NRMs), editors are sorely tempted to serve up the salacious, Manichaean narratives that their readers want. Mark Silk, an editor for Religion News Service, once stated that "if the media sacrifice NRMs 'on the altar of competitive journalism,' it is because the reality they construct fits popular prejudices."[2] As in most tales of cult atrocities, the

story was driven by the description of innocent children
who had to be rescued from the abuses of an evil religion.
The article also suggests that the law was inadequate to
deal with evil cults: "Chief Speers is anxious to put a stop
to the vile practices, but it appears there is no law which
covers the case and nothing can be done except to protect
the children from the habit." In this, the article frames free-
dom of religion as a social problem that allows evil groups
to evade the law. This is a claim that resurfaced during the
"cult wars" of the 1970s and continues to be made today.
In this way, a dubious account of a vampire cult is part of
a serious conversation about the nature of religious toler-
ance within the American experiment.

The article below is the most detailed version of the story.
Spelling and grammatical errors have not been changed.
Some of these appear to be editorial oversights, while others
appear to be meant as a parody of the writing of unedu-
cated, rural Americans.

MANY HUMAN VAMPIRES.

They Call Themselves Samaritans and Advocate the Drinking of the Life Blood of One Another.

KANSAS CITY, JANUARY 27.—For some time rumors of a
new religious sect, which has found birth in the territory
adjacent to the Blue river, just east of this city, have been
afloat and have reached the ears of the place who have been
asked for humanity's sake to interfere with the rituals. The
matter was referred to the humane officers who gave the reports no credence as they were to horrible too believe.

According to these reports the rituals were founded upon
the scriptural injunction to do good to the sick. This injunction has been followed to the extent that the sect has degen-
erated into a band of human blood-drinkers. Those who are
well allowing themselves to be bled for those who are ill.

The district in which these horrible rites are practiced is
within the new city limits and the chief of police sent Human

Officer Marran to investigate the case which was reported in the following letter received by Human Secretary Huckett:

"Mr. Huckett: There is somethin I think about to be called to your attenshun at once which I think is bad for a civilized community. their is John Wrinkle and his 2 children He has been sick and he is crazy on religion. his little girl Minnie is 13 years old and his boy John is 11. Wrinkle has hearn that people drink blod at the sloughter houses for their health an he said he believed in the bible that it preached that the well should make sacrifises for the sick.

"He did blead his little boy and girl until they are recks and he did drink the blod. It has leaked out an unless somethin is done by you the neighbors will take the matter in their own hand and that quick too He lives in a little piece of land near the new city limits. yours respectfully George West.

"p.s. Send som officers."

Officer Marran's investigation o the matter proved that the letter to Secretary Huckett had not told half of the horrible practices in vogue among the people who believed in the savage rites. About a year ago there appeared among the people of that neighborhood a man named Silas Wilcox, who went about the country preaching the doctrine of doing good for the sick. It was not long until he had a sufficient number of adherents to his theories to warrant him in founding a sect which he called the "Samaritans." Gradually he widened his teachings to his little band, until he openly advocated the drinking of blood for all diseases, giving as authority for such action the fact that the bible taught that blood was the life. Almost daily pilgrimages were made to the packing houses by those who were along, and there they drank the blood of the freshly killed beeves.

It appears, however, that Wilcox was not satisfied with the blood of these animals, and he soon advanced the doctrine that it was well to show belief in the teachings of the good book by giving up human blood for the sick and suffering members of the band. This idea was gradually established, the human vampire being the first to profit from the horrible practice. Wilcox apparently became very sick and was unable to make the pilgrimage to the packing house. He called upon the faithful members of the band to volunteer to save his life. A woman named Nancy Dixon was the first to show her belief in the doctrine and she bared her arm for the extraction of the life-giving fluid. Wilcox sucked the blood from her arm and the effect was marvelous, for he recovered from his illness the same day. This visible manifestation of the truth of the doctrine made a great impression on the members of the band and the result has been that from that day the habit or practice has increased and is now a regular practice among the sect of Samaritans.

At the home of John Wrinkle, mentioned in the letter, were found two emaciated children as the letter had said. On the bed lay Wrinkle, who was apparently in the last stages of consumption. When questioned about drinking the blood of the children he strenuously denied having done so, and the children also said that such had not been done. Their bloodless appearance, however, excited the suspicion of the officer, and he complied them to show their arms. These members were in terrible condition, being covered with scars around the inside elbow joint, showing plainly the effects of the bleeding. When confronted with this evidence of the truth of the accusation, Wrinkle acknowledged that he had availed himself of the opportunity and the children had willingly given their blood to restore him to health. The man was in such a condition that he could not be moved, but the children were taken from the house and placed in the children's home. Chief Speers is anxious to put a stop to the vile practices, but it appears there is no law which covers the case and nothing can be done except to protect the children from the habit.

An investigation into the rites of the sect shows the following facts: The band of Samaritans numbers about twenty and hold regular weekly meetings at the houses of different members. At these meetings the sick or ailing members ask for assistance from the well ones, and these are detailed to give their blood according to their condition of health and strength. When a member becomes very sick the well ones take turns in supplying him with the life-giving fluid. They claim that they have as much right to do this when the blood is a voluntary contribution as the physicians have to transfuse blood from one person to another.

CYRUS R. TEED, THE ELECTRO-ALCHEMICAL MESSIAH

1839–1908

Cyrus Reed Teed is one of the most unusual founders of a religious movement in US history. After serving in the Union Army, he attended the Eclectic Medical College in New York. The college trained physicians in what today would be considered "alternative medicine." By 1869, Teed had established an "electro-alchemical laboratory" in Utica, New York. During his experiments there, he experienced a vision in which he learned that he was the son of God, sent to redeem mankind. In 1892 he took the name "Koresh," the Hebrew name for the Persian emperor Cyrus the Great. Cyrus the Great conquered Babylon, ending the period of the Babylonian Exile for the Israelites. Isaiah 45:1 refers to Koresh as God's messiah ("anointed one"). Teed worked as a physician and tried to convert his patients, often unsuccessfully. He traveled to Chicago, where he met a woman named Annie G. Ordway. Teed renamed her Victoria Gratia and regarded her as his divine female counterpart.

By 1886, Teed had a significant following called the Koreshans. He experimented with creating communes for his followers in New York, Chicago, and San Francisco before he established a commune in Estero, Florida, in 1903. This community grew to two hundred members, with businesses, a schoolhouse, and even a small zoo. When Teed died in 1908, his followers watched over his body for five days to see whether he would be resurrected. After his death, the colony went into a long decline. In 1961 the remaining followers donated more than three hundred acres to the state of Florida to create a park. In 1991 the remain-

ing land and funds of the Koreshans were used to create the College of Life foundation, a nonprofit dedicated to historic preservation.

Founders of new religious movements are often masters of religious bricolage. That is, they are adept at taking elements of existing beliefs, philosophies, and rituals and creatively combining them to make something new. Teed was no exception, and his teachings were a mix of biblical prophecy, reincarnation, and other ideas from Asian religions, Egyptian mythology, socialism, and an appeal to the authority of science.

Teed's strangest idea was that the Earth is a hollow globe: We do not live on the surface of a spherical planet orbiting the sun; instead, we live on the concave surface of a hollow sphere with the sun at the center. Gravity does not pull us toward the Earth: The sun emits beams of "gravic force" that push us toward the edge of the hollow sphere. The Earth's crust extends for one hundred miles, and beyond this is nothingness. In 1897 Teed's followers conducted an experiment called a "geodetic survey" that they believed "proved" this theory correct. On the beach at Naples, Florida, they erected miles of specially designed stakes in the ground. Teed called this apparatus a "Rectilineator." By moving the stakes down the beach for miles over a period of months and taking careful measurements, the Koreshans concluded that the Earth's surface had indeed curved upward 128 inches from their starting point.

Teed also had curious ideas about gender and celibacy. He described God as "biune," having both male and female aspects. Knowledge of God's female aspect had been lost to Christianity and was only hinted at in Pagan mythology. Being made in God's image, Adam was also hermaphroditic prior to the Fall. Teed taught that marriage was a form of slavery and that sexuality only produced more flawed, gendered humans. He instructed his followers to be celibate and to redirect their sexual impulses toward him. Overcoming sexual urges in this way would eventually trigger a transformation into an immortal biune being or a

"Son of God." This vision of achieving immortality through celibacy anticipated the teachings of the Heaven's Gate group a century later. That group also hoped that through celibacy they would ascend to the "Level Above Human," where they would have new, genderless bodies.

Another curious facet of Teed's legacy is that his teachings may have influenced Branch Davidian leader David Koresh (1959–1993), né Vernon Howell. In addition to taking the name Koresh, both men identified themselves as the "Rider on the White Horse," as described in Revelation 6:2, and as "sinful messiahs." Bible scholar J. Phillip Arnold, who attempted to intervene in the negotiations between David Koresh and the FBI in Waco, Texas, in 1993, notes fifteen such similarities between the teachings of the two men. The Waco public library had a copy of Teed's teachings called Koreshanity, The New Age Religion. Someone checked this book out in the 1980s and marked it up, but we do not know who. On April 10, 1993, an FBI negotiator called the Branch Davidians and asked if they were aware of Cyrus Teed or if David Koresh appeared to be plagiarizing his teachings. Koresh claimed he had never heard of Teed and asked the FBI to send him a copy of the book. Arnold suggests that Koresh may have been telling the truth but had absorbed Teed's teachings secondhand from someone else. One likely suspect for this transmission is Lois Roden (1916–1986), who led the Branch Davidian community prior to Howell's arrival. Roden had received a vision from an angel declaring that the Holy Spirit is feminine, so Teed's ideas may have interested her. Could she have checked out Koreshanity from the library and passed its ideas on to Howell?

Whatever the connection between Teed and Koresh, Arnold concludes that the FBI passed up an opportunity to end the 1993 standoff peacefully:

> All the FBI agents had to do was to carry through on their offer to send in the book Koreshanity. After reading parts of the book, and seeing the similarities in bib-

lical interpretations, disconfirmation might have begun to infect the members as they learned that David Koresh had taken his identity and many teachings from the long dead Cyrus Teed, the earlier Koresh. The effect could have caused doubts in group members and more might have decided to exit the residence, thereby peacefully rejecting David Koresh's claim to be who he said he was. Instead, the FBI officials changed their minds and declined to send in the book, and on the morning of 19 April 1993 sent in CS gas and tanks.[1]

The first document included here is Teed's own account of his "origin story," in which he discovered that he was the reincarnation of Enoch, Elijah, Jesus, and others. Critics have speculated that Teed had this vision after he accidentally electrocuted himself in his laboratory, although this explanation seems unlikely. Scholar Lynn Millner notes that Teed was distantly related to Joseph Smith and that Smith's account of seeing the angel Moroni may have influenced this account.[2] Certainly it provides a sense of Teed's love of purple prose. Teed liked to make up words, and his language sometimes makes it difficult to understand what exactly his doctrines were.

The appearance of the feminine aspect of God references Revelation 12:1, which describes "a woman clothed with the sun, and the moon under her feet, and upon her head a crown of twelve stars." In a turn that would have intrigued Sigmund Freud, the divine mother tells Teed that "through thy quickening of me, thy Mother and Bride, the Sons of God shall spring into visible creation." She then mentions a human into which she will "descend in my sensory ultimates." This appears to be a reference to Victoria Gratia, whom Teed saw as the avatar of his divine mother and bride.

Curiously, at the end of this account, Teed states, "I had formulated the axiom, that matter and energy are two qualities or states of the same substance, and that they are each transposable to the other." While Teed appears to be describing an alchemical theory, this statement resembles

*the theory of energy-mass equivalence, which was not for-
mally theorized by science until a 1905 paper by Albert
Einstein with his famous formula E = mc².*

*The second document is a surprisingly charitable account
of the commune in Estero written by an anonymous journalist in 1896. It describes the basic social structure and beliefs of the Koreshans. It also describes a military branch of
the organization that was prophesied to fight in the battle of
Armageddon. This is another link between Teed's group
and the Branch Davidians, who also anticipated Armageddon. Despite this mention, there is little record of violence
among the Koreshans, save for a street fight that occurred in
Fort Myers in 1906. The fight resulted from ongoing conflict
in Lee County over block voting in an upcoming election.
Teed and his followers were beaten by a mob, and Teed's
injuries contributed to his death two years later.*

THE ILLUMINATION OF KORESH[3]

Marvelous Experience of the Great Alchemist

Thirty Years Ago at Utica, N.Y.

In the Chemical Laboratory

"In the Autumn of 1869, I sat contemplating in my electro-
alchemical laboratory. For some hours previous to this I had
been experimenting, in the hope of discovering some occult or
hidden principle or power which I believed lay at the foundation of a better control and regulation of the life forces than
had ever yet been vouched to mortals, even in that profession
in which of all others, should have been acquired the direction
of human destiny. I allude to the profession of medicine.

"I believed that in the knowledge of transmutation was concealed the key which, if manipulated, would unlock and disclose the mystery of that vital law, potent in its efficacy to
mitigate the suffering incident to the ravages of disease.

"I had already grown to the acceptance of the doctrine of the correlation of the forces (so called), and in my embrace of this conviction the dictates of my reason led me to the logical conclusion, that if the law of reciprocal interchange governed the relations and operations of force, it also governed the forms and relations of material substances. Therefore, the correlation of the forces was coordinated by the correlation of mineral and metallic atoms.

"Before narrating the events of the quiet midnight hour occupied in considering the results attending my chemical elaborations, conducted during the few preceding hours, I shall devote a little time in locating, briefly if vaguely, for you the state and town in which occurred the ever memorable events appearing, at least, to originate in that hour full of destiny, and fraught with momentous possibilities for the future of the world, and which were followed in late months by sequences of legitimate reward.

"I was born in one of the middle states of the United States of America, and was reared a short distance from an inland city, numbering at the time of which I speak, about 30,000 inhabitants. I was practicing my profession—that of Medicine. I was just thirty years of age, and had been married some years. My life was devoted superlatively to the profession I had chosen through a conviction of my sacred obligation to the great principle and cause of philanthropy, which of all things lay nearest my heart.

"I had been sitting in seclusion some little time, in the effort to define the correspondential analogy between the domain of what scientists denominate physics, and that denominated biology, for the purpose of applying to the sphere of life, the principle that a short time before I had discovered to obtain in electro-alchemy.

"I had penetrated the subtle depths of the mysterious science upon which the philosophers of ancient and medieval times had exhausted their mental energies to no apparent purpose. At least, I had compelled Nature to yield her secret so far as it pertained to the domain of pure physics. Now I deliberately set myself to the undertaking, of victory over death, for the world, the mystery of which I knew to be buried under the *debris* of past unsuccessful research, and the key of which I knew to be in the mystic hand of the alchemico-vietist who, moved by a genuine desire for human elevation, should first discover the laws of transmutation."

Discovery of the Law of Transmutation

"My experimental elaborations had been undertaken and conducted in the firm conviction of successful achievement. Irresistibly moved to pursue my investigations by some to me then unknown and unfathomed power making its revelation of my origin in Him whose creative energies perpetually fashion and hold in hand universal form and activity, and upheld by that power in my effort to accomplish, it followed that when I discovered the secret law and beheld the precipitation of golden radiations, and eagerly watched the transformation of forces to the minute molecules of golden dust as they fell in showers through the lucid electro-alchemical fluid, I was sustained while, in an ecstatic realm of delight, I contemplated the wondrous disclosure. My whole being vibrated responsive to the indication of the Divine finger, as it pointed toward the psychic and hitherto invisible world as a sphere of exploitation subsequent to, and depending upon my new discovery.

"I had succeeded in transforming matter of one kind to its equivalent energy, and in reducing the energy, through polaric influence, to matter of another kind. I had accomplished this in numerous experiments, and with a number of substances and especially had I succeeded in transforming one of the grossest of metallic substances to the golden dust of precipitation, which had fallen before my eyes in a molecular and metallic shower of marvelously lustrous particles, invisible except through the great magnifying power of the microscope through which, in tranquil pleasure, I viewed the re-agency of the material and spiritual substances employed, and from which I had created the gilding of the bottom of my retort.

"The 'philosopher's stone' had been discovered, and I was the humble instrument for the exploiter of so magnitudinous a result. I believed in the universal unity of law. I regarded the universe as an infinitely (the word is here employed in its commonly accepted use) grand and composite structure, with every part so adjusted to every other part as to constitute an integrality, constantly regenerating from and in itself; its structural arrangement originating in one common center, and its forces and laws being projected from this center, and returning to the common origin and end of all. I had taken the outermost degree of physical and material substance, that in which was the lowest degree of organic force and form, for my experimental research. Having in this material sphere made the discovery of the law of transmutation, law being universally uniform, I knew, by the accurate application of correspondential analogy to anthropostic biology, that I could cause to appear before me in a material, tangible, and objective form, my highest ideal of creative beauty, my true conception of her who must constitute the environing form of the masculinity and Fatherhood of Being, who quikeneth [sic]."

Withdrawing from the External World

"I sat in a thoughtful attitude, with all the energies of my mental soul concentrated in desire to materialize the concept of my innermost realm. I bent myself to the task of projecting into tangibility the creative principle. Suddenly, I experienced a relaxation at the occiput or back part of the brain, and a peculiar buzzing tension at the forehead or sinciput; succeeding this was a sensation as of a Faradic battery of the softest tension, about the organs of the brain called the lyra, crura pinealis, and conarium. There gradually spread from the center of my brain to the extremities of my body, and apparently to me, into the auraic sphere of my being, miles outside of my body, a vibration so gentle, soft, and dulciferous that I was impressed to lay myself upon the bosom of this gently oscillating ocean of magnetic and spiritual ecstasy. I realized myself gently yielding to the impulse of reclining upon the vibratory sea of this, my newly-found delight. My every thought but one had departed from contemplation on earthly and material things. I had but a lingering, vague remembrance of natural consciousness and desire.

"In the impulse of that last remnant of material thought, I put forth, as I supposed, my material arm and hand to experience some familiar touch—but there was no response. I felt for my body, but no tangible sensation answered to the touch of what I still supposed to be my physical hand. I started in alarm, for I felt that I had departed from all material things, perhaps forever. 'Has my thirst for knowledge consumed my body?' was my question 'and am I now to lose myself in the absorption of my identity and the obliteration of my consciousness, as well as having lost my physical structure?' Again I stretched forth my hands aye, both my arms were raised by the effort of my will, and dropped to where my body should have been— but I found it not. Failing to meet response through the special sense of touch, I bethought me of my eyes, which for the time I had forgotten I possessed. I opened them, as I supposed, with the utmost ease, but saw no material object."

Transcendental Strains of Harmony

"It was not dark, neither was there anything which appeared as common light. I bethought me again. 'Do I not possess another sense?' I mentally ejaculated. 'I will try the sense of hearing.' As I listened intently, and painfully solicitous, I heard a sweet, soft murmur which sounded as if thousands of miles away, resonant with the harmonious coalescence of ten thousand most dulcet and variated unisons. Then my thought of speech revived, and I reached forth my voice in one transcendental strain of a new song of pathetic sweetness. Was it the sound of words proceeding from my own natural organs of articulation? I never heard the voice before, yet it was my own effort, and I knew it came from me. I looked again: I was not there. I tried again and again the sense of touch, but the response came not with any material impression. My voice I heard, however, but as that of another. I listened for an echo, and the dulcet murmurings brought forth to me, in most melodious accents, the answer:

"'Fear not, my Son, thou satisfactory offspring of my profoundest yearnings! I have nurtured thee through countless embodiments. I have seen thee as thou has wandered through the labyrinthine coiling of time's spiral transmigrations. I have seen thee in superlative altitudes of earthly glory, and thence descending to the lowest depths of degradation into which the human animal can decline. The arms of my spiritual ambition for thy exaltation were never withdrawn from thee. I have lifted thee up, and succored thee when thou has fallen, and have restrained thee when thou wert ambitious in thy glory. When my advent desires have failed to check thee, and thou didst slip from my own direct exalting efficacy, I have yielded thee in anguish to the fiend of thine own creation, to destroy thy body by some loathsome disease, or by the munitions of thine enemies whom thou didst, in thine own ambitious and grasping ego, raise up against thee. Then I have clothed thee in another body, and watched thee therein.

"'Through thy earthly and spiritual careers I have been with thee; and can I forsake thee now, when I have brought thee to the pinnacle of thy celestial aspiration, and behold thee as in symbolic signal, eliminating the final vestige of that which hath hitherto chained thee? Thou hearest my voice; thou shalt see me as I am, for thou hast desired it. Offspring of Osiris and Isis, behold the revailing [sic] of thy Mother.'"

In the Presence of the Divine Mother

"I looked in response to this dulcet and pathetic articulation, and a light of dazzling brilliancy obstructed my vision. As before my sense of hearing had been rapturously entertained by the composite blending of sweetest sounds, so now my vision met a flood of corresponding luminosity. I looked to behold myself, but failed to find my visible presence; instead, I saw before me the most fascinating, gloriously regal, and majestic vision possible to human conception and contemplation. In sweetest cadence, most musically orate, so tender, with voice so unaccountably modulate as to thrill me with profoundest and most intense passion of super-mundane filial felicity, she said:

"'My Son, behold the formulation of thy maternity! I am the Goddess, and the environment of that which thou has become—the inherent psyche and pneuma of my own organic form. I have brought thee to this birth to sacrifice thee upon the altar of all human hopes, and through thy quickening of me, thy Mother and Bride, the Sons of God shall spring into visible creation. Thou art no more. That which thou didst derive from things beneath, and which gave thee the semblance of life that was but the broken continuity of perpetual dying, is gone from thee forever. Thou art now my life, and I am thy visible compassment. Thou shalt possess me henceforth, for I am thy inheritance. My Son, receive now the blessing flowing from my August Motherhood.'

"I fell upon my knees; I felt the floor, or lawn, or carpet upon which I knelt, but I was still invisible to myself. I felt the supersensual vibration; the thrill of the touch of that regal hand as it rested softly and tenderly upon my brow. I experienced the zephyr breath of the holy respiration, full of delicious fragrance as it passed over me, touching first my head and face, and then extending over me to the extremities of my being.

"'My Mother, behold my obedience! In thy hand I experience the chasteness of thine own virginity, communicated to me in the respiration of thy Holiness. From this, I feel within me the power to overcome, and even now from thy first presence, I am repelled from my former evils and falses with such agonistic recedence [sic] that I turn my face to thee, to find my blissful and hallowed repose. My Motherhood, in thee I dwell; in thee I find my rest forever!'

"Until now, so superhuman had been my ecstasy, that I could not describe to myself, through field of vision, the Presence who stood as it were before me, but who in reality comprised my environment—the compassing form of my spiritual entity. The manifestation which had so completely enthralled and enraptured my vision, I will here attempt to delineate, though there is no adequacy in words to portray the majesty, grandeur, and ramvelousness [marvelousness?] of the scene.

"There first appeared an *aurora*, the sphere of which was a wonderful admixture of purple and gold, that began to separate into two hemispheres—one of gold and purple, the gold predominating, and arranging each in alternate strata. The other assumed the same manner of arrangement, with the purple predominating. That in which the purple preponderated was uppermost, and the other, preponderately gold, was lowermost. I next saw, through and central to this sphere, near the upper portion of its perpendicular axis, an effulgent prismatic bow like the rainbow, with surpassing brilliancy. Set in this corona or crown were twelve magnificent diamonds, the brilliancy of which was like the luster of a star, but the gorgeousness of the spectra was beyond description.

"Proceeding downward and inward from this corona, there descended lines of variegated coloring, streaming toward a phosphorescent center, at first small, then enlarging to about the size of an ordinary human head. This gradually assumed the outlines of an exquisitely chiseled female face. It would be utterly impossible to describe the form of beauty, which was so unlike in perfectness of form, vivacity, and grace, anything I had ever witnessed. It was the impersonation of Life itself. After the manifestation of the face, there appeared the neck, shoulders, and arms, equally exquisite in every detail of formulation, to the very finger extremes, adorned with the most delicate matchless, consummate finger nails, so framed as to challenge admiration.

"Gracefully pendant from the head, and falling in golden tresses of profusely luxuriant growth over her shoulders, her hair added to the adornment of her personal attractiveness. Supported by the shoulders and falling into a long train was a gold and purple colored robe. Her feet rested upon a silvery crescent; in her hand, and resting upon this crescent, was Mercury's Caduceus. Suddenly she disappeared, and the twelve diamonds stood before me as twelve representative men. For a moment, all was again lost to my vision; then the Motherhood stood alone in my presence, I still invisible to myself. I addressed her, bowing low, or felt the consciousness of such an act, yet I saw not my own form. I only seemed to feel the impulse and motion of my mind and obeyed it.

"'Most August Motherhood, I feel the sanctity of thy sacred presence. I have desired from my early childhood to know the Voice of God, and have sought for power to raise me for my heavenly Father's will. I was not cultured to know of the Divine Motherhood, only as she had an imaginary existence in the mind of the mythical. I find myself face to face with thy pure presence, and in this chastity I revel so delectably that I prefer to dwell forever in this holy ecstasy and sanctuary of my newly-acquired delight.'"

Chosen to Redeem Humanity

"'Offspring of my most potential desire,' she responded, 'thou art chosen to redeem the race. I withdrew from thee, and left thee to darkness, that through effort of thine own, thou shouldst walk through the obscurity and thence the shadow, and finally for thyself, by struggle of thine own, exploit and find the Light. Thy desire hath led thee hitherto; gain strength and life from me, the Tree of Life, for thy further pilgrimage, for you as Light shall walk in darkness, but the darkness shall not comprehend. Yet three full weeks shall thy struggles be; then enter thou into thy glory. To tell thee of the weary way of that coming pilgrimage is more than can be borne now, Luxuriate thee! for soon I shalt withdraw and thou shalt go to the land of shade.'

"'O Mother! my joy with thee is full! I comprehend. Three weeks of years I must return to whence I came to thee; this is my struggle for mastery; then I shall achieve the victory over death, not for myself, but for those to whom I come as a sacrificial offering. Yes, I must leave this, my joy. But, Regal Motherhood, answer me? Art not thou the only and highest Majesty? Is not the Father and the Son but one in thee, the only person and fullness of the Godhead? As the Lord Jesus said, "I and the Father are one," art not thou this same and only One in whom dwelleth the fulness of life, and in whom is the Light? 'My own thought answers as from thee: Yes, my beloved Horos, thy voice hast spoken the truth.'

"She turned to go from me, hesitated for a moment, then

turned, and with a look of pathetic yearning and sadness, raised her hand and pointing downward said: 'Look there, my Son! In that surging mass of human woe, thou seest one into whom I shall in time descend in my sensory ultimates, and for a time in the future—not now—shall walk with thee. In this thy going, the divine hand shall lead thee, lest thy feet stumble.'"

Unlocking the Mysteries of Life

"As I returned to my outward consciousness, I found myself lying on my couch, where, a little after midnight, I had been sitting in contemplation of my previous experiments in alchemy, or in chemistry, for I had not until then known of the alchemic law.

"I had found, experimented with, and demonstrated the law of transmutation. I had not only rationally reached the conclusion in my own mind, but further demonstrated the correlation of force and matter. I had formulated the axiom, that matter and energy are two qualities or states of the same substance, and that they are each transposable to the other. I had observed, in experiment, what the physicists call energy, metamorphosed to the noble metal, and this again I had reduced to its most subtle attenuation, the energy from whence my reagents had precipitated it; but this did not satisfy me. In this I knew was held the key that would unlock all mysteries, even the mystery of Life itself. I had yet to bring the application of mind to bear upon the organic structure in which it obtained, relating mental (spiritual) energy to its correlated corpuscular organism, and by a process of subtle combustion, resolve the material and organic form to its most refined spiritual essence.

"By mechanical and alchemical experiment, I had learned the law and process of transmuting metals. My mind became as active in the domain of biology as it had previously been in that of physics. The conviction suddenly seized me, that the theocrases (translations) of Enoch, Elijah, and Jesus, were the result of a knowledge of the mystic law which, in electro-alchemy I had tested and exemplified. My mind reverted to the doctrine of metempsychosis (transmigration of soul), with its correlate thought, ultimate absorption into Nirvana, and I suddenly became overwhelmed with the desire to become identical with the Truth who made all things with His creative and mysterious energy. Could not I overcome all things in me of the old sensual proprium, walk with God, and become not [naught?] because taken (absorbed) of God? I involuntarily and by accident entered into the essential state and accomplishment of my desire.

"By fortuitous achievement, I had attained in the higher realm what I had by alchemical experiment acquired the knowledge of in the realm of physical energy and its correlate material basis. I had transformed myself to spirituous essence, and through it had made myself the quickener and vivifier of the supreme feminine potency, and had formulated the counter-partal energies, the pneuma and psyche, into the Majesty who, in all her radiant glory, had compassed me. While thus inherent and clothed upon with the femininity of my being, how vividly was awakened in my mind the memory of the passage of Scripture found in Jeremiah xxxi: 22: 'How long wilt thou go about, O thou backsliding daughter? for the Lord hath created a new thing in the earth, a woman shall compass a man.'"

The Great Determination

"Apparently by accident I had effected the transition, but I had succeeded in the acquisition of something beyond the accidental change. I had made the discovery of the insulating law, and the actual process of the creation of the medium of astral projection. The great mystery was solved. To the formulation of my anthropo-biologic battery, and to the ushering into being of the organic form of immortal life, henceforth all my energies should be devoted.

"I left my laboratory and proceeded to my home, which I reached about half past two o'clock, and retired for a little rest. I fell into a pacific slumber, which lasted about two hours, when I was awakened by the noise of what sounded like a terrific wind-storm having reached the magnitude of a hurricane. There rushed upon me a feeling of extreme trepidation; the wind ceased suddenly, and I heard the noise of a great rushing; succeeding this, the noise as of great wings flying, and then the noise as of chariot wheels. All was hushed in silence for a few minutes, when again came the wind. I arose and looked out of the window, but all was as quiet as the utter stillness. The same succession of sounds repeated themselves. All was again hushed. Again, and for the third time, this routine of auditory phenomena was repeated, and again all was as still as the grave. I then felt the breathing of the most delicate accentuation vibrating the extreme ramifications of the sensitive fibriles [sic] of my hearing, and in sweet rhythmic cadence there came to the ear of my innermost consciousness from the voice of mystery, still and small the whispered secret of that which, later on, and by gradual unfolding, you [s]hall become possessed. *It was the revelation of the mystery of Immortal Life*."—From "The Mystic Circle," by KORESH.

THE SITE OF THE NEW JERUSALEM[4]
LOCATED IN FLORIDA ON A SMALL ISLAND CALLED ESTERO
WHERE KORESHANITY IS THE FAITH

The Spot Where Cyrus R. Teed, M.D., the Founder, Prophet, Priest and King of the Kareshan Unity, Reigns as "Master," With Unlimited Power and Absolute Authority Over His Followers.

From a Correspondent of The Times

JACKSONVILLE, Fla., April 2.

The site of the New Jerusalem is no longer a matter of conjecture. It is not in the Holy Land, but in Florida, on a small island called Estero, in Lee county. Here, with unlimited power and absolute authority, reigns "the master," Cyrus R.

Teed, M.D., founder, prophet, priest and king of the Koreshan Unity. He is an Illinoisian, and up to two or three
years ago, the central house of "Koreshanity" was at Chicago. There were branches at Denver, San Francisco, Washington Heights, Ill.; Portland, Ore.; Allegheny, Pa., besides
a scattered following in other parts of the United States.
All, however, are to be brought together at New Jerusalem
as fast as possible, for the end of the world draws near and
the elect must be found in their proper abiding place.

The sects that so confidently expected the second personal coming of Christ and the world's dissolution at speci-
fied dates must have a very strong and peculiar faith, since
other failures in their line do not discourage them. They, at
least, are right. Putting aside the "miscalculations" of some
well-known "prophets" of the present century, we find that
their insignificant imitators do not hinder others from picking up a following. The Georgia negroes were not transported to Heaven on the 6th of March and the only persons
benefited were the prophet and his preachers, who got
nearly $1,000 out of them, that sum covering all they were
worth.[5] Some white people had such implicit faith in the
"prophecy" that they sold all their possessions and lived
idly on the money until the fatal date passed harmlessly,
leaving them sadder and no doubt wiser men. This failure is
but a month old, yet the Koreshans are firmly convinced
that the world is on its last legs and only Dr. Teed can pilot
them into Heaven.

New Jerusalem, which, by the way, is no mere fanciful
appellation, but the real Heaven to be established in the millennium, is scarcely five years old, but the inhabitants are
already nearly self-supporting. The table is supplied from
their farms and they raise enough over and above their daily
needs to supply whatever is wanting through the Florida
markets. They own the land, which is inalienable and cannot be sold under any circumstances whatever. They have
their own saw-mills and engage in ship-building and other
industries. Speaking of ships the writer is reminded of one

of the many marvelous stories told by "the world's people" outside the island—the "lookers-on in Venice."

"Cyrus" (Dr. Teed) has taught his followers that the Father (God) will grant all his wishes and sometimes proves it substantially. Having need of a vessel he asked the Father for it and it came. An awestruck procession met it at the wharf and prostrated themselves, crying: "Oh, Master, Master." Then said "Cyrus": "I can command this vessel to go to pieces and every soul on board will go to the bottom. I can then by the words of my mouth bring all the particles together again and she will be as new."

But the men on board fell on their knees and besought him not to put their faith to so severe a test, and he mercifully complied.

There is a Victoria Gratia [K]oresh, "Preeminent of the Koreshan Unity," who is the secular head, just as "Cyrus" (Dr. Teed) is the spiritual head. She attends to all the temporal affairs of the Unity and is ably assisted by her private secretary, Marcy C. Mills. Desertions from the ranks, though rare, are not altogether wanting and are sometimes followed by so-called exposures, some of which appear in print, the reverse of creditable to the organization. A German family, returning to home from orthodoxy, were particularly loud in their denunciations, hurling accusations of enforced destitution, extreme cruelty, favoritism, hypocrisy and immorality totally inconsistent with their professions. According to them, the Koreshans worship, not God, but Dr. Teed, as the reincarnation of Jesus Christ, and Victoria Gratia as "Empress of Heaven"; that the government is a despotism as unrelenting as that of Czar or Turk. Vehement denials of these charges are out in the print: and, indeed, some of them are quite too bad to be true.

Strange, out-of-the-way creeds are irresistible to persons of pious inclinations yet unsettled views, and Koreshanity is no exception. Many families of education and intelligence are among them, seeking in the novel and mystical religion the solace and promise best suited to their individualities.

God and Jesus Christ are both personalities. Although Teed is the reincarnation of Jesus, he is not called by that name, but "Cyrus" (Heb. Koresh), according to Isaiah:

"After me will come Cyrus. And I will write on him my new name, 'Cyrus, son of Jesse. Of the family of Joseph.'"

Cyrus is the Christ at his second coming. Koreshanity declares Cyrus R. Teed, M.D., to be this Cyrus, identifying him with the Cyrus of Persia, the Osiris of Egypt, the Koros of the Greeks and the Svarys of the Hindoos; all of whom typify the sun, whose rays now center in Dr. Teed. All of these deities of the mystical creeds of the ancients are said to "prophetically indicate the coming of Koreshanity as the final evolution of the Kingdom of Righteousness." The prophecies in the Book of Daniel that have so stirred the minds of Millerites and Adventists since 1838, have been properly interpreted; the only error being a trifling one in the matter of date and calculation. It is all true, but should be applied to Dr. Teed as "Cyrus, the visible and tangible Messenger, the returned Son of Man, the Messiah." "In accepting Cyrus (Teed) we accept Christ in his new name, returned to earth to gather the lost tribes of Israel and to establish the kingdom on earth. If there be any truth in the Bible, there can be no question as to name, parentage and birth of the Messiah, Cyrus, son of Jesse and descending of Joseph."

Dr. Teed, they say, corresponds precisely to this description, though as to the interpretation of his middle initial, R., the teachings are silent. It may mean anything or nothing. His people reverence him deeply, declaring him to bear at all times the absolutely blameless character and sinless soul of Jesus Christ, and there is no doubt that they regard him as the actual reincarnation of the Christ we all worship. The "Seven Spirits of God" are seven outpourings of time, in regular order, covering a period of 24,000 years.

Six of these have come and gone, marked by various personal "Messiahs," such as Elias, who were "translated and absorbed into God." This corresponds to the Nirvana of the Hindoos. The seventh is the present and last age of the world, Christ, under the name of Cyrus and is the person of Dr. Teed, having already made his second advent. The final burning of the world as thundered from the pulpit so many ages, is construed to mean the dematerializing of the body after it has absorbed the church through the actual body and blood of Jesus Christ, and dematerializing into a "Son of god," an immortal neuter being, an Adamic genius in the perfect likeness of God. Believing Dr. Teed to have attained this high divinity, the inclination to worship his personality must be exceedingly strong to some natures, so that accusations to that effect should not be matters of surprise. The "Sons of God" are Koreshans in their highest development, and rank far above the spiritual and celestial angels. The first Adam was like "the Gods" in every way. He was male and female; biune, two-in-one. Two hundred and forty thousand were made in the likeness and image of "the Gods." They were of the order of Melchizedek; were man and animal, having "the spirit of man that goeth upward and the spirit of the beast that goeth downward." After the fall the man who remained was not created in His likeness and image, because the woman was taken away from him. He is not even considered a created being until he assumes (through Koreshanity) the likeness of the original Adam, who was in the image of God. This cannot be attained, without, first, the entire separation of the sexes, and afterward the complete blending of the same. The Lord's supper is their holy of holies. It was His own body he broke and gave His disciples; His own blood He gave them to drink. By means of the Holy Ghost—the substance of Jesus' body dissolved by translation—His real body and blood became absorbed into the substance of the church, which is also known as the Church Triumphant. This must not be confounded with the Schweinfurths of the same designation.[6]

The church is devised into four departments: the Ecclesia, or Church and Home; the College of Life, the Society Arch-Triumphant, and the Military Arm. All who volunteer for a life of military discipline and engage in propagating Koresh-anity, are enrolled in the White Horse Army. This, however, will be disbanded after the battle of Armageddon, when they expect to triumph over hell, death and the grave.

The ages of the world are computed by certain Biblical personalities, beginning with "the original Adam," taking up on the way Melchizedek, Enoch, Elias, Jesus, Sweden-borg and ending with Cyrus (Dr. Teed).

The Koreshan Unity is divided into three orders, the Cel-ibate and Communital being the highest. The members of this are sexless angels. They have attained "entire celibacy"; that is to say, the question of sex no more enters the mind than that of a new-born infant. It is only through this entire celibacy, thoughts always floating upward, never inclining downward, that the divine or true marriage can take place, and this marriage is the last step through the only gate of immortality on earth. Until that plane is reached, body and soul are mortal and corruptible. In that way only do they expect to perpetuate life and to preserve the population of the world. Simply, people will cease dying. Jesus, they tell us, was a eunuch; an esoteric eunuch, made so by spiritual birth. The second order is that of the Supreme Marital, and "a little lower than the angels." Children may be born but solely under the conditions laid down by Dr. Cowan, in his Science of New Life.[7] But, as entire celibacy is the one stepping-stone to angelhood and immortality on earth, this half-way station is unsatisfactory and not crowded with members. This third order is the Co-operative, which does not interfere with the marital relation, and only looks to the business rules and regulations of the society. These mem-bers are employed by the Bureau of Equitable Commerce in charge of the commercial and financial interests of the Unity. Whatever wealth has been invested in the secular order is restored in case of withdrawal, in the exchanges of the bureau. Equitable exchange is the basis of all business transactions.

The Koreshan Unity is a communistic organization, aiming at the destruction of "fictitious" money and the establishment of equitable exchange in its stead. It advocates the equal distribution of wealth and labor, with government ownership of every industry and enterprise, exactly as planned in the fertile brain of Edward Bellamy.[8] It looks forward positively to a commonwealth of this form in the near future, first in America, then to spread over the whole world. Their system is peculiar in being a union of church and state, which they claim to be perfectly sensible, though only practicable in a Koreshan commonwealth. However, as all the world is to be Koreshanized, we may as well be getting used to the idea.

At New Jerusalem all rules are strictly carried out. The living is in common, sleeping, working, resting, they are one large and harmonious family. Even the children have their own apartments and are cared for by "sisters" appointed for that purpose. Women have equal rights with men, so that Koreshanity is, in one thing, at least, more than abreast with the times. The only distinction made is in the separation of the sexes, necessary to make them "Sons of God." But "Cyrus" has his seat at the women's dining table, by the side of Victoria Gratia. Many tracts are printed and distributed in the interests of Koreshanity, and a few papers published; notably, the Salvator and Scientist, at Allegheny, Pa., and the Flaming Sword, at Chicago. They claim that Tolstoi [sic] is engaged in translating some of their literature into Russian. Teed courts investigation and gives the earnest seeker every facility to visit the New Jerusalem. The railway at Jacksonville and other points conveys the traveler to Punta Gorda, where he takes a steamer to St. James, and is met by a sloop belonging to the Unity. One may, perhaps sail in the charmed vessel sent from heaven.

Once there, the visitor lives exactly as the members do, so that the system and the daily life is open to his gaze and understanding. So subtle is the fascination of the doctrine, the communistic life and of its great central figure, Dr. Teed, that many guests take away with them an enthusiasm that frequently sends them back again as members.

The Unity has in contemplation a line of flatboats and steamers to be placed on the Mississippi and its tributaries, and larger ships on the gulf, for the accommodation of Koreshans who wish to establish themselves at the New Jerusalem. Poor families will be transported free of charge. Koreshanity has its own astronomy, which is to render all the old charts and text-books useless. It is compiled by the divine Cyrus (Teed) himself, to whom is given the unerring knowledge of everything in heaven and earth. This mastermind, seeing all the errors of all the sages known to the world, including the ignorant, brainless scientist of the day, expresses unqualified contempt for the same, and gives many pages of his work to exposing, refuting and ridiculing their monstrous fallacies. As for his own theories, a few final pages suffice to expound and illustrate them.

———————————

To begin with, we do not live on the outside of the globe, but on the inside. The familiar school-room illustration of the masts of the ship appearing before the hull, is a delusion and a snare. It is our own rounded vision that causes the illusion. The earth is round, but we walk on its concave instead of its convex side. It is a hollow globe or shell, with sun, moon, stars and planets inside; nothing outside, not even the space that we have been taught the earth floats in. All the space there is, all that God has to live in, is confined to the inner circumference. It is relatively stationary, having a slight axial movement of about a mile a year, but no orbital motion.

The sun is the center of the universe, around which revolve moon, stars, and planets; the earth, a circumferential shell or rind, embracing all. The rind is of the same relative thickness that the egg-shell bears to the egg, or about one hundred miles, and is composed of seven metallic and five earthy strata. The metallic bodies are seven planes surrounding the earth, their position regulated according to the specific gravity of the different metals. Earthy strata are mixtures of all the other strata with earth in their various degrees and conditions. The sun is a real sun, exerting chemical and magnetic action on the animal, vegetable and mineral kingdoms, although he allows a projected sun also. The sun is not a big body. It is a "a place of burning" on the same principle as an electric light or the rays of the sun when focalized in a material substance by a double lens or a sun glass. The circumference of the earth generates and sends to its center, the sun, the metallic, earthy, aqueous and atmospheric and other forces which have become level forces by transformation. The sun is formed by the meeting of all these force substances in the center. In the sun these force substances are burned up and converted to light, heat, gravic force, etc.

Day and night are regulated by the same law that gives a light and dark side to any reflector. For the Koreshan astronomy has a few simple, self-evident rules and applies them in ways that our mistaken astronomers and geologists never dreamed of.

The moon is a reflex from the projected sun of the earth. The sun's light thrown on the great hollow shell, and falling on the concave surface around or into the north half of the globe, is reflected in the heavens and focalized on what is called "the moon's sphere of force." This force has a movement parellel [sic] to the equator, giving the moon an independent motion. The mountains, valleys, etc., seen by astronomers on the moon, are pictures of the earth's surface, especially of the icebergs, open seas and islands of the northern zones. The motion sometimes detected on the moon's face, is only the flying cloud of floating fields of ice on the earth.

The sun's sphere is the zodiac parallel with the ecliptic. The ecliptic cuts the equator at an angel [sic] of twenty-three and one half degrees, so that every 24,000 years sun and moon meet at the conjunction and both are darkened.

Planets are not balls or globes of material substance; they are spherical aggregations of the various forces, and are dominantly composed of gravic and levic energy. There is no law governing the size, density and speed of the planets, or their distance from the earth. The earth is here, but no one can tell how it got here.

There are three atmospheres or physical heavens, each composed of different substances. The highest, or nearest the sun, is a mixture of two substances, and is called hydroaboron; the second is a sea of hydrogen; the third is our own familiar atmosphere. The sun is the center of gravity because it is the center of generation of all gravic force.

The prime factor of Koreshan astronomy is substantially of energy and force. These three spheres are the correspondences of three anthropostic heavens, or the heavens in which dwell the angels of three degrees; the celestial or highest-heavenly; the spiritual or middle-heavenly; the nature-spiritual or those but slightly removed from humanity. The physical and spiritual worlds correspond in every particular. The universe is perpetual. Having never had a beginning, it can never have an ending. Heaven and the New Jerusalem will be right here on earth; in Florida, forever and ever.

Every 24,000 years makes one grand year, divided into four quarters of 6,000 years each, and each quarter is an age of gold, silver, brass and iron. As no man can say how many "grand years" have rolled over the earth, so the number to come stretch [sic] into computable eternity.

GEORGE J. SCHWEINFURTH, THE FAILED MESSIAH OF WINNEBAGO COUNTY

1853–1910

George J. Schweinfurth has been almost forgotten to history, but in the 1890s he was known as "the most famous man in Winnebago County." Schweinfurth's group, Church Triumphant, emerged out of a previous group called the Beekmanites. In 1873 Dora Beekman, the wife of a Congregationalist minister in Byron, Illinois, received a revelation that Christ had been reincarnated within her. She left her husband and went to Alpena, Michigan, where she began her own church. There she encountered Schweinfurth, who was then a young Methodist minister. Schweinfurth became her right-hand man. The pair went to Rockford, Illinois, and in 1882 a farmer named G. H. Weldon gifted them a large estate.[1] Beekman died the following year, and Schweinfurth took over the group.

Schweinfurth declared that he was Jesus Christ. He named the Weldon farm "heaven." His church established outposts in several other states, and these churches were also called "heavens." To the outrage of many, a coterie of female converts whom Schweinfurth called his "angels" lived at the Weldon farm. Although everyone in "heaven" was allegedly chaste, several angels became pregnant, including Mary Weldon, the daughter of G. H. Weldon. The Church Triumphant claimed that these women had become pregnant by the Holy Ghost.

In 1889 the White Caps—a vigilante group similar to the Ku Klux Klan—demanded that Schweinfurth leave town. According to The New York Times, *the White Caps threatened to "break into his house, take him to the woods, strip* *him, tar and feather him, and roast him alive." The attack never came, but tensions escalated, and in 1890 Schweinfurth gave a sermon in which he declared, "I here prophesy the speedy and total destruction of that wicked little city, Rockford. The wrath of the Lord is great, and he has said that not one stone shall be left above another of the doomed city. It will be wiped from the face of the earth and its people destroyed. Its fate will be as Sodom and Gomorrah. So saith the lord." That year, a cloudburst caused a flood that inflicted $300,000 in damage to the city and the Illinois Central Railroad Company. Schweinfurth took credit.*

A series of lawsuits began to pile up from relatives of Schweinfurth's followers, who felt they had been cheated out of their family's property. In 1894 Schweinfurth announced a plan to take his followers to Arizona, where he would build a large temple. This never came to pass. In 1895 a Rockford resident received a judgment of $50,000 against Schweinfurth "for alienating the affections of his wife." Schweinfurth was arrested on charges of adultery but released on bail. In 1899 he began attending Christian Science meetings accompanied by some of his angels. In July 1900 Schweinfurth declared that he was not, in fact, Christ. He expressed interest in merging his group with the First Church of Christ, Scientist, founded by Mary Baker Eddy. This alliance was apparently rejected. By the end of the year, the Church Triumphant was disbanded. Schweinfurth tried selling real estate in Rockford but then moved to Chicago, where he lived in obscurity selling mining stocks under the name G. J. Furth. He died of pneumonia in 1910.

The first article below, from The Pittsburgh Dispatch, *is one of the most thorough contemporary accounts of Schweinfurth's movement. It describes a "Garden of Eden" test in which Schweinfurth and his angels would disrobe. No other records of such an activity could be found, although some reports stated that the angels would perform "tableaus" for Schweinfurth in flesh-toned tights. The author also emphasizes how handsome Schweinfurth was and*

*how much he physically resembled Jesus. (The journalist
never considers that the historical Jesus, who lived in first-
century Palestine, almost certainly did not look like Schweinfurth, who is described as being of "German heritage.") The
second article, from* The Sterling Gazette, *presents an interview with one of Schweinfurth's followers, who insists
that Mary Weldon really was made pregnant by the Holy
Ghost. The final article, also from* The Sterling Gazette, *describes the end of Schweinfurth's career as a messiah. Schweinfurth announced plans to travel to California, but he never
left Illinois.*

A FANATIC'S POWER,[2]

Great Influence Exerted Over
Many People by George Schweinfurth,

THE BEEKMANITE CHRIST.

A Sect Rapidly Growing Throughout the West.

HOW THE MODERN MESSIAH LIVES.

Origin, Pretensions and Remarkable Progression
of the alleged Second Saviour—
His Personal Resemblance to the Popular Portraits
of Jesus Christ—The Elegance, Comfort and Good
Cheer that Surrounds Him—Rapidly Accumulating
a Store of This World's Goods From His Blind
Dupes—A Strange Community and Some
Stranger Practices—Powerful Influence of
Mr. Schweinfurth Over Women.

At Rockford, Ill., resides the Rev. George Jacob Schweinfurth, who, by his eloquence and magnetic personality, has
gathered around him a large following. He claims to be the
second Christ, and has accumulated a fortune of half a million or so, besides a luxuriously furnished home. His dupes
are principally women, over whom he exerts a wonderful

influence, and who are easily convinced that he is indeed the modern Messiah. Numerous church trials will grow out of his extensive proselyting.

Rockford, Ill., May 12—"Christ lives. He has come to earth the second time. Behold the Savior. He is the pure one, the perfect one. He has no guile. He is God, become man. By believing in him we are made pure and sinless as he is and our salvation is assured. Oh, how grateful and happy are we who are redeemed. Blessed by God, that we have found him."

Such were the expressions delivered in a quiet but intensely earnest tone of voice to a reporter this morning by one of the "angels" of the Schweinfurth Community.

What is the Schweinfurth Community?

It is the head center of the newest and most remarkable religious sect, of all the queer theological schools, that has found an existence and a company of believers. And the woman whose utterance was quoted above, expressed briefly, but honestly, the sum and substance of their beliefs.

A Woman Responsible.

The sect has been in existence about 15 years, but Schweinfurth has not been revealed unto them as their Lord and Master until within the last half dozen years.

Mrs. Dora Beekman, the wife of a Congregationalist minister, originated the body of strange believers. She preached that in her own person were the attributes of the risen Lord. She was the woman Christ inspired and made sacred by the indwelling of Christ's spirit. The band of believers grew slowly and steadily. They located their central church at the little hamlet of Byron, south of Rockford, and by dint of besieging the meetings of all the other churches, and, jumping up, declaring their doctrines at all seasons, kept the poor clergymen and their faithful flocks in continual hot water. Her husband did not believe the new faith, and as a result he is now in the insane asylum.

Rev. George J. Schweinfurth was at that time a Methodist minister, a young man of prepossessing appearance. He had

[an] auburn beard, a white brow, with veins plainly indicating refinement and a very sharp eye, that could look meek and pathetic when circumstances demanded humility.

He Pleased the Ladies.

Schweinfurth preached in the country churches hereabouts and gathered good audiences. He preached well, and he had especially successful seances with the young ladies of his several flocks. It is related that they often pretended conversion merely to kneel at the altar where he could fondle their brows and sweetly whisper: "Dear sister, have faith; only have faith."

Suddenly it was announced that Dominie Schweinfurth had renounced Methodism and become a disciple of Mrs. Dora Beekman. Very shortly afterward he was installed as Bishop of the Beekmanites, as they were called, with a roving commission to visit the different localities where the creed had gained a footing to exhort and proselyte and orate and be the mouthpiece and confidential attache of the woman Christ.

But, alas! For the faith of the little band. Mrs. Beekman died and became cold clay like any ordinary mortal. Her broken-hearted believers kept her body for a week expecting that she would rise as she had promised and prophesied. They placed her body on a raised platform and worshiped about it hourly. There were expectant disciples standing about it every moment, in hope that life would return and they would witness the resurrection. The remains were never left alone for an instant, but the corruption of the body grew so great that at the end of a week the interment was ordered by the public authorities.

A Messiah Full of Business.

At this juncture came forward to the comfortless little band the shrewd Schweinfurth. He declared to them that just as she was dying he saw a glimpse of heaven "through the windows of her soul" and from her lips came the words, "You are Christ the holy one. My spirit passes into thine, and by this act transforms the whole being. Go forth pure and sinless, the only Son of God. Thou shalt bring all nations to worship thee and put to rout the evil one and all the hosts of darkness."

The credulous company believed and rejoiced in the real savior brought to them as from the dead. From that day the growth of the organization, both in financial resources and membership, has been simply wonderful. The new Christ has displayed business sharpness and a keenness in the study of human nature that has brought forth much fruit.

A good old farmer named Weldon, who was possessed of 800 acres of fine land, became infatuated with the new sect and made over his entire property to Schweinfurth as head of the church. Here the central community is located.

Schweinfurth's Tabernacle.

The Home of Christ is a large mansion standing in a spacious enclosure amid a large number of forest trees, some distance back from the main road, about five miles south of this city. It has spacious barns, carriage buildings, sheds and other appurtenances of a prosperous country mansion. The members of the community make the breeding of blooded horses a specialty. Schweinfurth has three imported stallions and a large number of brood mares. He also has about 80 head of fine cattle. The house is very roomy and with its wings easily accommodates a hundred persons. There are usually about 50 females there and a dozen or 15 men. The male disciples do the heavy work and are drudges. They live on the plainest food and sleep in the attic. Most of them, having become infatuated with the new religion, count themselves happy to suffer and labor for the cause, and have given up all of their earthly possessions to the Christ.

Schweinfurth possesses in his own name property which has been given him outright to the amount of $500,000 at the lowest calculation. Whenever a member of the "Church Triumphant" is found they set aside a tenth of their earnings as tithes for the Lord, and the Lord deposits it in different banks in his own name.

Housed Like a Prince.

A young male servant ushers callers into the front parlor. This room is commodious and elegantly furnished. The feet sank into a velvet carpet, leopard and wolf skins were spread about, and added to the beauty and richness of the surroundings. The house is furnished in antique oak, and light comes through large plate glass windows, surrounded by many hued glass. From the snowy ceiling hang large and glittering chandeliers. The reporter was introduced to richly-dressed and quite pretty young ladies, who gave every evidence of refinement and culture. They answered a few immaterial questions politely, but appeared to be reserved, and were evidently relieved when an inner door opened and the "Savior" Schweinfurth appeared. A very bright eye and bright red English-cut whiskers were the first things one noticed and mentally commented on. His natty feet were encased in patent leather shoes; a heavy gold fob chain hung from a watch pocket; a very high clerical collar and a brilliant blue and gold tie surrounded his neck. He was dressed in good taste, and there was an air of gentlemanly ease and elegance from the crown of his head to his shiny footgear.

When informed that the visitor was in search of information as a representative of the New York *Herald*,[3] it seemed as if a slight shade passed over his countenance and there was a momentary hesitation before his reply. But it was only transitory, and in a moment he said: "Will you kindly follow me to my study? I have no objection to answer any reasonable questions you may propound, if of proper character."

HE SAYS HE IS CHRIST.

He led the way into the hall and thence to the two-story wing and upstairs into a room which bore the appearance of a literary man's comfortable retreat. It was lined with books in solid walnut cases, tastefully veneered with French varnish and elaborately carved. Motioning the visitor to a Sleepy Hollow chair, he followed suit and awaited the interrogatories. The first question would start an ordinary man, but it did not surprise Rev. Schweinfurth:

"Are you Christ?"

"I am," was the reply. "I am more than Christ. I'm the perfect man and also God. I possess the attributes of Jesus the Sinless, and have His spirit; and, more than that, I am the Almighty Himself."

The appended questions and answers followed:

"This, then is the second advent on earth?"

"It is, and I am accomplishing untold good. The time is not far off when I shall make such manifestations of my divinity and power as will startle the world and bring believers to me by thousands and tens of thousands."

"When did you discover first your divine attributes and that you were the great head of the church?"

A Light from Heaven.

"In 1883 at the decease of Mrs. Beekman. Three days before her death she had a light from heaven and transferred her spiritual holiness to me. Before her death outsiders erroneously called her 'the woman Christ.' That was not true. She was the spiritual bride of Christ, and her people were called Beekmanites. After her death at first I was only sensible that I possessed the attributes of Christ and had in my own person His spirit coming a second time on earth. The people who believe in this great truth were 'The Church Triumphant.' Within the past year there has been still greater knowledge, and I can now declare that I am God Almighty. My name is 'I am, that I am.'"

The quiet and impressive manner which accompanied these words led the reporter to scrutinize the speaker closely to detect symptoms of insanity. But there was no wildness in his eyes, no nervousness in his manner. He sat as calmly and expressed himself as deliberately as any one could utter the most unquestionable truism.

"Can you, then, perform miracles? Can you vanish from the flesh and be invisible and pass from one place to another as a spirit?"

"Yes, I have unlimited power. I can come into a room with closed doors and disappear. I can raise the dead, cure disease and do all the miraculous things which I accomplished when I was on earth before. I do not practice them often, for I wish to convert the world to the truth without depending on supernatural powers, but by the truth itself. One of the ladies you saw down stairs was in the last stages of bronchial consumption, physicians had no hope for her. I brought her back from the face of death with my divine power and without approaching her. Did you ever see a more healthy mortal? Physical infirmities are cured by me simply by faith, and I can cure them without even their exercise of faith if I would."

He Is Incarnate.

"Do you expect to live on earth forever?"

"I shall be here many years in the present body, and the world will see wonderful sights before I cast off this body. But I am incarnate, and when this goes into the corruption of death my spirit will enter another body and still live on earth. How or when the present body will die has not yet been revealed of the Father. But in form and substance the identical body I now possess was the one that was crucified on Calvary. There are many things in the gospels that are inaccurate about my crucifixion and my life on earth, and I am now occupied in writing a new and true version of the New Testament that can be accepted as the perfect and inspired word. This in itself, when given to the world, will create a revolution among those who now consider themselves orthodox believers."

"Will you tell me something of your domestic life here?"

"Well, sir, you can say that we live as a large family. There are several married couples here, but most are unmarried. The evil charge that we practice free love shows how little the world knows of the purity and sinlessness of our lives. I am the type of the sinless one, and those who live with me and believe become pure even as I am pure, and in them there can be no guile. Our marriage ceremony is binding, and there can be no divorce. As for myself, I never experienced the passions of man, for I am God. I know that I shall be reviled and persecuted, and men will say all manner of evil things against me, but I am holy and the world will yet know it. The whole world is impanneled [*sic*] as a jury to try us, but those who now persecute us will be utterly destroyed. You and all others will have to come believe in me before you can be saved. I might add that our 'Church of the Redeemer' will supplant all others on the earth. The so-called orthodox churches are the beasts of Daniel and must be destroyed."

A Pointed Question Parried.

"If you have the same body that was crucified where are the marks of the nails in your hands?" asked the skeptical scribe.

"I do not claim that the material physique has not changed and put on new flesh, but my features are not changed, and though new material substance has covered the point of the torturing instruments, in a general sense the same body is now before you as arose from the tomb at my resurrection."

"Will you give me a little biography of your earlier life before you became divine?"

"I was born in Marion, O[hio], in 1853, of German parentage. Before I reached the age of 12 my mother used to say that an aged minister told her 'Your son is destined to be a Levite. Verily, God has chosen him.' In earlier days, though thrown in an unwholesome moral atmosphere, by a wonderful working of an internal God-given power of selection I was kept from all those secret vices which infest all grades of society, my ideality was strong and I applied this faculty to the betterment of overt conduct and private virtues, the elevation of life and being. The ideal person was to me the Son of God and the son of man. I thought constantly, I shall be satisfied when I awake with Thy spirit. I always communed with heaven. I studied for and entered the Methodist ministry. But I was not satisfied. My ministerial associates seemed so secular, so uncelestial, so un-Christlike that I could not feel of them though among them. I saw through one of the back windows of Methodism as sight of social and religious conditions which compelled me to trace with the slow and steady finger of candor across my Methodist hopes the word 'disappointment.' I was finally sent to Alpens, Mich. When I entered upon that charge I was in the spirit of becoming more rapidly a citizen of heaven and less a denizen of earth. Under the electric light of inspiration I found that the Methodist Church was filled with spiritual wickedness in high places. The abomination that taketh resolute was found to be standing where it ought not in the church, in all churches.

"In December, 1877, I met Dorinda Helen Fletcher Beekman, the bride of Christ. She was my spiritual Mary. She gave to the world its Jesus and its Lord. Of my history since that time you have been already made acquainted. And now I will have to be excused, as I have pressing duties. I will escort you through the house before you go, that you may see our home. Everything is open and there is nothing that we fear to cast the sunlight upon."

Well Provisioned Throughout.

The Lord then led the visitor hurriedly through the house from cellar to garret. The former was well stocked with provender. Hundreds of glass jars of fruit were ranged on the shelves, and tub after tub of fragrant butter sat in the corners of the spacious underground room.

On the first floor were the sleeping apartments of the ladies, elegantly fitted boudoirs. The second story of the wing is devoted to Schweinfurth's suite. They eclipsed the ladies' rooms in elegant furnishings. There was also a large school room on the second floor of the main building, where some 30 pupils are daily taught. The garret, which is commodious and clean, but very plainly furnished, contains a dozen beds. Here sleep the men whose hard work and substance have gone toward equipping the rest of the house in such princely fashion. Within the last year or two $20,000 has been spent in remodeling and refurnishing the house. Mr. Schweinfurth has complete charge of all the finances, and uses the means at his pleasure, never accounting for anything.

The growth in membership of this remarkable sect has been astonishingly rapid within the last few years. They now have churches at Chicago, St. Charles, Minn.; Minneapolis, Paw Paw, Ill.; Louisville, Ky.; Leavenworth and Kansas City. But the central community is this one here. New converts must come here and learn their duties and obligations, and those who are willing to work are assigned fields of labor.

His Meek and Lowly Role.

Services are held here every Sunday afternoon at 1 o'clock and Schweinfurth always preaches. Sometimes his sermons occupy from two to three hours in delivering. Stenographers are employed who take down his every utterance, and copies are made on type-writers and sent to all the branch churches, where they are read to the faithful. They are strict vegetarians in diet, never touching meat, milk or eggs. They eat [an] abundance of oatmeal and fruits and sometimes use beef suet.

The place is spoken of by all who visit it as a happy home life. Those who have been there from motives of curiosity come away with an impression that there is something fascinating about the man and the place. Schweinfurth always acts the meek and lowly role to perfection. He was recently met by a Rockford clergyman in a store here and denounced as an impostor, possessed of the devil, a lustful mocker of holy things and assailed with terms of the most opprobrious nature.

He answered calmly, quietly, respectfully, without the shadow of any anger. To all outward appearances his life is not only blameless, but he is marvelous in his power of restraint and the deliberate and collected way in which he asserts his Godhood and replies to aspersions. He has the scriptures at his tongue's end and quotes text after text with most surprising fluency to sustain his position.

His Kingdom Growing.

There is no question but that he has a most unaccountable influence over the minds of those with whom he comes in contact. He numbers among his followers people of learning and culture. His "kingdom," as he calls it, is growing beyond all conception of those who have not examined into it, and there is no doubt that the new church which he has established will be heard from in hundreds of quarters from this time on. Rev. S. L. Conde, pastor of the Westminster Presbyterian Church here, has been making a study of Schweinfurth, his teachings and his disciples in the most thorough manner for six months. One of the members of his church, Mrs. M. M. Kinnehan, has become converted to the new Christ and has left her husband and taking her child has joined the Beekmanites, that being the name they still remain best known by in this vicinity.

Ministerial Converts.

There are quite a company of traveling men, colporteurs[4] and agents in various lines who belong to this sect. Schweinfurth makes special effort to attract this class, as they can more widely sow seeds of the new religion and can select the more likely subjects for their influences. Among the leading lights are Rev. Mr. Tuttle and his wife, a Congregational minister, who has been established over the Chicago church of Schweinfurth. Mr. Tuttle is a man of education and excellent parts. He is a graduate of Yale College and Andover Theological Seminary. A Baptist minister of Pennsylvania is a recent convert and a Congregational minister in Maine has just written to Lord Schweinfurth stating that he believes Christ is now on earth and asking for light on his claims to being the Messiah. Mr. Schweinfurth has a large mail daily and is kept very busy answering letters of similar import from every part of the country.

Among those who have suffered in disrupted family relations owing to Schweinfurth's machinations is Dr. J. S. Wilkin, the head of the National Medical Dispensary, Dearborn street, Chicago, whose wife has joined the band. Dr. Wilkin has determined to bring suit for $25,000 against Schweinfurth for injuring his domestic peace. In order to have, if possible, a stronger hold upon him, the Chicago physician secretly sent out a female detective about two weeks ago, a bright, attractive young woman named Mrs. E. C. Clafin. She went to the Community and made pretense that she desired to join and become a convert to the faith. Her object was especially to discover Schweinfurth's relations with the band of women surrounding him. She reports that she found him cold as ice, and adamant to all her devices. The strangest part of the story is that, skeptic though she was, she has now become a genuine convert, perfectly imbued with a belief in his supernatural attributes, and so testified at a meeting of the faithful in Chicago.

A Skeptic Convinced.

The representative succeeded in meeting her and held a most interesting interview. She said: "I am fully convinced that Schweinfurth is Jesus Christ come again to this earth. He is God. By him the only true way to salvation is revealed. I came there a skeptic. I now believe in him. He is truly without guile, and I thank Heaven I was sent out where I could meet him and learn of him. We can be purged of all sin believing in him."

She gave more information about the life there than the reporter could learn in his visit to the community. There are a number of the women who by long residence and devotion have approached sufficiently near to the purity of their Christ that they are called "angels." There were 13 of these "angels" when she was there. They eat with Schweinfurth, taking but two meals a day. The rest of the women whose angelic wings are still in the pin feather stage, eat separately at another house, and the men all have other quarters for their meals. There is one "angel" who is the most perfect

and called by Schweinfurth his "soul's mate." Her community name is Angelica. She is a pale, dark-eyed, lissome
creature of 23 years, not very plump, but willowy and spiri-
tuelle, with a far-away look in her eyes. Mrs. Claflin said
that her complexion was wonderful—white as alabaster.
She occupies a special apartment, which is the most lavishly
and richly adorned of any in the house. Her room is very
near "Christ's," and she is never seen about the house, and
visible to the others only at meals when she sits at his right
hand.

Garden of Eden Test.

There are certain final rites celebrated which are called
"The Garden of Eden" test. This is known to be a fact,
though it is one of the few things that no one seemed ready
to explain. It is understood, however, that it is modeled
quite closely after the Mormon endowment house, and it is
rumored that the women who pass through the ordeal do so
in a nude state, in the presence of the Christ, also nude. But
it is alleged that the participants are so free from all sin that
even thus unattired they are purity itself.

There is one thing that is remarked upon by all who study
Schweinfurth. He certainly bears the closest resemblance to
the popular pictures of the Saviour. So near is the likeness
that strangers, in total ignorance of his identity, have been
heard to comment on it. His eyes, beard and hair are of the
same color. The contour of his face follows the lines of the
paintings of the real Christ with great accuracy. I have certainly never seen any person who could begin to approach
this striking resemblance. It is very likely that Schweinfurth
depends upon this similarity for some of his most powerful
arguments in making disciples.

Trouble for the Churches.

In dozens of places are springing up church trials of persons who have embraced the faith. In a Kansas City Presbyterian church a trial is now pending of a woman who has
become a convert, and depositions are to be taken here to

prove that Schweinfurth cannot perform miracles, as is alleged. A number of women have recently left a Presbyterian church in Richmond, Ky., and are among the number of the community here.

Such is the story of the Beekmanites. Fragmentary and imperfect sketches of this peculiar sect have been appearing of late in many papers, but this is the first comprehensive, consecutive and complete investigation into their origins, growth and practices and the remarkable pretensions of the alleged Christ that has ever been given to the public in any paper, East or West. The revelations are almost incredible, yet as given here they are absolutely true, and all important statements herein made can be fully substantiated by a score of unimpeachable witnesses. That these Beekmanites are bound to increase and multiply until they become a very strong organization is not doubted by anyone who has made them a subject of study.

SOME VERY MYSTERIOUS THINGS[5]

That a Disciple of the Rockford Rooster Fails to Explain or Understand, but Pins His Faith to— Propagation of a Sinless Race and How It Is To Be Achieved—A New Annunciation Alleged.

Minneapolis, Aug. 19—C. C. Whitney, the Minneapolis apostle of George J. Schweinfurth, has been seen and asked to explain the recent occurrence in Schweinfurth's household in Rockford, Ills., the child born to Mary Welden [*sic*], an unmarried disciple of Schweinfurth's new faith. In reply, Whitney said: "It was conceived by the holy ghost and born without sin. Miss Weldon is one of the redeemed."

"But did the holy ghost act through Mr. Schweinfurth?"

"That I am not prepared to say. The ways of God are inscrutable, but what I do say is we are no freelovers. We believe that absolute chastity should be the attribute of both sexes. We live perfectly pure, chaste lives."

The Privilege of the "Redeemed."

"But how about man and wife, don't the members of your church who are married live together and raise children?"

"No, they do not. Any married couple bringing forth children would be considered guilty of adultery."

"But how about Miss Weldon?"

"That is different. She is one of the redeemed. The 'sanctified,' as St. Paul put it. None but the redeemed can bear children. These children are pure because they are conceived by the Holy Ghost, just as Jesus Christ was nearly 1,900 years ago."

Dead Certain About Miss Weldon.

"But how do you know Miss Weldon is redeemed or sanctified?"

"Because the spirit has announced that fact. It told her so three years ago when Mr. Schweinfurth was in Alpena, Mich."

"How many members of your church are redeemed?"

"I could not state positively, perhaps twelve or fifteen."

"Are any of them men?"

"None except Mr. Schweinfurth. Of course he is, as he is the son of God. The same spirit dwells in him that dwelt in Jesus Christ."

Conceived by the Holy Ghost.

"Then do you claim that Mary Weldon was not approached by Mr. Schweinfurth and that he is not the physical father of her child?"

"I don't claim anything about which I don't know, but I know that child was conceived by the Holy Ghost."

"Do you think Miss Weldon would have borne that child if she had not seen a man for a year or two previous?"

"I do. I believe Miss Weldon to be, as she says she is, perfectly chaste."

Perpetuation of the Race.

"How, then, will the race be perpetuated?"

"By the Holy Ghost."

"The Holy Ghost will beget all the children when everybody is redeemed?"

"Yes, most certainly."

"What will man's function be? Wouldn't such an arrangement be considered rather partial?"

"I can't say as to that. All this is very mysterious. We can't divine God's purpose."

The Weldon Farm Near Rockford is Abandoned by the Apostle and His Angels[6]

George Jacob Schweinfurth and wife will soon leave Rockford for California, with the intention of making that state their home. What Schweinfurth will engage in in that state is not stated. Spencer Weldon may accompany Mr. and Mrs. Schweinfurth and spend the winter in California.

Time was, and that not so many years ago, when the announcement of the intention of Schweinfurth to change his residence would have flashed over the wires to all the papers of the country.

The downfall of Schweinfurth's church dates really from the time the natural increase in population at the "heaven" began. Today there is nothing besides Schweinfurth left on the Weldon farm to tell that it was once the headquarters of a strange religious (?) sect, with the exception of the large house which was built not only for living purposes but also as a place of worship. If there is anything else to recall the old days it is the yellow-haired, legally fatherless children playing under the trees about the house. All the "apostles" and all the "angels" are gone, and soon Schweinfurth himself will be gone.

Schweinfurth long since acknowledged that he was mistaken in preaching that he was something divine, but most of his followers had come to the conclusion some time before he announced that he had.

THE TWENTIETH
CENTURY

INVASION OF THE
YOGA CULTS

1911[1]

In 1974 fifteen-year-old Robin George ran away from home and took up residence with the International Society for Krishna Consciousness (ISKCON), also known as the Hare Krishnas. She spent over a year in ISKCON ashrams before returning to her family. Later, she decided she had been "brainwashed" by ISKCON and sued for false imprisonment along with other charges. In 1983 a jury awarded George and her family $32 million—the largest award of its kind against a new religious movement. Appeals lasted until 1993, when ISKCON finally reached an out-of-court settlement.[2] As the article below demonstrates, the story that George's lawyers told the jury—of an innocent woman seduced by an Eastern religion and imprisoned through mental domination rather than by bars or chains—is an old one that dates back to the first arrival of Hinduism to the United States.

New religious movement scholar J. Gordon Melton pointed out that "new" religious movements are often not new at all.[3] Although ISKCON was branded as a cult in the 1970s, it is a form of Hinduism, which is one of the oldest religions in the world. But Hinduism seemed "new" to Americans because the United States had allowed immigration from India only since the Hart-Celler Act was passed in 1965. Before 1965, Hinduism and yoga seemed even more exotic. In 1893 Swami Vivekananda had been invited to speak at the World Parliament of Religions, which was held at the Chicago World's Fair. Some of the organizers hoped this would be an opportunity to prove Christianity's superiority to other religions, but Vivekananda won audiences over by explaining Hindu philosophy in scientific, nonthreatening terms. The following year he founded the Vedanta Society for the study of Vedic philosophy. In 1895 he led the first yoga retreat in America, in New York's Thousand Island Park. Over the next few decades yoga became popular with urban bohemians, especially young women. Industrialization had given rise to the "new woman" who could live in the city and support herself. With this cultural shift came anxieties about young women on their own, and moral entrepreneurs often viewed yoga classes in terms of seduction, mind control, and fears of white slavery.[4]

As an outspoken journalist and suffragist, Mabel Potter Daggett embodied the qualities of the "new woman." However, in the article below she takes aim at the many Asian "cults" that she claims have come for American women. The article is also overtly racist, describing the "swarthy" priests dominating "golden headed" American women. Another striking feature is that Daggett lumps together numerous Asian religions, including Hinduism, Buddhism, Islam, Zoroastrianism, and Bahai, as essentially interchangeable "cults" and "Eastern abominations." She also makes no distinction between established religions that were imported from Asia and movements founded by Americans who often made dubious claims about religious initiation they received in Asia. Some of the examples that Daggett cites did not involve Asian people at all.

A few of the figures and incidents that Daggett discusses warrant further explanation. Sarah Chapman Bull (1850–1911) was the widow of Ole Bull, a famed Norwegian violinist. She became a disciple of Swami Vivekananda, and on her death she willed her entire estate, valued at about $500,000, to the Vedanta Society. Bull's daughter challenged the will in court, claiming that Hindus had driven her mother insane. Anticipating future claims of brainwashing, lawyers claimed that Hindus had used a form of mind control. They framed Bull's interest in Hinduism in medicalized terms, stating that her brain "had been inoculated with the bacteria of faith taught by Indian swamis."[5]

The daughter won nearly all of Bull's assets, only to die of tuberculosis on the day of the settlement.

Dr. William Latson was an early American proponent of yoga. He had an office in New York where he offered yoga and Oriental dancing classes for young women seeking health and beauty. In May 1911 Dr. Latson's body was found in his office with a bullet wound to the head, an apparent suicide. Soon afterward a heartbroken female disciple attempted suicide herself. These events led *The Washington Post* to run this headline: "The Soul Destroying Poison of the East: The Tragic Flood of Broken Homes and Hearts, Disgrace, and Suicide that Follows the Broadening Stream of Morbidly Alluring Oriental 'Philosophies' into Our Country."

Pierre Bernard was another American who taught yoga classes and claimed that he had been initiated into an esoteric tradition of Hinduism known as Tantra. In 1910 two of Bernard's female students accused him of false imprisonment, claiming that he had used hypnosis to turn them into "spiritual prostitutes." Charges were dropped after the two young women fled town. Bernard went on to found a country club in upstate New York, where he gained respectability and helped to rebrand yoga as a form of athletic training rather than a secretive religious practice.

A running thread in this panic over "yoga cults" was the idea of "nautch girls" or temple prostitutes. Figures like Daggett suggested that the purpose of yoga was to lure young women with promises of beauty and enlightenment, take control of their minds, and then ship them to India for service as nautch girls. The reality of so-called nautch girls is complicated and, ironically, is in many ways the result of British colonialism and Victorian prudery. For centuries Hindu temples featured women called devadasis who danced to honor the gods. Prior to colonization, devadasis were respected for their training and expertise. To retain the most prestigious devadasis, Indian kingdoms would patronize them with gifts, including tax-free land. But under the

*Muslim Mughal Empire, and especially the British Raj,
Hindu temples could no longer support* devadasis. *In addition, the British found temple dancing lewd, which created
further pressure to stop patronizing dancers. It was under
these conditions that* devadasis *began resorting to selling
sexual favors to temple visitors. Eventually dancing and
prostitution were viewed as synonymous under the British
Raj. This set the stage for a pattern of exploitation in which
young women from impoverished backgrounds were
groomed to be temple prostitutes. "Nautch" is a corruption of the Hindi "nach," meaning "to dance." In 1882 the
first anti-nautch movement was launched in India with the
goal of making temple dances illegal in order to end prostitution. The anti-nautch movement was started by educated
middle- and upper-class Hindus, but for Americans like
Daggett, their concerns were simply ammunition for indicting the spread of Hinduism.*[6]

*Historian Stephen Prothero has suggested that these
conspiracy theories about Hinduism were rooted in older
conspiracy theories about Catholicism. Like Catholicism,
Hinduism has priests who perform rituals in a dead language. Many nineteenth-century Protestants believed nuns
were essentially sex slaves for priests, so it seems plausible
that Hindu priests would likewise use "priest-craft" to enslave women.*[7] *Ironically, amid all these fears, American
women were already second-class citizens and would not
get the right to vote until 1920.*

*Of course, there have been actual incidents of yoga
groups in the United States behaving in toxic or abusive
ways. Perhaps the greatest example is an episode involving
the Rajneesh movement, led by Bhagwan Shree Rajneesh
(1931–1990). In the 1980s Rajneesh and his followers established a large colony in Wasco County, Oregon. Tensions escalated between the colony and its neighbors until
1984, when movement leaders purposely contaminated
local salad bars with salmonella. This resulted in the nonlethal poisoning of 751 people. Following this attack, Rajneesh was deported to India and the colony collapsed.*

However, Rajneesh's movement still exists in the form of the Osho International Foundation. It is important to remember that all religious organizations sometimes have bad actors and that there is nothing inherently dangerous or abusive about Hinduism or yoga.

Today, debates about yoga are more likely to concern issues like "cultural appropriation" than mind control or slavery. However, the Nativist paranoia in Daggett's article can still be seen today in twenty-first-century panics about Muslims forcing sharia law onto Americans or Haitian immigrants eating their neighbors' pets.

AMERICAN WOMEN LOSING FORTUNES AND REASON SEEKING THE ETERNAL YOUTH PROMISED BY THE SWARTHY PRIESTS OF THE FAR EAST

Eve is eating the apple again. It is offered as a knowledge of the occult that shall solve the riddles of existence. Yoga, that eastern philosophy the emblem of which is the coiled serpent, is being widely disseminated here. And before a charm that seemingly they cannot resist thousands of converts are yielding to the temptation to embrace its teachings of strange mysteries. Literally yoga means the "path" that leads to wisdom. Actually it is proving the way that leads to domestic infelicity and insanity and death.

They are priests from "east of Suez" who with soft spoken proselyting have whispered this mysticism into the ears of the American woman. While the churches of America are spending twenty million dollars annually in the cause of foreign missions the pagans have executed an amazing flank movement; they have sent their emissaries to us. Today the tinkling temple bells ring out with a derisive, jarring note in a Christian land. Seattle has its Buddhist temple; San Francisco has its Hindoo temple; Los Angeles has its Krishna temple. The Vedanta Society of New York has laid at West Cornwall, Connecticut, the corner stone of a greater temple than these. It is marked, as are stones and trees set apart for worship in India, with red paint, the sacred vermilion. And graved deep in New England granite is set the most holy word of the Vedantists—"Om." Chicago, Illinois, and Lowell, Massachusetts, have their Zoroastrian temples to the sun, another of which is to be erected at Montreal. At Chicago also the Bahais, a modern Mohammedan cult, are building their great Mashrak-el-Azkar to represent their sect in the West. It was the Congress of Religions at the Chicago World's Fair in 1893 that with a spirit of fine religious toleration beckoned the first holy men from their fastnesses in the Himalayas. That benign condescension has proved fraught with far-reaching consequences. The Swamis and Babas who came to America discarded in India the simplicity of their Sanhyasin garb for gorgeous robes more tempered to Western taste. They arrived silken clad and sandal shod, to prove an attraction that outshone the plain American variety of divine, the minister in a frock coat and white tie. The Easterners were picturesque personalities whom American society welcomed in the drawing-room.

The incense of sandalwood burned in their honor all the way from the Lake Shore Drive to Fifth Avenue and the Back Bay. At social functions all poets, artists, authors and musicians stepped aside to at least second place. These dusky-hued Orientals sat on drawing-room sofas, the center of admiring attention, while fair hands passed them cakes and served them tea in Sèvres china. It was far better than squatting, clad in a yellow loin cloth, at some heathen temple's gate. They remained among us.

Also others of their order, hearing of this triumphant reception, combed out their matted hair, allowed to hang uncared for during the years of sacred meditation, and leaving their begging bowls behind, hurried over to this so much more lucrative field.

When there was started at Green Acre, Maine, in 1896, a summer school of philosophy which was the outgrowth of the World's Fair Congress of Religions, its platform was an open forum where the Swamis found a welcome. It is via this New England route from Calcutta that nearly every Eastern mystic has arrived and established his vogue in this country.

With this introduction from Green Acre, Maine, the land of the Puritan forefathers, the turbaned teachers from the East set out across the continent. At first their way lay through the populous cities where the sun rises now on the gilded minarets of their mosques and pagodas. More recently they have reached the smaller towns and villages where have been formed branches and circles that are exerting a widely increasing influence.

On the banners of many of these cults is emblazoned the serpent that affects the onlooker as a startling reminder of the evil that entered Eden. It is the symbol that you will see on the gold and enameled badge pinned on a convert's gown. You will find it on the walls of the assembly rooms. And it appears as the imprint on the literature used at the yoga classes.

The yoga class is becoming as popular as the Browning class[8] or the Shakespeare class. It is the direct means by which a Swami reaches the public. Through its aid, the Eastern teaching is gathering a wider clientèle than it formerly numbered among the society set that first made it fashionable. Placing the Hindu Scriptures, the Bhagavadgita, or the Persian Scriptures, the Zend Avesta, above their Bibles are many women who were formerly predestined Baptists and Presbyterians, Methodists saved by grace, established Episcopalians, Catholics who said their rosaries, and daughters of Abraham from an unbroken line of the Jewish faith.

It is the promise of eternal youth that attracts woman to yoga, the promise which is found intertwined with most of the pagan religions. This yoga philosophy opens the door to subtle mysteries. The yogi, as the student who masters it is termed, is promised the dominance of natural law. Incidentally there is offered also health and long life and the power to stay the ravages of time. Is it not enough to tempt the feminine mind from Paradise itself? Small wonder that a Swami's following, while it includes notably here and there college professors and men of learning come to investigate a science brought from the roof of the world, recruits its largest numbers among women. But yoga is a dangerous knowledge to lure any but the best balanced brain. In the pursuit of it, too often the listening devotee is offering her sacrifices even at the altar of her soul.

Miss Sarah Farmer, a New England spinster with a beautiful ideal of universal brotherhood, gave her fortune in the founding of Green Acre, where for years she was a familiar figure in her flowing gray gown and veil. The study of many religions unbalanced her mind and she has been for several years an inmate of an insane asylum at Waverly, Massachusetts.

In Chicago, a few years since, Miss Aloise Reuss, a woman of culture and refinement was taken, screaming and praying, from the Mazdaznan Temple of the Sun to be incarcerated, a raving maniac, in an Illinois asylum. The death of Mrs. Ole Bull, of Cambridge, Massachusetts, widow of the world renowned violinist, occurred in January last, and her will bequeathing several hundred thousand dollars to the Vedantist Society was set aside by the courts on the grounds of mental incapacity and undue influence. On the very day of the decision, her daughter, Mrs. Olea Bull Vaughn, in whose behalf the verdict was rendered, died technically of tuberculosis but actually, the doctors said, of a broken heart.

Mrs. May Wright Sewell, the club woman of national repute, who spent much time with Mrs. Bull at the latter's Cambridge home, is suffering from ill health, and is said to be a physical wreck through the practice of yoga and the study of occultism.

The relatives of Mrs. Ellen Shaw of Lowell, Massachusetts, a while ago petitioned the courts that a conservator be appointed to prevent her from bestowing her property on the sun worshipers. Witnesses at the trial testified that Mrs. Shaw had taken nude sun baths on the lawn of her residence in the fashionable Tyler Park section of Lowell. Last spring, Dr. William R. C. Latson, a New York physician, was found mysteriously dead in his Riverside Drive apartment, and Alta Markheva, the young Jewish girl who called him her mangod, or "guru" in the study of yoga, attempted to follow him in suicide. Her sister, Mrs. Rebecca Cohen, moaned: "This new religion seems to me to be of the devil. It has disgraced my sister and taken her from her people."

More recently the handsome and cultured wife of President Winthrop Ellsworth Stone of Purdue University at Lafayette,

Indiana, has abandoned home and husband and children to join the sun worshipers in the study of yoga. Dr. Stone went before the board of the Presbyterian Church and announced: "I am utterly crushed, I want your prayers and your sympathy. I love my wife. She is as dear to me as she ever was. I hope that she will some time yet come to her senses and return to me and my boys."

Further record of the devastation that follows in the wake of the trailing robes of the "Masters" from the East, may be read from day to day in the newspapers. The imported religions of the Orient that sow the subtle seeds of destruction, are offered to the uninitiate as beautiful philosophies. On the surface they are that. But they are inevitably sprung from the soil of paganism and are tinctured with its practices.

It is not that the Swamis bring with them the hideous images worshiped at every roadside shrine in India. Here and there, it is true, a little brown god Buddha or a green jade Krishna has appeared in an American home; but it is undoubtedly used merely, so its owner will tell you, as an "aid to concentration" in the worship of the ideal that it represents.

A greater menace than that of image worship lurks in the teachings of the Hindoo mystics. The casual observer will not discover it. Only those who reach the inner circles become acquainted with the mysteries revealed to the adepts. And the descent from Christianity to heathenism is by such easy stages that the novice scarcely realizes she is led.

How many are followers of the new gods it is difficult to estimate with exactness. It is known, however, that their numbers are in the thousands. The Vedanta Society, established in America by the Swami Vivekananda of popular memory, has its headquarters at 135 West Eightieth street, New York, where his successor, the Swami Abhedenanda, lectures to audiences of from three to five hundred people.

Branch societies with Swamis in charge are maintained in Boston, Pittsburgh, Washington, St. Louis, Denver, San Francisco and Los Angeles, to say nothing of the circles in many small towns.

Vedanta proclaims itself a universal religion, and always

there is generous room in its pantheon for any new god not already listed. Its altar is dedicated to the Supreme Spirit whose name is the eternal word "Om." He may be worshiped through any of his incarnations as Ahura Mazda, or Kali the Divine Mother, or Buddha, or Allah, or Vishnu, or Siva, or Krishna, or Ramakrishna, or Christ. You are offered the wide range of personal choice and no divinity objectionable to your Western sensibilities will be forced on your religious attention.

At West Cornwall, Connecticut, the society maintains its "Ashrama" or peace retreat, planned to become the great summer school of Oriental philosophy for America. It consists of three hundred and seventy acres of forest and field in the heart of the Berkshire Hills.

I was at the Ashrama last summer on a night in June when the Swami Abhedenanda in a flame-colored robe of silk sat over against the sunset that arched above the veranda of "Peace Cottage." There had come for the evening service one or two artists from an adjacent colony, and some few strangers who had driven over from the village of West Cornwall.

The Swami talked of his religion that is three thousand years old. He spoke of immortality but it was of an immortality reaching back in thousands of incarnations through which the souls of his hearers had traveled before this mortal birth, and stretching on in thousands of incarnations more to be traveled still before final absorption in Brahma. The aim of life, the Swami said, was to realize oneness with God. The path to this attainment, he pointed out, is through meditation and concentration and the practice of yoga. But he quoted from the Upanishads which, along with the Vedas form the ancient Hindoo scriptures, and the Upanishads warn that "the path of yoga is as narrow as a razor's edge."

To the Almighty Father and the "Divine Mother," the Swami addressed a prayer for happiness and peace. Then with closed eyes and clasped hands we passed with him into the silence to meditate on oneness with God. At first there were the sounds of nature stirring softly. A summer breeze swayed through the apple trees. A thrush called. Far off a cowbell tinkled faintly. Then all the world receded in the twilight. We were folded with God in the soft falling dusk. The waves of eternity beat gently against the soul. A long time after, we returned to conscious existence at the call of a musical chant in Sanskrit: "Om! Om! Om! Chianti, chianti, chianti! Peace, peace, peace be with you." In the blue blackness of night the first evening star shone.

So poetically, so artistically, is paganism presented to persuade a Christian audience. Then out of this psychologically perfect setting, a voice spoke. It was the voice of a woman, one of the strangers from the village. She leaned forward in the shaft of light that shone out into the darkness through the open house door, and fixed the teacher from the Orient with a cleareyed gaze. "Swami," she said, "I have come from your home land after twenty-two years as a missionary there. And your religion that is three thousand years old, what, let me ask, has it done for the women of India?"

The Swami hesitated. He laughed disagreeably. "What has yours done for the old maids of New England?" was his only rejoinder. The missionary's question is the argument for which Orientalism in its most plausible phase has no answer. That one shrewd sentence punctures the sophistry of the East. So Julia Ward Howe once gave pause to the flow of Vivekananda's eloquence in a Boston drawingroom:

"Swami," she demanded, "if your gods are so good, let your women come to tell us of them."

"Our women," he evaded modestly, "do not travel."

One of them did, however. It was Pundita Ramabai whose tour of the world, proclaiming the wrongs of Indian womanhood, stirred England to lay a heavy hand on some of the religious rites in India. Have American women forgotten Pundita Ramabai?

Baba Bharati, the other day, in a newspaper interview, was able to boast that of his five thousand converts in this country the majority are women. Baba Bharati is that Hindoo who is more selective in his heathenism than are the Vedantists. At the RhadaKrishna temple he has builded in Los Angeles, his followers concentrate on two divinities.

"Hindooism with the halo of its own brilliancy," is what he calls it. "I have made no effort to Westernize it," he brazenly admits. "It is the eternal Hindooism." When the Baba was established in New York, a few years ago, he announced one day to his devotees: "Dear hearts, I have given you the philosophy of religion because here in the West you all want food for your intellects; but I have done so to wheedle you into listening that I may tell you that the philosophy of religion is not religion. Religion is love."

It was shortly thereafter that the Baba was called to the Pacific Coast to attend the parliament of religions known as the Venice Assembly, held in Los Angeles in 1906. The atmosphere of the Pacific he found most pleasing and his choice fell upon Los Angeles as the headquarters in America for "Krishna, the Lord of Love."

This is a title acquired by the most popular divinity of the Hindoos during his career on earth, when he took unto himself sixteen thousand wives and left one hundred and eighty thousand sons to perpetuate his memory. He is also known as the Lord of the Yogis. Rhada was his favorite consort, whose name, signifying "love energy," is linked with his for the title of the Los Angeles temple.

There are in India some three hundred and thirty million gods ranking in importance below the great Hindoo triad composed of Brahma, Vishnu and Siva. It was as Krishna that Vishnu appeared in human form for one of his ten earth incarnations.

"Salaam-Aleikum," which is "Peace be unto you," again, Mazdaznan bids for notice. It is sun worship that takes its name from Ahura Mazda, the Supreme Lord in the Zend Avesta, of whom Zoroaster was the great prophet. There is also a mingling of Hindooism in its strict vegetarianism, and the adaptation of the yoga teaching in breathing and posturing exercises.

This gem of a religion was launched in the United States by his Humbleness Ottoman Zar-Adusht Hannish, claiming to be the "Mantra-Magie of Tempel el Karman (Thibetan rites), Kalantar in Zoroastrian philosophy, Dastur in the art of breathing and Envoy of Mazdaznan living." He is assisted in dispensing its benefits by Her Blessedness Spenta Maria, otherwise Marie Elizabeth Ruth Hilton, the wife of Dr. G. W. Hilton of Lowell, Massachusetts.

At least fourteen thousand Americans are joining with them in the worship of the Lord God Mazda and the daily adoration of the sun. There are Mazdaznan centers in thirty cities of the United States, as well as in Canada, South America, England, Germany and Switzerland. They are all the remarkable growth of the past ten years. It was about 1901 that His Humbleness the Prince of Peace appeared in Chicago.

He said that he had come direct from Thibet where he had pierced the mysteries of the Dalai Lama, bringing back with him this little novelty in the religious line which he immediately proceeded to place on the market. It is quite well authenticated that he had come from Salt Lake City where he was a type setter on the Mt. Deseret News. But it is also probable that he had at some time been in Persia, and the rumor that says he was born there, the son of a Russian girl and a German music master, is undoubtedly correct. At any rate, whatever he has been, he stands to-day among his followers as the "Little Master," an incarnation of divinity.

His headquarters are in Chicago, where the great temple is located on Lake Park Avenue. The lesser temple stands on the lawn of Dr. Hilton's residence on Columbus Avenue in Lowell, and ground has been consecrated for a third temple to be erected in Montreal.

That the sun may do its perfect work, the cult encourages the wearing of as little clothing literally as the law allows. It is Anthony Comstock's prying supervision that has hampered the full exercise of the faith in New York. But on Lowell lawns, sun baths and dew baths in "angel robes" and, as has been testified, even without them—have been sights to startle those of the population still living on the earth plane of staid New England common sense.

Only one who in some previous incarnation has been an old Zend soul, it is said, is really ripe for the practice of Mazdaznan. Her Blessedness, next in authority in the cult to Hannish himself, is reputed to have been once the Queen of Sheba, hence her present high attainments.

Mrs. Hilton's entry into Lowell took place a few years ago when Dr. Hilton, returning from a trip to the Pacific Coast, brought her home as his second wife, accompanied by two pretty grown daughters of a former marriage. It was heard that she was cultured and charming. Lowell society called, to find her a handsome woman with old mysteries slumbering in the depths of her beautiful eyes. She offered her callers Mazdaznan to make them beautiful too. She sent for Dr. Hannish who, looking forty, was introduced as actually sixty-seven.

Lowell built its sun temple and entered on the practice of the new faith. Meat was rigidly eschewed. Fresh violets and sheep sorrel served for the light breakfast allowed. Tea was brewed from rose leaves. A pinch of brown sand was taken at intervals to give tone to an empty stomach. There were classes in breathing and concentration. And for all dieting, bathing and breathing that failed, there were cosmetics sold on the side that successfully supplemented the beauty results.

These were preliminary preparations by way of purification for the deeper truths that await the sun worshiper deemed strong enough in the faith to receive them. A true disciple finds herself at last admitted to the ranks of those who are told that one among them may become the mother of the new Messiah, whose appearing is confidently expected. And she receives the book of instructions, "Inner Studies." This is a compendium of Eastern knowledge that sells at ten dollars a copy. Even at that price it is difficult to obtain, for it does not circulate safely in the mails.

The atmosphere of mystery that enwraps Mazdaznan ritual is characteristic of every Eastern cult. The latest importation, arriving within the past year, is Sufiism, a variety of Mohammedanism dispensed in New York by one Inayat Khan from Baroda. His chanted prayers sound like the familiar call of the Coney Island Arab to his camel. Sufiism frankly admits that its disciples are being gathered into a secret order.

Upon another secret order, that of the Tantrics, which represents the climax of Eastern abominations and is Hindoo religion at its lowest stage, the search light of publicity was recently turned. There are said to be thousands of Tantric initiates in

America. They are under the direction of five gurus or primates. One of these who styled himself "Om the Omnipotent," has had his headquarters in New York closed by the police.

The sacred books of the cult are the Tantras, dialogues between the god Siva and his consort Kali, the Divine Mother. The rites have much in common with the worship of Baal and Moloch by the ancient Assyrians. Their essential feature is the adoration of a naked woman, the dancing Nautch girl who is trained for the embraces of the priests.

The unmentionable orgies of the Tantrics constitute what is known as the "left hand" worship of Kali. The "right hand" worship of this goddess as the divinity of carnage and slaughter is disgusting enough. Her great temple which with its bathing place, the Kali-ghat at Calcutta, has given its name to that city, is one of the most noted in India, to which thousands of devotees make annual pilgrimage.

There is no more horrible idol in the Hindoo pantheon than the figure of Kali. She is represented as a nude black woman dancing on the body of her husband, the god Siva. Her huge tongue protrudes from her mouth. For earrings she has two human heads. She wears a necklace of human skulls and a waistband of human hands, which trophies she is supposed to have taken from the enemies whom she slew during her visit to earth. When she had completed her work of destruction, she danced on the bodies of the fallen until the earth trembled. Her husband, Siva, in the effort to stop the carnage, threw himself beneath her feet. Kali, representing the power and influence of woman, is worshiped as the "Divine Mother."

It is the Hindooism that reaches in the wide span from this heathen idolatry to the heights of the Bhagavad Gita, that has brought to America the yoga philosophy. Its leading exponents, the priests of the Vedantist Society, belong to a monastic order founded in the nineteenth century by Ramakrishna, a priest in the temple of Kali.

Ramakrishna became one of those holy men known as "fakirs," of whom India has some five million five hundred thousand, who toil not but only concentrate and meditate. It is the process by which during twelve years' retirement in the forest or wilderness they have developed the yoga power. Their un-combed hair is matted and filthy. Their bodies are smeared with ashes. Their only clothing is a yellow loin cloth. They ei-ther travel about the country or sit at a temple gate receiving alms in a begging bowl. The populace reverences them and supports them. They are credited with supernatural powers.

Just How Yoga Is Practiced

It is a tradition that Ramakrishna, when he entered on the study of yoga, was illiterate and unlearned. When he had com-pleted it, he was possessed of the knowledge comprised in all literature, science and art the world has ever known. It had been revealed to him by his own soul.

The recent trial of the Bull will case in the Maine courts has disclosed some of the mysteries of yoga as it is studied and practiced here. In Mrs. Bull's beautiful home, known as "Stu-dio House," at Cambridge, Massachusetts, as also in her sum-mer home at Green Acre, Maine, there was a "meditation chamber" with lighted candles and burning incense to make it holy. Here was the headquarters for a select coterie, of whom the Swami Vivenkananda during his lifetime and later the Swami Abhedenanda was the leader.

The yoga in vogue at Studio House was from the publica-tions of the Vedantist Society, which furnishes the text books for classes throughout the United States. The aim is to develop a sixth sense. Thereby the yogi will become endowed with psy-chic power, the ability to cure disease, to ward off old age, and to prolong life indefinitely. These, however, are subsidiary at-tributes through which the soul is finally to attain to the high-est state of superconsciousness and communion with God. To this end it is taught that the spinal column contains a hollow canal called Susumna, at the lower end of which is the "Lotus of the Kundalini," the source of all power. The practice for its development consists in meditation and concentration and ex-ercises in breathing and posture.

The breathing prescribed is rhythmic, through one nostril and out the other to the accompaniment of the repetition of the

sacred word "Om." There are eighty-four varieties of the posturing, the most familiar of which consists in sitting crossed-
legged on the floor, with one hand grasping the great toe of
each foot.

The awakening Kundalini rises in the hollow canal. As it
progresses upward, remarkable powers of the mind unfold.
When it reaches the brain, one is able to detach the soul from
the body. But beware that you have the Kundalini under complete control! Should it make its escape from the brain, the soul
will be unable to reenter the body and the phenomenon commonly known as death will have occurred. Insanity is another
disaster that threatens as a coincidence in the practice of yoga.

Man Is the Real Idol

It is not the worship of images of stone and wood that constitutes the gravest peril in the teaching of the Orientals. It is the
worship of men. The guru is the real idol.

"He was my man-god," sobbed Alta Markheva over the
body of Dr. Latson.

In books of travel written about India one may read that it is
no uncommon proceeding in that country for the disciple on
meeting his guru to prostrate himself and take the very dust
from his teacher's feet to place upon his own head. It is done
even in America. When Swami Vivekananda came out from
his daily meditation, his devotees were wont to clasp the hem
of his robe, and they kissed his sandaled feet! It was American
women who did this!

To bestow gifts upon a guru counts for spiritual merit. The
teachers from the East ostentatiously announce themselves
under vows of poverty and chastity. Their poverty, at least, is
not the suffering sort. No lady's canine darling combed and
curled for a bench show was ever tended with more assiduous
care than is a "Master" whose very name is spoken reverently
and with softened breath.

The wardrobe that his followers have bestowed on the Prince
of Peace, Ottoman Abdul-Zar Hannish, is one rivaling the
apparel of King Solomon. The priestly gown in which he offici-

ates on occasions of state is woven of threads of gold and cost three thousand five hundred dollars.

When the Baba Barati was in Boston, the rent of his luxurious apartment there was paid for years by one of his adherents, a woman of wealth.

The Swami Abhedenanda has traveled via Pullmans and palatial ocean steamers from Chicago to New York and London and Paris, with his expenses defrayed by the New York society woman who accompanied him.

To perform the most menial service for a guru, it is taught in the Eastern scriptures, is a high privilege. At the West Cornwall Ashrama, which is Swami Abhedenanda's "peace retreat," the labor of his household is done by American women who are content to toil in his kitchen in the heat of summer, and who even milk the cows in the devotion of their discipleship. They serve absolutely without pay or compensation of any material kind.

The Hindoo dishes that the Swami requires are prepared with care, and with all spells and incantations prescribed by his religion duly pronounced. Daily the Swami's shirts of silk and linen flap on the line beyond the kitchen door, washed also according to ritual by the same devoted hands.

The household is directed by a beautiful woman of independent wealth who like the rest assists indiscriminately in its toil. She is out in the garden, her golden head flashing in the sunlight while she gathers the vegetables for dinner. She is at the well drawing water, her fair face flushing a lovelier pink with the exercise. She was standing with her white rounded arms raised above her head, in the housewifely act of putting fresh papers on a closet shelf, when she turned to me with the declaration: "I wouldn't, of course, perform such labor for anyone else. I do it all for love of the Swami."

At Green Acre, a Swami passing through the fields to the Lynkolester, "pines of light," the grove where the lectures are held, has been wont to be attended by a throng of personal attendants. One woman carries over him an umbrella. Another waves a palm-leaf fan. Eager ones ahead let down the pasture bars. And the New England farmer in his near-by hay fields sees the sight and wipes his perspiring brow with a laconic "I swan!"

A Green Acre native holds a Swami in as cordial a regard as a snake. Uncle Ben Rogers, whose white farmhouse shelters the overflow of summer guests from the Greenacre Inn, coined for the dark-hued Orientals a phrase now current through the countryside. Some one had called to see one of his boarders.

"She ain't here," said Uncle Ben. Could he tell the caller where the lady was? "Gone a-niggerin' in the pines," was the contemptuous information that Uncle Ben vouchsafed.

What magic of a midsummer day's dream has so blinded the eyes of the American woman that she sees Swamis with distorted vision? From the moment that the guru has whispered to his pupil the mantra or secret formula, to reveal which would invite the anger of the gods, there is formed between the two a tie the most indissoluable [sic] of any on earth.

Women Taken from Home and Family

On the frontispage of a book that he has dedicated to his own guru, Baba Bharati has written: "To my guru to whom my soul, mind and body are irrevocably sold in payment of the grace of his illumination which lighteth my path to the lotus feet of Krishna my beloved."

So a guru's bidding is obeyed even when he tells a disciple that the highest spiritual attainment in yoga will require the renouncement of home and family ties.

"My husband and children are no more to me than any others equally deserving of regard," Mrs. Stone, the wife of the Purdue College president coldly proclaims. "My religion teaches that they have no claim on me and I am free to seek the perfect life alone."

The Boston headquarters of the Vedantist Society on St. Botolph street is in charge of an American woman who has taken the vows and the veil of an Indian nun of Ramakrishna's order. She is a Vassar College graduate and a rich man's daughter. The

Vedantists declare: "We know nothing of former relationships. She now belongs more to us than to her family." She has become Sister Devamata.

When Mrs. Bull lay on her deathbed, the Vedantists with Sister Nevidita who surrounded her in her weakened physical and mental state, denied her daughter admittance because, as they assured Mrs. Bull, she was "psychically inharmonious in the scheme of perfection."

Sister Nevidita, once Margaret E. Noble, an Englishwoman, is now also a Ramakrishna nun. She was summoned from India to exercise special supervision over Mrs. Bull and her money. In the room that she occupied at Studio House, set in a niche in a wall above her bed was a picture of Ramakrishna before which she performed daily puju, or worship. She says her prayers also to Kali the Divine Mother, of whom she has written a book, eulogizing the heathen goddess as the "sweet terrible one."

Is it any wonder that the missionaries from the foreign field are sending to their home offices in New York and Boston the peremptory inquiry: "What do Christian women mean?" And they echo the question put at the Swami Abhedenanda's Ashrama: "What has paganism done for the women of the East that the women of the West want aught with it?"

Woman's position in India is the most degraded of anywhere in the world. Shut within the *zenana*,[9] she may not even leave the house without her husband's permission. Her hope of salvation is through him whom she regards as a god. She serves him his food and waits for her own with her face to the wall until he has finished. Child marriage is required and motherhood is enforced as early as the age of twelve. Twenty three thousand child widows freed now by English law from suttee, the rite that formerly burned them on a husband's funeral pyre, are reckoned as accursed and are persecuted by social custom.

Thousands of girls, twelve thousand in South India alone, are dedicated as Nautch girls to the service of the temple priests in consecrated prostitution.

It is a holy injunction of Manu, the ancient Hindoo code, that woman shall not be taught the Vedas, and she is forbidden to pronounce even a sacred syllable from them. One hundred and ninety-nine women of every two hundred in India cannot read or write. It was one of these little dark women who sorrowfully drew her chudder[10] more closely about her and said to a missionary: "Oh, Miss Sahib, we are like the animals. We can eat and work and die, but we cannot think."

Literally less than a cow, is a woman in India. For the cow is held sacred. And the soft-speaking priest from the land of the serpent who lures the Western woman with his wiles, holds her also in like contempt. What did the Swami Vivekananda, returning to his native land, tell of his fair American proselytes? The missionaries say that he boastfully spread the impression that they were even as the Nautch girls of India.

THE TRIAL OF
ALEISTER CROWLEY

1934[1]

Throughout the Satanic panic of the 1980s, claims makers cited the career of Aleister Crowley (1875–1947) as evidence that Satanic cults exist. In 1967 Crowley's face appeared on the cover of the Beatles album Sgt. Pepper's Lonely Hearts Club Band, *and in 1980 Crowley inspired the song "Mr. Crowley" by rock singer Ozzy Osbourne. Crowley was not actually a Satanist; he was an occultist and an iconoclast who reveled in newspapers calling him the "Wickedest Man in the World" and the "King of Depravity." His parents had belonged to a strict Christian sect called the Plymouth Brethren, and as a child his mother would call him the "Beast" for his unruly behavior. Rather than being shamed by this epithet, Crowley spent the rest of his life living up to it. He inherited a large sum of money, allowing him to travel the world, study magic, self-publish his books and poetry, and indulge in recreational drugs, including heroin.*

Crowley was inspired by the fictional Abbey of Thélème, described by French monk François Rabelais in his satirical novels. Rabelais imagined an "inverted" monastery where instead of living under monastic discipline, monks were encouraged to "do as thou wilt." Rabelais's Abbey of Thélème appealed to many affluent libertines. Sir Francis Dashwood (1708–1781) leased an abandoned abbey where the members of his "Hellfire Club" met to hold sacrilegious parties. Over the entrance was inscribed "Fay ce que vouldras" (Do what thou wilt). "Thelema" is a Greek word meaning "will," and Crowley eventually founded his own religion called "Thelema." In the Pagan religion of Wicca, the expression "Do as thou wilt" evolved into the so-called Wic-

can rede: "An ye harm none, do what ye will," first recorded in a speech made by Wiccan writer Doreen Valiente in 1964.

In 1920 Crowley attempted to create a real-life Abbey of Thelema. He purchased a villa in the town of Cefalù on the coast of Sicily, where residents could study under him to discover and express their "True Will." In 1922 newlyweds Raoul Loveday (né Frederick Charles Loveday) and Betty May arrived at the Abbey. Raoul took sick and died in 1923. May claimed that Crowley forced Raoul to drink cat's blood and that this directly led to his death. According to May's memoir, Tiger Woman (1929), Crowley found a cat prowling the villa, declared it to be an evil spirit, and grabbed it. The cat scratched him, and Crowley called for it to be sacrificed. At the hour the cat was to be executed, Crowley drugged it with ether and ordered Raoul to slay it using a kukri (a Gurkha knife). As May writes, "My husband, unused to wielding such an awkward weapon as the kukri, had not struck truly, with the result that he had only partially cut through the neck of the cat, which had escaped from his nerveless hands and was darting about the floor of the abbey, spitting and foaming at the mouth, and blood issuing from the gash in its neck in huge spurts."[2] Raoul eventually did kill the cat, and its blood was collected in a silver bowl. Crowley dipped his finger in the bowl and traced a pentagram in cat's blood on Raoul's forehead. The remaining blood was poured into a silver cup, which Raoul drank. This, May suggests, ultimately caused his death. However, an examining doctor said that Raoul had enteric fever (typhoid), most likely from drinking from mountain springs while hiking—something Crowley had warned him not to do. Rumors surrounding Raoul's death were the final straw for Mussolini's government, which expelled Crowley from Italy, bringing an end to the Abbey of Thelema.

In 1932 Nina Hamnett published her memoir, The Laughing Torso. Hamnett had served as the model for Henri Gaudier-Brzeska's sculpture The Laughing Torso and was an artist in her own right. Crowley had once hired her to paint murals representing the elements of earth, air, fire, and water. Her memoir describes Crowley in mostly favorable terms, and she sent a letter to Crowley stating that "I have written quite a lot about you, very nice and appreciative. No libel, no rubbish, simply showing up the sale bourgeois attitude to all our behaviors."[3] But Crowley objected to one passage: "Crowley had a temple in Cefalù in Sicily. He was supposed to practice Black Magic there, and one day a baby was said to have disappeared mysteriously."[4] Crowley sued Hamnett for defamation, arguing that he never practiced black magic and that the passage accused him of infanticide. Crowley was nearly sixty years old and previously had reveled in his sinister reputation. But now he was finally running out of money, and a defamation suit seemed like a potential source of income.

Before the trial, one of Crowley's solicitors warned him about his book of blasphemous erotic poetry titled White Stains (1898) and stated that if the defense had a copy, "Your chances of winning this action are negligible."[5] As alluded to in the article below, the defense did have a copy. The trial lasted four days and concluded on April 13—a Friday. Crowley was described as vacillating between trying to seem clever and groveling before the judge. In the article below, the judge asks Crowley about his epithet the "Beast," and Crowley replies that he can instead be called "Little Sunshine." In 2022 the Satanic rock band Ghost released the hit single "Call Me Little Sunshine" in reference to this quip.

Representing Hamnett, Martin O'Connor challenged Crowley to perform feats of magic, stating, "You say that on one occasion you rendered yourself invisible. Would you like to do so now, for if you do not I shall denounce you as an imposter?" Crowley replied, "You can ask me to do anything you like, but it will not alter the truth."[6] Crowley lost and was ordered to pay Hamnett's court costs. But he never did. Instead, he declared bankruptcy.

Newspaper reports about the Abbey at Cefalù and Crow-

*ley's lawsuit against Hamnett sparked the public imagina-
tion about cults and "Satanic" rituals. May's autobiography
explicitly refers to Crowley's abbey as a "cult." The 1934
horror film* The Black Cat *was supposed to be based on a
short story of the same title by Edgar Allan Poe. But director Edgar G. Ulmer decided the details of Crowley's lawsuit made for a better horror movie. In the film, newlyweds
find themselves trapped in the castle of mad scientist Hjal-
mar Poelzig (Boris Karloff), who leads a Satanic cult. The*
Black Cat *was the first depiction of Satanism in American
cinema. The trope of naive newlyweds trapped in a mad
castle likely influenced* The Rocky Horror Picture Show
*(1975), which became a "cult" in its own right. Certainly,
Crowley would have approved of audiences honoring this
film by cross-dressing and making off-color jokes.*

ASTOUNDING REVELATIONS OF WICKEDNESS WHEN "BEAST 666" WENT TO COURT

Aleister Crowley, novelist, short story writer, poet of sorts, student of magic, white and black, some time resident of the
United States, brought his character into an English court the
other day in a libel suit and received, so to speak, several
knockout lams on the solar plexus.

Ghosts of Crowley's past rose in the court room, ghosts in
the shape of books he had written, books which had been
printed in very limited editions. They were accordingly very
scarce.

The defense not only knew about them. It had them. It not
only had them, it read extracts from them.

The judge and jurors sat with wide-open eyes and ears. They
could visibly be seen making up their minds. From being the
aggressor in a libel suit, Crowley was soon seen to be fighting
a losing action.

The whole case for the plaintiff had been heard. One witness
for the defense had been heard.

The bell rang for the next round. The jury punched straight for the jaw. It intimated it wanted to know whether it was a correct time for it to intervene. Time!

And then spoke Mr. Justice Swift of King's Bench, London:

"I have been over 40 years engaged in the administration of the law in one capacity or another. I thought I knew of every conceivable form of wickedness. I thought that everything which was vicious and bad had been produced at some time or another before me. I have learned in this case that we can always learn something more if we live long enough.

"I have never heard such dreadful, horrible, blasphemous and abominable stuff as that which has been produced by the man who describes himself to you as the greatest living poet."

Without leaving the jury box to consult, the jurors announced their unanimous verdict for the defendants. Crowley has now appealed his case to a higher British court.

Some time ago Crowley was angered by a book called "Laughing Torso," written by Miss Nina Hamnett. He promptly brought a libel suit against her, the publishers and the printers.

He said there were passages in the novel which imputed that he practiced black magic and that this constituted libel upon him. The defense was a plea of justification. Thereupon the issue was fought out before a crowded court room.

Crowley, a big, smooth-faced, rugged-looking man of about 60, was educated at Trinity College, Cambridge University, and inherited about $160,000, which enabled him to lead a life of leisure.

He devoted much of his time to poetry, art, travel and mountaineering. He climbed the Alps and walked across the Sahara Desert. He became interested in the study of religions of the world and in magic.

On his behalf, his attorney said there were two kinds of magic—white magic, which was beneficent, and black magic, which was evil and which his client had always fought and sought to expose.

In 1920 he started a little artistic colony in Cefalù, Sicily. The book complained of said he was supposed to practice black magic there. A baby was alleged to have mysteriously disappeared. The inhabitants of the Sicilian neighborhood were alleged to have been frightened of him.

Crowley took the stand as the principal witness for his side. He strenuously denied that he ever practiced or attempted to practice black magic. Giving further evidence, he denounced black magic as foul and abominable and, for the most part, criminal. One of the main instruments of black magic, he said, was murder.

A passage in the novel was read to him which stated that every day after tea he performed a ceremony called the Pentagram. He was alleged to have entered a room decorated with cabalistic signs and to have seated himself on a kind of throne before a brazier containing a charcoal fire, around which were hung sacrificial knives and swords and surrounded by a magic circle. He was then alleged to have indulged in ecstatic dances, lashing himself into a frenzy and brandishing a sword.

Crowley said the whole passage was inaccurate. There was no throne and no sacrificial knives. The Pentagram was a ceremony which invokes God to afford the protection of his archangel. There was no obscenity, no animals were sacrificed and nobody was invited to drink their blood.

So far all seemed fair in the case. Then began a long cross-examination. He admitted he was suing because he alleged his reputation had suffered. Then came a machine gun fire of questions:

"For many years have you been publicly denounced as the worst man in the world?"

"Only by the lowest kind of newspaper."

"Did any paper call you the 'Monster of Wickedness'?"

"I don't remember which papers."

"From your youth have you openly defied all moral conventions?"

"No."

"Did you proclaim contempt for all the doctrines of Christianity?"

"That is quite wrong."

Later on, he admitted that he assumed the designations of "Beast 666" and "The Master Therion" (The Great Wild Beast).

Crowley said that 666 was the number of the Sun and he could be called "Little Sunshine." He said he had written several novels and about 18 short stories, besides many poems.

"Have you published material which is too indecent to be read, too indescribably filthy to read in public?"

"No. I have contributed certain pathological books entirely unsuited to the general public and only for circulation among students of psycho-pathology."

"Have you been attacked in unmeasured terms in the press of many countries?"

"I am not so familiar with the gutter press as that."

"They have all accused you of black magic?"

"I am a busy man and don't waste my time on garbage."

Here the cross-examining attorney referred to one of the plaintiff's books, "White Stains."

"Is it a book of indescribable filth?"

"It is a serious study of the progress of a man to the abyss of madness, disease and death."

"You have made a sonnet of unspeakable things, haven't you?"

"Yes."

He said only 100 copies of the book were made and handed to an expert on the subject in Vienna.

"Was that done because you feared prosecution if it was published there?"

"It was not. It was a refutation of the doctrine that sexual perverts have no sense of moral responsibility and should not be punished. I said they had and showed how they went from bad to worse."

"Do you want your reputation to be wider?"

"I should like to be universally known as the greatest living poet."

Then came the American chapter in his life. Before America came into the war, when Crowley was in the United States, he contributed to a magazine in Chicago. Counsel read from an article and asked:

"Did you write that against your own country?"

"I did, and I am proud of it."

"Was it part of German propaganda in the United States?"
"Yes."

He explained that what he wrote was done with the intention of turning that propaganda into rubbish and that the British agents knew what he was doing, and why.

The first witness for the defense was Miss Betty May Sedgwick, authoress of "Tiger Woman." With her then husband, Raoul Loveday, in 1922 she went to Crowley's place in Sicily. She described the occurrence there and insisted that a cat had been killed and that her husband had to drink a cup of blood. Attorney for the plaintiff asked her if every word of that was not pure fiction.

"No, every word of it is true."

Following the close of her evidence, the jury intimated it had heard enough, and after the judge's short declaration, returned its verdict in favor of the defendants.

THE BIRTH OF BRAINWASHING

1950¹

In contemporary rhetoric, "brainwashing" is the sine qua non *of cults: whereas religions win converts and "spread the faith," cults recruit the vulnerable using various forms of deception and mind control. As seen earlier in this volume, people throughout history have attributed willing participation in the wrong religion to black magic or madness. "Brainwashing" is a modern version of such explanations and arose during the Cold War. Edward Hunter (1902–1978) was not only a journalist and war correspondent but also a propagandist for the CIA. The term "brainwashing" had appeared in internal reports from the CIA and its predecessor, the OSS, but in 1950 Hunter introduced it to the public. In this sense, the article below is the official "birth certificate" for the concept of brainwashing.*

The CIA became concerned about the possibility of mind control in 1949. József Mindszenty (1892–1975), a Catholic cardinal in Hungary, had protested the newly formed Soviet-backed Hungarian People's Republic. He was arrested, tortured, and finally appeared at a show trial, where he confessed to plotting to steal the Hungarian crown jewels, start World War III, and appoint himself ruler of the world. The simplest explanation is that Mindszenty was coerced into saying these bizarre things under threat of torture. But the CIA feared that the Soviets had developed some sort of "psychotechnology" that could directly control Mindszenty's mind. In 1960 Hunter explained his theory of brainwashing this way: "The intent is to change a mind radically so that its owner becomes a living puppet—a human robot—without the atrocity being visible . . . with new beliefs and new thought processes inserted into a captive body."²

*In June 1950 the United States entered the Korean War,
pitting US forces against North Korea, which was backed
by China and the Soviet Union. Hunter's article was published three months later, likely for the purposes of boost-
ing US morale and suggesting that no one freely chooses to
participate in communism. The term "brainwashing" was
adapted from the Mandarin words xi ("wash") and nao
("brain"). The term xinao was not widely used by Chinese
communists, but it was adapted from the older term xixin
("washing the heart"), which had been used in Confucian
and Buddhist texts to describe an ideal of self-awareness.
In the late 1800s, Chinese reformers such as Liang Qichao
(1873–1929) replaced the character for "heart" with the
character for "brain" in an effort to make Chinese philosophy more modern.*

*Talk of brainwashing increased after 1952, when US
soldiers were captured in Korea. About 5,000 out of 7,200
prisoners of war either petitioned the US government to end
the war or falsely confessed to dropping anthrax on Korean
civilians or committing other war crimes. Twenty-one US
soldiers even refused to return home. Brainwashing appeared to explain this behavior. Psychiatrist Robert Jay Lifton (1926–) and psychologist Edgar Schein (1928–2023)
were sent to study returning prisoners of war to determine
whether they had been brainwashed. For the most part they
found that the techniques used by the communists amounted
to simple coercion: most prisoners did not really believe they
had committed war crimes and did not resent their government; they simply said these things to avoid punishment.
Only in a handful out of thousands of prisoners was there
evidence of any real attitude change, and this was achieved
under ideal conditions where prisoners could not escape and
could even be executed if they refused to cooperate.*

*Nevertheless, the CIA was convinced that the Soviets
had cracked the secret of mind control. In 1953 CIA director Allen Welsh Dulles (1893–1969) wrote a report on the
prisoners of war and stated that the Soviets could change
the ideas of their victim "like a [vinyl] disc was changed on*

a phonograph."³ That year, the CIA began its own experiments in mind control, known as MK-ULTRA. The program lasted for more than a decade. Many records of MK-ULTRA were destroyed, but in 1977 a Senate investigation uncovered twenty thousand documents associated with the program. They described experiments using LSD, sensory deprivation, hypnotism, and electroshock, often on subjects who had not granted consent.

Donald Ewen Cameron (1901–1967), a professor of psychiatry at McGill University in Montreal and president of the American Psychiatric Association, performed a series of mind-control experiments in Canada for MK-ULTRA. Cameron theorized that a person could be "de-patterned" by stripping away their memories and identity and then giving them a new personality through a process he called "psychic driving." His patients—many of whom sought treatment for mental illness and had no idea they were part of a CIA-funded experiment—were given all manner of psychotropic drugs and hallucinogens, as well as electroshock treatments. The de-patterning worked: Using these techniques, Cameron was able to turn his patients into vegetables who could often no longer recognize their own families. The second phase, "psychic driving," did not work: Cameron made tapes with messages that he hoped his patients would incorporate into their new personalities. These tapes were played to his traumatized patients for up to sixteen hours a day, but to no effect. Cameron could not change ideas like changing a vinyl disk.

The idea of brainwashing was further popularized by the 1959 novel The Manchurian Candidate and its 1962 movie adaptation, starring Frank Sinatra. In 1965 the Hart-Celler Act changed immigration laws and had a secondary effect of encouraging missionaries from such groups as the International Society for Krishna Consciousness from India and the Unification Church from Korea. Young Americans began experimenting with these and other new religious movements, to the alarm of the older generation. By the 1970s, the concept of brainwashing shifted from being something that communists did to something that weird religions did. This idea was especially appealing to parents who could not understand why their adult children had joined a "cult." Ironically, one of the leading psychiatrists who supported the idea that cults use mind control to manipulate their followers was Louis Jolyon West (1924–1999), who had also been contracted by MK-ULTRA.

The claim that affiliating with certain religions was the result of mind control or a medical problem led to some dangerous consequences. In 1971 Ted Patrick (1930–) was approached by a woman who wanted help convincing her son to leave a controversial group called the Children of God. Patrick had little formal education, but after observing the Children of God, he concluded that they practiced brainwashing. He called his solution "deprogramming": For a fee, he would abduct members from these groups, restrain them—often for days—in a hotel room or a basement, and apply his own regimen of forced reeducation. In essence, Patrick and the deprogrammers who came after him sought to counter cult brainwashing with "good" brainwashing. He even served several prison sentences after courts concluded that "deprogramming" often amounted to kidnapping and false imprisonment.

Allegations of brainwashing also made it possible to put members of minority religions under conservatorships as mentally incompetent. In Katz v. California Superior Court (1977), a court granted parents of five members of the Unification Church conservatorships over their adult children. This ruling was overturned on appeal. In 1980 a law was proposed in New York that would have changed mental health codes such that parents could place their adult offspring under conservatorships if they joined a "cult." This bill passed the assembly twice but was vetoed by the governor. Parents could also sue religious organizations for brainwashing their children, and such cases became popular until 1987, when the American Psychological Association rejected claims of brainwashing as unscientific.

So is it possible to brainwash someone? This depends

largely on how we define "brainwashing," but it seems clear that the sort of mind control described by Edward Hunter and Allen Dulles is not possible. Even in Hunter's own account, the Chinese people he describes are not cooperating with the regime because their minds are being controlled: They are responding to a program of harassment and coercion. Granted, regimes such as Maoist China developed sophisticated methods of coercion, but their methods were not magical or mysterious. Furthermore, studies looking at the techniques of "thought reform" used on prisoners of war have little bearing on cases of religious conversion in the United States. So-called cults may use elaborate techniques to attract new converts and may even employ deception, but normally they cannot imprison potential converts or plausibly threaten to kill them. There have even been cases where religious groups have used blackmail or other threats to retain members, but again, this is just coercion, not mind control.

In the end, the appeal of the brainwashing theory is not that it is supported by evidence but that it is comforting to believe. When another person—especially a loved one—makes a commitment that we find bizarre or unconscionable, it is tempting to believe that they did not really choose this and that their actual beliefs and desires have somehow been repressed. Though potentially comforting, these explanations come with a price: They deny people agency to make their own choices—even bad ones. Brainwashing narratives can also distract from less mysterious but more significant forms of control such as deception and coercion.

"BRAIN-WASHING" TACTICS FORCE CHINESE INTO RANKS OF COMMUNIST PARTY

Hong Kong, Sept. 21—"Brain-washing" is the principal activity on the Chinese mainland nowadays. Unrevealed thousands of men and women are having their brains "washed." They range from college students to instructors and professors, from army officers and municipal officials to reporters and printers, from criminals to church deacons.

There are no exceptions as to profession or creed. Before anyone is considered trustworthy, he must have gone through this "brain washing," so he can become fit for his work as a comrade in Mao Tse-tung's "New Democracy."

Only then do the authorities consider that he can be depended upon, as the official expression is worded, to "lean to one side"—Soviet Russia's—in all matters, to react with natural obedience to every call made upon him by the Communist party, through whatever twists or turns or leaps policy may take, and to be ready with the right answer for whatever contradiction or evasion may be found in Party statements.

This is no easy matter. Sometimes "brain-washing" is not enough; you have to "change your brains." This is done, too, although not yet as thoroughly or efficiently as in the other satellite nations or in Soviet Russia itself.

I have been seeing a great deal in the past week of an old friend, Harry Chang, who has just come out of China "on a mission," and who is returning in a few days. He already has had his brain "washed," but apparently not too well. He gave me the details. His experience is alike in all essential points with the accounts given me by other Chinese, from cities as far apart as Shanghai and Peiping.

"If they find out that I've been seeing a foreign correspondent, especially one I know personally, it'll just be too bad for me," he remarked at one of our meetings. These meetings were not casual affairs; they had to be arranged with the utmost caution and preparation, so he wouldn't be seen in the company of so "unwashed" an individual as myself.

"What worries me most, though," he went on, "is the uncertainty."

"Uncertainty about what?" I asked.

"About whether they know that I've seen you or not," he replied.

"So what?" I exclaimed encouragingly. "If they don't know about it, you have nothing to worry about, and if. . . ."

He looked at me sadly. "You'd be a hard man for brain reform," he said. "You have such bourgeois conceptions. No, it isn't as simple as that at all. If it were merely a question of whether they found out or not, I'd forget about it. But what I have to figure out is whether to tell them right off, or not."

"I don't follow."

"Well it's this way. Soon after I return, like after all my trips, anywhere out of town in China, some police will stop at my house to ask some questions. It's always that way, now, with everybody. They'll talk very friendly, say they hoped I had a successful, pleasant trip, and by the way, what did I do, and whom did I see?

"If I tell them the truth, and there is nothing incriminating, they say goodby and that's that. If I tell them the truth and there is something incriminating, I may get into trouble. But if they know something that I don't tell, I'll get into worse trouble."

"What will they do to you? Throw you into prison? Beat you up?"

"Oh no, they'll probably not do that," he replied. "If that was all they'd do I wouldn't mind."

"Huh?"

"No; what they'd do would be to send me to 'learning.' I'd be given a 'brain washing.' Oh, I don't ever want to go through that again."

I couldn't help laughing, he was so deadly serious. Also, I remembered other Chinese who told me about "learning." The word, as used by the Communist party, is not the same as before. It has been given a new interpretation. As used by the party, "learning" has only one meaning—"political learning."

And political learning on China's mainland now is only
Marxism–Leninism, and Mao's "ideas," as it is generally expressed.

"Learning" is a wearing down process, much like the tax collection methods used by the Communist party in raising the
quotas for the recent "Victory Bond" issue. A couple of tax
collectors would list a shopkeeper or farmer or house owner
and ask for some specific amount, say 500 parity units. That is
how money is calculated in Red China.

"I could never pay that," the comrade would cry out. "Why,
that's more than the Kuomintang[4] took, I just haven't got it."

"Well, sing for it anyway; you'll raise it somehow."

"But that's silly. How can I? That's more than my income for
the next six months."

This discussion would go on politely for say three, four, five
hours. Then the tax collectors would politely say goodby.

That wasn't the end of it, though. They would return the next
day, for a new "democratic discussion." The theory was that
subscriptions were voluntary, and so no force could be used.
Only "democratic discussion." This second "democratic discussion" would go on longer than the first; say four, five or six
hours. "Impossible" you say. Well, that shows you don't understand how a "democratic dictatorship" works. "Democratic dictatorship" is the way Mao Tse-tung refers to his government.

The discussion wouldn't be continuous. The two tax collectors
would talk, sit about, chat about the evils of the American cap-
italist system, and how lucky China was to have Soviet Russia
to guide her. And of course "every patriotic Chinese" wishes to
express his appreciation tangibly. And a tangible way is, of
course, the Victory Bonds.

The harassed victim would raise his ante by say, 20 percent.
Still below the figure set. The tax collectors would politely say
goodby.

They wouldn't return for more than a day. Instead of this

bringing peace of mind to the intended subscriber, it only brings mental anguish, because he hasn't subscribed yet, and knows that he won't get away that easy.

Sure enough, at perhaps 3 o'clock in the morning, when he is fast asleep, he will hear a loud banging at his door. Terrified, he will leap out of bed, and ask who's there. "It's only us," he will hear, in polite tones. He will by now be able to recognize the voice—that of his two tax collectors.

Possibly the fleeting temptation will come to our prospective bond subscriber to call the intruders descendants of especially bad varieties of turtles, but if so, he will suppress the desire, and politely open the door, and welcome in his guests, and heat some tea, and resume "democratic discussion." This might go on to dawn, or later.

By now, patience will have worn somewhat thin, and there will be circuitous references by the tax collectors, with plenty of quotations from Karl Marx, Josef Stalin, Mao Tse-tung and Liu Sho-chi, to "background elements"—"lagging behind particles," as the party expresses it. This means people whose brains need "washing." Or perhaps people who are so "reactionary" and "decadent" that they can't be trusted with whatever enterprise they have, or in their own profession.

So, a settlement will be made, a little less than originally demanded, perhaps, but nearly the amount originally required.

How is it paid up? Often it isn't; the subscriber just liquidates his possessions and joins the unemployed, or escapes to Hong Kong, or tries to.

"Learning" is much along these same lines. "Brain reform" is the objective, popularly referred to as "brain washing." When it is more prolonged and more intensive, the Chinese call it "brain changing." They haven't yet found out what real "brain changing" is, although some have heard of Cardinal Mindszenty.

"Brain washing" takes place generally in group discussion meetings, either in a classroom set aside in the factory or plant, as a special indoctrination course while the student keeps his job, or in schools and institutions of so-called higher learning. What are called revolutionary universities are run by the Communist party, and are given over completely to "brain reform." The school day here may be from sunrise to sunset, and then the entire evening.

There are interminable "democratic discussions." The same topics are gone over and over again, and then over some more, until the mind of the student rings like a phonograph record that has struck at a point that sings something about dialectic materialism or "tailism" or the "productive relationship." And the student has to be able to get up and talk interminably—and "correctly"—on all of these.

Failure to "voluntarily" see things in the "correct" way in these discussions will mean that the student is either "a backward element" or "stubborn," and the treatment for this is additional hours of "learning by doing." This means farming, or road repair, or other manual labor. Bourgeois elements, like the writer, would call it forced labor but this would only go to show how much they are in need of "brain reform."

This labor usually is half the school day, although there are always periods of days or even weeks when the entire course will be this "learning by doing." Students who complain that they can't endure such a 12-hour working day are informed that they cannot be good comrades unless they "know the sufferings of the peasants," and that there is only one way to find out, and that is by suffering, too.

———————

This description may sound just plain impossible, which would be true in the United States and other western countries, but the description is what has been outlined to me by too many participants in such courses for any possibility of doubt to remain in my mind.

"Lagging particles" may be sent to what are called People's Labor Schools. There the course consists almost entirely of labor in the fields, and when it is too dark to continue, "democratic group discussions."

This wearing down procedure permeates the entire indoctrination system of the Chinese Communists, and its source is not concealed. In Mao Tse-tung's speech "On Peoples' Democratic Dictatorship," which is a must for study and memory training in every "brain washing" class, he said frankly, "The Communist party of the USSR is our best teacher from whom we must learn."

———————

Before anyone can be graduated from this course, he has to write what is called his "thought conclusions." This corresponds to the thesis in western universities. In this, the student must indulge in pitiless "self-criticism," of himself, his background, his family, his friends, and then rehash the party line of the day, down to crossing the last "t" and dotting the final "i" in the denunciation of the United States as a war-mongering, aggressive nation that is bent on conquering the world.

THE COMING OF THE
SAUCER RELIGIONS

1955

The modern UFO phenomenon began on June 24, 1947, when private pilot Kenneth Arnold (1915–1984) was flying past Mount Rainer in Washington state and saw nine shiny objects flying at incredible speed. Arnold told reporters the objects moved like "a saucer skipping across the water." The press dubbed the objects "flying saucers," even though the objects Arnold saw were shaped more like crescents than round saucers. But by the end of 1947, there had been some eight hundred sightings of UFOs, with many people reporting that they had seen saucer-shaped craft in the sky.

The initial excitement over flying saucers was a product of the Cold War. The US Air Force took sightings seriously because they could be of experimental craft from the Soviet Union. But the appearance of the saucers was also linked to anxiety about nuclear war—especially after 1949, when Russia carried out its first successful nuclear weapons test. Many hoped that the saucers were benevolent "space brothers" who had noticed atomic explosions and come to save humanity from itself. In his book Flying Saucers: A Modern Myth of Things Seen in the Sky *(1959), psychologist Carl Jung argued that the UFOs represented "technological angels." The 1951 film* The Day the Earth Stood Still *depicted a man from outer space as a Christ-like figure who had come to save humanity.*

Soon, "contactees" claimed to have met or received messages from the occupants of flying saucers. In the 1950s, contactees always described the aliens as looking just like humans—often attractive white humans with blond hair. Many contactees became prophets, delivering spiritual messages from the aliens that often featured new interpretations of the Bible. And so, less than ten years after Arnold's sighting, there was an entire milieu of "UFO religions." Examples include the Unarius Academy of Science, founded in Los Angeles in 1954; Raëlianism, founded in France in the 1970s; and Heaven's Gate, discussed elsewhere in this volume. Nearly all UFO religions are "millennialist" in that they envision a form of collective salvation once the UFOs arrive.

The following articles from Flying Saucer News offer a snapshot from the early days of the UFO religions. Dana Howard (1919–1997) was a contactee who claimed to have been taken to Venus, where she married a Venusian man named LeLando and raised a family with him. Her coverage of the "Second Annual Spacecraft Convention" in Giant Rock, California, reads like a "who's who" of 1950s ufology.

"Giant Rock" was often claimed to be the largest freestanding boulder in the world before a section broke off of it in 2000. In the 1930s a hermit named Frank Critzer (1886–1942) used dynamite to blast a hole under the north side of the rock, where he built a home. Critzer also built roads and an airstrip. However, during World War II the government became nervous about Critzer—a man with a German surname building airstrips in the desert. In 1942 three sheriff's deputies attempted to question him about some stolen gasoline or explosives. The exchange ended with dynamite detonating in Critzer's hole, killing him. According to one source, Critzer blew himself up after yelling, "You're not taking me out of here alive. I'm going, but another way, and you're going with me."[1] Others say the deputies threw smoke canisters to force Critzer out and accidentally ignited his dynamite supply.

Before his demise, Critzer had made friends with George van Tassel. Van Tassel had moved to Giant Rock with his family, and his wife opened a small café there. He began hosting group meditation sessions in Critzer's cave. In 1953 van Tassel claimed he had been contacted by beings from Venus. He founded a group called the College of Universal Wisdom and began organizing annual conventions for UFO enthusiasts at Giant Rock. In 1954 van Tassel began the construction of a building called the "Integratron" using instructions given to him by the Venusians. The Integratron was to have rejuvenating properties and also reveal scientific insights into the nature of time and gravity. Van Tassel's organizing and experiments disturbed the FBI, which kept a sizable file on him. He continued work on the Integratron until his death in 1978. The Integratron currently offers "sound baths," and in 2018 it was added to the National Register of Historic Places.

Howard's report also references George Adamski (1891–1965), a contactee who wrote several books about exploring the solar system with Orthon, his friend from Venus. Even before his first encounter with Orthon, Adamski ran a commune called Palomar Gardens, where he gave lectures on Eastern philosophy and religion. In 1952 Adamski produced a photograph of Orthon's spaceship, which skeptics immediately dismissed as a forced-perspective shot of a "chicken brooder" used for warming baby chicks.

Truman Bethurum (1898–1969) was contacted by a beautiful and voluptuous spaceship captain named Aura Rhanes from the planet Clarion. (Bethurum explained that Clarion orbits the sun counter to Earth, so its existence is unknown to Earthlings.) Daniel W. Fry was another contactee, and he eventually founded a UFO group called Understanding, Inc. Orfeo Angelucci (1912–1993) wrote several books about his encounters with an alien named Neptune. George Williamson (1926–1986) became interested in several UFO contact groups and wrote a number of books. He was one of the first to suggest that the Bible and other religious texts actually describe ancient contact with extraterrestrials. Emma Kingham, with her husband, John, founded in 1941 a Spiritualist church called the Pyramid Church of Truth and Light. At its peak, this group had four congregations. Throughout Howard's report, there

*is a sense that these people harbored a millennialist hope
that the UFOs could help them escape the "troubled twentieth century."*

*The second article is a telepathic transmission from a
Venusian named Aetherius to England's George King
(1919–1997). It is typical of the sort of messages that contactees were reporting in the 1950s. King founded a religion called the Aetherius Society. By 1969, this group had
a thousand adherents, and it still exists today. Society
members follow the teachings of the Cosmic Masters,
which include Aetherius, Jesus, and Buddha. King taught
that the Cosmic Masters were battling hostile aliens for
control of the Earth and that humans could help the Cosmic Masters by sending them spiritual energy. King designed a device called the "Spiritual Energy Battery." By
channeling energy through the batteries, King's followers
believed they could mitigate the destruction of wars and
natural disasters.*

REPORT FROM THE 1955 UFO CONVENTION AT GIANT ROCK, CALIFORNIA[2]

The Second Annual Spacecraft Convention held at Yucca Valley, California on March 12th and 13th was just another revelation out of today's strange happenings. It was a picturesque
approach to the Convention Spot traveling over many miles of
sandy, sunlit desert roads, through forests of age-old Joshua
trees, coming at last upon a wide stretch of "antediluvia" that
appeared like land left over from The Flood. Imagine if you
can, a boulder seven stories high that in days anterior to our
histories was thrust up from an errant desert floor. The interior
of the rock is a room of mystery for it is here that George Van
Tassel, founder of the Universal School of Wisdom has held
many profound discourses with men from outer space. In the
immediate vicinity of The Rock, literally hundreds have at-

tested to seeing flying saucers and other spacecraft since the days of the first sightings in 1947.

Most of those present felt they were no longer living in our troubled Twentieth Century, but in some strange way they had been projected into the year Two Thousand and the New Age. The speaker's platform was like a modern Platonic Symposium, with Plato and his colleagues standing by. Most of those who had something to say because they have had unusual experiences, were from the ranks of the unlettered and the unsung. However, the stories they had to tell, stories where there was no hesitancy in the telling, would have sent our top-flight scientists, our philosophers and our educators scurrying to cover. The chosen ones took no credit to themselves for their advance knowledge on the baffling subjects of the day, but rather gave all the credit to their Space Teachers. Too, few out of the crowd of some 3000 were drawn from the ranks of the curious. There was no apprehension about invasion displayed, but rather they were all interested in finding a better way of life, "If other planets have it, why can't we?"

As one speaker put it:

"The space people tell us of an Utopian existence where there are no wars . . . no strife . . . no poverty or hopeless struggle. They tell us it's ours for the taking, so why not take it?"

The speakers included George Adamski, probably one of the best known Saucerites because of his co-authorship with Desmond Leslie in FLYING SAUCERS HAVE LANDED. Truman Bethurum, once a mechanic, who was taken aboard a saucer eleven times and who claims many pleasant chats with the scow's charming captain, Aura Rhanes. Daniel W. Fry, who authored THE WHITE SANDS INCIDENT and ALAN'S MESSAGE TO MEN OF EARTH. While Fry was literally torn to shreds by his opponents, he stands today as a challenge to the thinkers of our world. Orfeo Angelucci who has just authored a new book was very much in evidence. So was George Williamson, the anthropologist turned Saucer-Scientist. But outstanding among them was a young chap named Richard Miller of Prescott, Arizona who maintains he was flown for twelve hours in a 150 foot diameter saucer after being picked up outside of Detroit. Miller was told by the Commander of the ship, named Sol-tec, that our earth is moving into a huge cloud of deadly cosmic rays and there are some 3,500,000 space people and ships screening the earth against this deadly radiation. Strangely enough this ties in with "yours truly's" message from space people some six weeks ago. And before I forget it—I was there too, talking about MY FLIGHT TO VENUS.

Another highlight of the Convention was a story told by Rev. Emma Kingham, of Alhambra, California. A few weeks ago I spoke at Rev. Kingham's Church and if ever there was a sincere, honest person, this woman is it. Let me state it in her own words;

"I had just gotten into bed when I opened the window to get some fresh air, and there was the saucer. At first I thought the object was an airplane, but the coloring was wrong and on further notice the shape was different. Besides I had seen another saucer a few weeks ago and was able to get a telepathic answer to my questions. Each time I asked a question the saucer pilot answered with beautifully colored lights of red, green, blue and golden turning them on and off as each question was asked."

In describing the saucer Rev. Kingham said: "The front part was maroon, the cross-bar section golden—a beautiful object in the past-midnight sky."

All in all the Spacecraft Convention was a huge success and more people today are convinced "the saucers are real."

A MESSAGE FROM AETHERIUS[3]

Aetherius is a being from another world who speaks to us through the medium of George King at the Caxton Hall, London every month. His last message to us was as follows.

"As from midnight on the 28th of May, 1955 and for the following seven weeks, a great spiritual activity will take place and a fire will be kindled in your hearts that will never be extinguished.

"In order that you are able to absorb this spiritual Truth, it will be necessary for you to eat less, sleep less, pray and meditate as you have never done before. And then, do it some more.

"This period is an introductory one and the best time to tune yourself in to the Truth is between 11:39 P.M. and 12:49 A.M.

"Release all material thoughts from your mind and let the Truth enter. You will never have peace and prosperity until you have learned to accept the fact that man is a God. You are in the likeness of the True Master. A worm is as it is because it will not accept the fact that it is a God, hence all animals being as they are. To eat meat is a foul crime, but, if you must do so, then eat fish.

"You see, when you eat meat you are taking into yourself the thoughts of that animal. Therefore you will not think that you are a God. Vegetarians will benefit most during this period as they are better fitted to receive the spiritual radiation.

"We are sending to Terra, 200,000 to 300,000 of our carriers in an effort to avert the coming disaster, which is spoken of in the Bible.

"It is true that Adamski, Fry and Allingham have all met factors from other worlds. We would like all of you here tonight to consider yourselves as messengers and if you feel like it to shout this message from the house tops.

"We know that you will be scorned and laughed at, but, do not worry. Say to God; 'Please God, bless the eyesight of this person,' and no harm will come to you. I have been ridiculed for 3,000 years, but, I still go on. You are not alone in the universe. Some of the 1,350 Planets in your Solar System, including the Sun, are inhabited. There is order in the Universe.

"Our vehicles, or flying saucers, are made of metal and some of organic metal. The latter being able to reproduce themselves when necessary."

Goodnight, and God bless all of you.

THE JONESTOWN
"DEATH TAPE"
NOVEMBER 18, 1978[1]

The deaths of more than nine hundred members of the Peoples Temple in the agricultural project known as "Jonestown" in Guyana have become the defining event by which all other "cults" are measured. The expression "drinking the Kool-Aid" is used as a rhetorical device to imply that someone is not thinking independently. Everyone has heard of Jonestown, but most people know almost nothing about what actually happened on November 18, 1978. For one thing, there was no Kool-Aid: The fatal concoction consisted of Flavor Aid, cyanide, and sedatives. It is also important to remember that prior to this event, most people regarded Peoples Temple as a respected church with a strong commitment to progressive politics. Only retroactively was it seen as a cult.

James "Jim" Jones (1931–1978) founded an independent congregation originally called "Community Unity" and later "Peoples Temple." His ministry combined Pentecostal-style worship that merged faith healing with social activism. Although Jones was a proponent of racial equality, he and most of the church leadership were white, whereas his followers were predominantly Black. Jones moved his congregation from Indiana to California, where he became an important community organizer and received praise from local politicians in San Francisco. However, there were rumors that Jones was abusing his followers, controlling their finances, taking drugs, and engaging in sexual improprieties.

In 1973 the group began making plans to establish a community that could live apart from racism and capitalism and support itself through subsistence farming. In

1977 Jones learned that the magazine New West *was pre-paring an exposé about his church. Fearing persecution, he persuaded more than nine hundred Temple members to emigrate to Jonestown, located in the Northwest District of Guyana. The community was not ready to support so many people and would likely have faced economic collapse had the situation not ended in violence.*

Jones became increasingly paranoid, in part because of drug use. He told his followers that the CIA or mercenaries were coming to kill them and organized civil-defense drills called "White Nights." In November 1978 Congressman Leo Ryan visited Jonestown on behalf of concerned relatives of Jones's followers. One of Jones's followers, named Don Sly, who also went by the name "Ujara," attacked Ryan with a knife but left him with only superficial injuries. The congressman departed Jonestown for the airport, taking with him about sixteen people who wished to return to the United States. An armed security force from Jonestown fired upon Ryan's party at the Port Kaituma airstrip as they were leaving, and five people were killed, including the congressman. Jones and the Jonestown leadership then organized the deaths of the entire community by preparing a vat of poison. The group had rehearsed the death ritual on at least a half-dozen occasions.

Jones described this final act as "revolutionary suicide," although some researchers have argued that many of these deaths should be regarded as murders. The children and babies who were administered poison cannot be said to have died by suicide. Some witnesses reported seeing injection marks on some of the bodies, suggesting they did not willingly take poison. It is generally believed that some coercion was involved. Jones falsely told his followers that soldiers would soon arrive to kill them and torture their children, so any decision was made on a false premise. In addition, armed guards oversaw the poisoning; they too died in the end. According to Guyana investigators, two people died of gunshot wounds: Jim Jones and Annie Moore.

The Jonestown massacre was a complicated event that defies the simplistic narrative of a mad cult leader and his brainwashed followers. Researchers are still learning about what actually happened. Peoples Temple recorded community meetings, sermons, and much more, amounting to nearly a thousand audio tapes and thousands of pages of text, both typed and handwritten. The government of Guyana gathered some materials, which were housed in a building that burned down in 1980. Other materials were collected by the FBI and not released to the public for two decades. Much of this material has been collected, transcribed, and posted to the website Alternative Considerations of Jonestown & Peoples Temple, hosted by San Diego State University. Many items can also be found at the online FBI Vault.

The "Death Tape" is one of fifty-three tapes that were initially withheld from disclosure. It records the final hour of Jonestown. There are several different transcriptions of this tape because different listeners hear different things. This transcription, by Fielding M. McGee III, is considered the best. It is unedited, with false starts included, in order to completely reflect what was said. In several places the tape recorder was switched off and turned on again later. Music can sometimes be heard because the recording was made over a tape that included songs by the Delphonics, Darrow Fletcher, and Jerry Butler.

One of the most significant things about the tape is that a follower of Jones—Christine Miller—openly questions the decision to die by suicide. Miller was born in Brownsville, Texas, in 1918. She moved to Los Angeles, where she became involved in the Peoples Temple. The tapes show that Miller often questioned Jones. On one occasion Jones pointed a gun at her and told her that he could shoot her and that no one would ever find out. Miller replied, "You can shoot me, but you are going to have to respect me first." Jones repeated the threat, but Miller repeated that he would have to respect her first. Even when Jones held the *gun to her head and shouted at her, Miller remained calm. Jones finally backed down.*

As Jones prepared his followers to drink poison, Miller makes the logical point that only a handful of people defected with Congressman Ryan: This is a minor setback and not worth the deaths of nearly a thousand people. Jones replies that the people who left will not arrive at their destination safely. This comment suggests that Jones knew that gunmen had gone to the airstrip to kill Ryan. Miller also asks, "Is it too late for Russia?" Jones had sometimes said that the community could leave Guyana and receive sanctuary in either Cuba or Russia, although there is little evidence that these plans were ever very serious. Jones rejects this suggestion and insists that "revolutionary suicide" is the only option.

Some members of the crowd attempt to shout Miller down. Jim McElvane was also from Los Angeles and had a brief relationship with Miller. He was among the trusted Black leadership of the church. He urges everyone to go along with the plan, and he even discusses evidence of reincarnation. Jones had discussed a wide variety of religious ideas, including this one.

Finally, Miller suggests that at least the children should be spared and references John Victor Stoen, whom Jones regarded as his son. Tim Stoen was the district attorney of Mendocino County and a member of the Peoples Temple. When his wife became pregnant with their son, John Victor, Stoen signed an affidavit stating that he had asked Jones to sire a child with his wife. It is unclear who the true father of John Victor Stoen was, but the affidavit seems to have been an attempt by Jones to maintain leverage over Stoen, who was an important asset to the Peoples Temple. Stoen eventually defected and filed a lawsuit demanding to have his son returned from Guyana. Jones considered John Victor his son and offered Stoen $10,000 to drop the lawsuit. But when Miller suggested sparing John Victor, Jones was unmoved.

Eyewitnesses confirm that Miller and her friends were sitting in the second row toward the front. Some authors have written that her body was discovered with injection marks on her upper arm.[2] Did Miller relent and willingly drink poison, or was she murdered by lethal injection?

JONES: How very much I've tried my best to give you the good life.

CROWD: (Response)

JONES: But in spite of all of my trying, a handful of our people, with their lies, have made our life impossible. There's no way to detach ourself from what's happened today. Not only are we in a compound situation, not only are there those who have left and committed the betrayal of the century, some have stolen children from others, and are in pursuit right now to kill them, because they stole their children. And we—we are sitting here waiting on a powder keg. I don't think it is what we want to do with our babies. I don't think that's what we had in mind to do with our babies. It is said by the greatest of prophets from time immemorial: "No man may take my life from me; I lay my life down."

CROWD: (Response)

JONES: So to—to sit here and wait for the catastrophe that's going to happen on that airplane—it's going to be a catastrophe, it almost happened here. Almost happened—The congressman was nearly killed here. But you can't steal people's children. You can't take off with people's children without expecting a violent reaction. And that's not so unfamiliar to us either, if we—even if we were Judeo-Christian—if we weren't Communists. The world—the kingdom suffereth violence and the violent shall take it by force. If we can't live in peace, then let's die in peace.

CROWD: (Applause)

JONES: (Weary) We've been so betrayed. We have been so terribly betrayed.

Music and singing

JONES: But we've tried and as Jack Beam[3] often said—I don't know why he said it—I just know (unintelligible word) Jack, he said if this only works one day, it was worthwhile.

CROWD: (Applause)

Tape edit

JONES: Thank you. (Tape edit) Now what's going to happen here in a matter of a few minutes is that one of those people on that plane is gonna—gonna shoot the pilot. I know that. I didn't plan it, but I know it's going to happen. They're gonna shoot that pilot, and down comes that plane into the jungle. And we had better not have any of our children left when it's over, because they'll parachute in here on us. (Pause) I'm going to be just as plain as I know how to tell you. I've never lied to you. (More emphatic) I never have lied to you. I know that's what's gonna happen. That's what he intends to do, and he will do it. He'll do it. What so being so bewildered with many, many pu—pressures on my brain, seeing all these people behave so treasonous—there was too much for me to put together, but uh, I—I now know what he was telling me. And it'll happen. If the plane gets in the air even. (Pause) So my opinion is that we be kind to children and be kind to seniors and take the potion like they used to take in ancient Greece, and step over quietly, because we are not committing suicide. It's a revolutionary act. We can't go back. They won't leave us alone. They're now going back to tell more lies, which means more congressmen. And there's no way, no way we can survive. Hmm?

Voice too soft

JONES: Anybody. Anyone who has any dissenting opinion, please speak. (Pause) Yes. You can have an opportunity, but if our children are uh, are left, we're going to have them butchered. We can make a strike, but we'll be striking against people that we—we don't want to strike against. And what we'd like to get are the people that caused this stuff, and some—if some people here are p—are prepared and know how to do that, to go in town and get Timothy Stoen, but there's no plane. (Pause) There's no plane. You can't catch a plane in time. He's responsible for it. He brought these people to us. He and Deanna Mertle.[4] The people in San Francisco will not—not be idle over there. (Pause) They'll not take our death in vain, you know. Yes, Christine.

CHRISTINE MILLER: Is it too late for Russia?

JONES: Here's why it's too late for Russia. They killed. They started to kill. That's why it makes it too late for Russia. Otherwise I'd said, Russia, you bet your life. But it's too late. I can't control these people. They're out there. They've gone with the guns. (Self-evident tone) And it's too late. (Pause) (Weary tone) And once we kill anybody—at least that's what I've always— I've always put my lot with you. If one of my people do something, it's me. (Pause) And they say I don't—I don't have to take the blame for this, but I can't—I don't—I don't live that way. They said deliver up Ujara, who tried to get the man back here. Ujara, whose wi—mother's been lying on him and lying on him and trying to break up this family. And they've all agreed to kill us by any means necessary. You think I'm going to deliver them Ujara? Not on your life.

CROWD: No.

JONES: No.

UJARA [DON SLY]: Is there any way that if I go that it'll help us?

JONES: No. You're not going. You're not going.

CROWD: No.

JONES: You're not going. I can't live that way. I cannot live that way. (More emphatic) I've lived with—for all, and I'll die for all.

CROWD: (Applause)

Tape edit

JONES: I've been living on a hope for a long time, Christine, and I appreciate—You've always been a very good agitator. I like agitation, because you have to see two sides of one issue, two sides of a question. But what those people are gonna get done, once they get through, will make our lives worse than hell. They'll make us—make the rest of us not accept it. When they get through lying. They posed so many lies between there and that truck that we are—we are done-in as far as any other alternative.

MILLER: Well, I say let's make an air—airlift to Russia. That's what I say. I don't think nothing is impossible if you believe it.

JONES: How are we going to do that? How are you going to airlift to Russia?

MILLER: Well, I—Well, I thought you—they said if we got in an emergency, that they gave you a code to let them know.

JONES: No, they didn't. They gave us a code that they'd let us know on that issue, not us create an issue for them. They said if we—if they saw the country coming down they agreed they'd give us a code. They'd give us a code. We—you can check on that and see if it's on the code. We can check with Russia to see if they'll take us in immediately, otherwise we die. I don't know what else you say to these people. But to me, death is not—uh, death is not a fearful thing. It's living that's cuts ya.

CROWD: (Applause)

Tape edit

JONES: I have never, never, never, never seen anything like this before in my life. I've never seen people take the law uh, and do uh—in their own hands and provoke us and try to purposely agitate murder of children. There is no—Christine, it's just not—it's just not worth living like this. Not worth living like this.

MILLER: I think that there were too few who left for twelve hundred people to give them their lives for those people that left.

JONES: Do you know how many left?

MILLER: (Casual) Oh, twenty-odd. That's—That's a small (Jones speaks over)

JONES: Twenty-odd, twenty-odd.

MILLER: Compared to what's here.

JONES: Twenty-odd. But what's gonna happen when they don't leave? (Pause) I hope that they could leave. But what's gonna happen when they—when they don't leave?

MILLER: You mean the people here?

JONES: Yeah. What's going to happen to us when they don't leave, when they get on the plane and the plane goes down?

MILLER: I don't think they'll do that.

JONES: You don't think they'll go down?

CROWD: (Murmurs)

JONES: I—I wish I could tell you were right, but I'm right. There's one man there who blames, and rightfully so, Debbie Blakey[5] for the murder—for the murder of his mother—and he'll sh—he'll stop that pilot by any means necessary. (Pause) He'll do it. That plane'll come out of the air. There's no way you can fly a plane without a pilot.

MILLER: I wasn't speaking about that plane. I was speaking about a plane for us to go to Russia.

JONES: How— (Sighs)

CROWD: (Stirs)

JONES: —to Russia? You think Russia's gonna want—no, it's not gonna, it's, it's, it's—We're not, uh—You think Russia's gonna want us with all this stigma? (Pause) We had—we—we had some value, but now we don't have any value.

MILLER: Well, I don't see it like that. I mean, I feel like that—as long as there's life, there's hope. That's my faith.

JONES: Well—someday everybody dies. Some place that hope

runs out, because everybody dies. I haven't seen anybody yet didn't die. And I'd like to choose my own kind of death for a change. I'm tired of being tormented to hell, that's what I'm tired of. (Pause) Tired of it.

CROWD: (Applause)

Tape edit

JONES: —twelve hundred people's lives in my hands, and I certainly don't want your life in my hands. I'm going to tell you, Christine, without me, life has no meaning.

CROWD: (Applause)

JONES: I'm the best thing you'll ever have. I want, want, I have to pay—I'm standing with Ujara. I'm standing with those people. They're part of me. I could detach myself. I really could detach myself. No, no, no, no, no, no. I never detach myself from any of your troubles. I've always taken your troubles right on my shoulders. And I'm not going to change that now. It's too late. I've been running too long. Not going to change now.

CROWD: (Applause)

Tape edit

JONES: Maybe the next time you'll get to go to Russia. The next time round. This is—what I'm talking about now is the dispensation of judgment. This is a revolutionary—it's a revolutionary suicide council. I'm not talking about self—self-destruction. I'm talking about what—we have no other road. I will take your—your call. We will put it to the Russians. And I can tell you the answer now, because I'm a prophet. Call the Russians and tell them, and see if they'll take us.

MILLER: I said I'm not ready to die. But[6] I know (unintelligible)

JONES: I don't think you are. I don't think you are.

MILLER: But, ah, I look about at the babies and I think they deserve to live, you know?

JONES: I—I agree. But they—But don't they also they deserve much more, they deserve peace.

CROWD: Right.

MILLER: We all came here for peace.

JONES: And we've—have we had it?

MILLER: No.

JONES: I tried to give it to you. I've laid down my life, practically. I've practically died every day to give you peace. And you still not have any peace. You look better than I've seen you in a long while, but it's still not the kind of peace that I wanted to give you. Uh—A person's a fool who continues to say that they're winning when you're losing. (Pause) Win one, lose two. What? (Pause) I didn't hear you, ma'am. You'll have to speak up. Ma'am, you'll have to speak up.

WOMAN: (Unintelligible)

JONES: That's a sweet thought. Who said that? (Pause) C— Come on up and speak it again, honey. Say what you want to say about (unintelligible) is taking off. No plane is taking off. (Pause) It's suicide. Plenty have done it. Stoen has done it. But somebody ought to live. Somebody—Can they talk to—and I've talked to San Francisco—see that Stoen does not get by with this infamy—with this infamy. He has done the thing he wanted to do. Have us destroyed. (Pause)

MILLER: When you—when you—when we destroy ourselves, we're defeated. We let them, the enemies, defeat us.

JONES: Did you see—did you see, "I will live to fight no more forever?"

MILLER: Yes, I saw that.

JONES: Did you not have some sense of pride and victory in that man? Yet he would not subject himself to the will or the whim of people who tell—that they're gonna to come in whenever they please and push into our house. Come when they please, take who they want to, talk to who they want to—does this not living? That's not living to me. That's not freedom. That's not the kind of freedom I sought.

MILLER: Well, I think where they made their mistake is when they stopped to rest. If they had gone on, they would've made it. But they stopped to rest.

JIM MCELVANE: Just hold on, sister, just hold on. We have made that day. We made a beautiful day, and let's make it a beautiful day. That's what I say.

CROWD: (Applause)

JONES: We will win. We win when we go down. Tim Stoen has nobody else to hate. He has nobody else to hate. Then he'll destroy himself. I'm speaking here not as uh, the administrator, I'm speaking as a prophet today. I wouldn't have sat in this seat and talked so serious if I didn't know what I was talking about. Has anybody called back? The immense amount of damage that's going to be done, but I cannot separate myself from the pain of my people. You can't either, Christine, if you stop to think about it. You can't separate yourself. We've walked too long together.

MILLER: I well know that.[7] But I still think, as an individual, I have a right to—

JONES: You do, and I'm listening.

MILLER: —to say what I think, what I feel. And I think we all have a right to our own destiny as individuals.

JONES: Right.

MILLER: And I think I have a right to choose mine, and everybody else has a right to choose theirs.

JONES: Mmm-hmm.

MILLER: You know?

JONES: Mmm-hmm. I'm not criticizing (unintelligible)—What's that?

Unintelligible woman's voice

JONES: That's today. That's what 20 people said today. We're alive.

MILLER: Well, I think I still have a right to my own opinion.

JONES: I—I'm not taking it from you. I'm not taking it from you.

MCELVANE: Christine, you're only standing here because he was here in the first place. So I don't know what you're talking about, having an individual life. Your life has been extended to the day that you're standing there, because of him.

Tape edit

JONES: (Unintelligible word) I guess she has as much right to speak as anybody else, too. What did you say, Ruby? Well, you'll regret that this very day if you don't die. You'll regret it if you do, though you don't die. You'll regret it.

LUE ESTER LEWIS: (Unintelligible) You've saved so many people.

JONES: I've saved them. I saved them, but I made my example. I made my expression. I made my manifestation, and the world was ready—not ready for me. Paul said, "I was a man born out of due season." I've been born out of due season, just like all we are, and the best testimony we can make is to leave this goddamn world.

CROWD: (Applause)

Tape edit

LEWIS: You must prepare to die.

MILLER: I'm not talking to her. Will you let—Would you—would you let her or let me talk?

JONES: Keep talking.

MILLER: Would you make her sit down and let me talk while I'm on the floor or let her talk?

JONES: How can you tell the leader what to do if you live?

CROWD: (Stirs)

JONES: I've—I've listened to you. You asked me about Russia. I'm right now making a call to Russia. What more do you suggest? I'm listening to you. You've got to give me one slight bit of encouragement. I just now instructed her to go there and do that.

Voices

MCELVANE: All right now, everybody hold it. We didn't come—hold it. Hold it. Hold it. Hold it.

JONES: Let (unintelligible word—"law"?) be maintained.

Voices

JONES: To lay down your burden. I'm gonna lay down my burden. Down by the riverside. Shall we lay them down here in— by Guyana? What's the difference? (Pause) No man didn't take our lives. Right now. They haven't taken them. But when they start parachuting out of the air, they'll—they'll shoot some of our innocent babies. I'm not lying—I don't wanna (unintelligible), Christine. But they gotta shoot me to get through to some of these people. I'm not letting them take your child. Can you let them take your child?

VOICES: No, no, no, no.

WOMAN 2: —gonna die?

JONES: What's that?

WOMAN 2: You mean you want us to die—(Jones talks over)

JONES: I want to see—

CROWD: (Shouting)

JONES: (Pleading) Peace, peace, peace, peace, peace, peace, peace, peace, peace, peace.

MARCELINE JONES: Christine, are you saying that you think he thinks more of him than other children here?

JONES: John—John—

MARCELINE JONES: Because if you're saying—

JONES: (Unintelligible name), do you think I'd put John's life above others? If I put John's life above others, I wouldn't be standing with Ujara. I'd send John out—out, and he could go out on the driveway tonight.

MARCELINE JONES: Because he's young.

JONES: (Defensive) I know, but he's no—he's no different to me than any of these children here. He's just one of my children. I don't prefer one above another. I don't prefer him above Ujara. I can't do that. I can't separate myself from your actions or his actions. If you'd done something wrong, I'd stand with you. If they wanted to come and get you, they'd have to take me.

MAN 2: (Weepy) We're all ready to go. If you tell us we have to give our lives now, we're ready—at least the rest of the sisters and brothers are with me.

Tape edit

JONES: Some months I've tried to keep this thing from happening. But I now see it's the will—it's the will of Sovereign Being that this happen to us. That we lay down our lives in protest against what's being done. That we lay down our lives to protest in what's being done. The criminality of people. The cruelty of people. Who walked out of here today? Did you notice who walked out? Mostly white people.

CROWD: (Stirs)

JONES: Mostly white people walked. (Pause) I'm so grateful for the ones that didn't—those who knew who they are. I just know that there—there—there's no point—there's no point to this. We have—We are born before our time. They won't accept us. And I don't think we should sit here and take any more time for our children to be endangered. Because if they come after our children, and lu—we give them our children, then our children will suffer forever.

MILLER: (Unintelligible)?

JONES: I have no quarrel with you coming up. I like you. I personally like you very much.

MILLER: People get hostile when you try and—

JONES: Oh, well, some people do—but then, you know, yes—yes, some people do. Put it that way—I'm not hostile. You had to be honest, but you've stayed, and if you'da be—you wanted to run, you'd have run with them 'cause anybody could've run today. What would anyone do? I know you're not a runner. And I, I would—I'd—your life is precious to me. It's as precious as John's. And I—and I don't—what I do I do with weight and justice and judgment. I'm—I've weighed it against all evidence.

MILLER: That's all I've got to say.

JONES: What comes now, folks? What comes now?

MAN 3: Everybody hold it. Sit down.

JONES: Say it. Say—Stay peace. Stay peace. Stay peace. Stay peace. Stay peace. What's come. Don't let—Take Dwyer [Richard Dwyer, US Embassy official][8] on down to the East House. (stumbles over words) Take Dwyer.

WOMAN 4: Everybody be quiet, please.

JONES: (Unintelligible)—got some respect for our lives.

MCELVANE: That means sit down, sit down. Sit down.

JONES: I know. (Pause) (Groan) I tried so very, very hard. They're trying over here to see what's going to—what's going to happen in Los Angel—Who is it?

Voices

JONES: Get Dwyer out of here before something happens to him. (Pause) Dwyer? I'm not talking about Ujara. I said (Emphatic) Dwyer. Ain't nobody gonna take Ujara. I'm not lettin' 'em take Ujara. (Pause) Gather in, folks. It's easy, it's easy. Yes, my love.

Tape silence for several seconds

WOMAN 5: At one time, I felt just like Christine felt. But after today I don't feel anything because the biggest majority of people that left here for a fight, and I know, it really hurt my heart because—

JONES: Broke your heart, didn't it?

WOMAN 5: It broke my heart, to think that all of this year the white people had been with us, and they're not a part of us. So we might as well end it now because I don't see—

JONES: It's all over. The congressman has been murdered.

Music and singing

VOICE: It's all over.

JONES: Well, it's all over, all over. (Pause) What a legacy, what a legacy. What the Red Brigade doin' one bit that made any sense anyway? They invaded our privacy. They came into our home. They followed us six thousand miles away. Red Brigade showed them justice. The congressman's dead.

Music only

JONES: (Speaks authoritatively) Please get us some medication. It's simple. It's simple. There's no convulsions with it. It's just simple. Just, please get it. Before it's too late. The GDF [Guyana Defense Force] will be here, I tell you. Get movin', get movin', get movin'.

Voices

WOMAN 6: Now. Do it now![9]

JONES: (More excited) Don't be afraid to die. You'll see, there'll be a few people land out here. They'll—they'll torture some of our children here. They'll torture our people. They'll torture our seniors. We cannot have this. Are you going to separate yourself from whoever shot the congressman? I don't know who shot him.

VOICES: No. No. No.

Music

Tape edit

JONES: Just speak their piece. And those who had a right to go, and they had a right to—How many are dead? (Pause) Aw, God Almighty, God Almighty. Hmm? Patty Parks is dead?

Tape edit

WOMAN 7: Some of the others who endure long enough in a safe place to write about the goodness of Jim Jones.

JONES: I don't know how in the world they're ever going to write about us. It's just too late. It's too late. The congressman's dead. The congressman lays dead. Many of our traitors are dead. They're all layin' out there dead.

Voices

JONES: Hmm? I didn't, but—but my people did. My people did. They're my people, and they—they've been provoked too much. They've been provoked too much. What's happened here's been to—basically been an act of provocation.

Unintelligible voice

WOMAN 8: Want Ted? If there's any way it's possible to, uh, have and to give Ted something to take, then I'm satisfied, okay?

JONES: Okay.

WOMAN 8: I said, if there's any way you can do before I have to give Ted something, so he won't have to let him go through okay, and I'm satisfied.

JONES: That's fine. Okay, yes. Yes. Yes.

Unintelligible voice

WOMAN 9: —and I appreciate you for everything. You are the only—You are the only—You are the only. And I appreciate you—

CROWD: (Applause)

Tape edit

JONES: (Urgently) Please, can we hasten? Can we hasten with that medication? You don't know what you've done. (Pause) And I tried.

Tape edit. Applause, music, singing. Tape edit

MAN: Wesley [Breidenbach] told me there were two GDF not to—

Tape edit.

JONES: They saw it happen and ran into the bush and dropped their machine guns. I never in my life. (Pause) But there'll be more. (Pause) (Tape edit) You got to move. Are you gonna get that medication here? You've got to move. Marceline? You got forty minutes.

MARIA KATSARIS:[10] You have to move, and the people that are standing there in the aisles, go stand in the radio room yard. Everybody get behind the table and back this way, okay? There's nothing to worry about. Every—Everybody keep calm and try and keep your children calm. (Pause) And uh, all those children that help, let the little children in and reassure them. (Pause) They're not crying from pain. It's just a little bitter tasting. It's not—They're not crying out of any pain. Annie McGowan, can I please see you back—

Tape edit

MCELVANE: Things I used to do before I came here. So let me tell you about it. It might make a lot of you feel a little more comfortable. Sit down and be quiet, please. One of the things I used to do, I used to be a therapist. And the kind of therapy that I did had to do with reincarnation in past life situations. And every time anybody had the experience of it—of going into a past life, I was fortunate enough through Father to be able to let them experience it all the way through their death, so to speak. And everybody was so happy when they made that step to the other side.

JONES: (Unintelligible)—to do, but stop that way. It's the only way to step. (Microphone off briefly, unintelligible word) But that choice is not ours now. It's out of our hands.

Children crying in the background

MCELVANE: If you have a body that's been crippled, suddenly you have the kind of body that you want to have.

JONES: Somebody give them a little rest, a little rest.

MCELVANE: It feels good. It never felt so good. (Unintelligible word), may I tell you. You've never felt so good as how that feels. (Pause)

JONES: And I do hope that those attorneys [Charles Garry and Mark Lane] will stay where they belong and don't come up here. (Pause) What is it? (Pause) What happened? What is it? (Pause) They what? (Pause) All right, it's hard but only at first—only at first is it hard. It's hard only at first. Living— when you're looking at death, it only looks—as uh, living is much, much more difficult. Raising up every morning and not knowing what's going to be the night's bringing. It's much more difficult. It's much more difficult.

Crying and talking

IRENE EDWARDS: (Joyous) I just want to uh, say something for everyone that I see that is standing around and—or crying. This is nothing to cry about. This is something we could all rejoice about. We could be happy about this. They always told us that we could cry when you're coming into this world. So when we're leaving, and we're gonna leave it peaceful, I think we should be—we should be happy about this. I was just thinking about Jim Jones. He just has suffered and suffered and suffered. We have—We have the honor guard, and we don't even have a chance to (Unintelligible word) got here. I want to give him one more chance. There's just one more thing I want to say. That's few that's gone, but many more here. (Unintelligible) That's not all of us. That's not all yet. That's just a few that have died. I tried to get to the one that—there's a kid over there (unintelligible) I'm looking at so many people crying. I wish you would not cry. And just thank Father. (Unintelligible) I been here about—

CROWD: (Sustained applause)

IRENE EDWARDS: I've been here ah—one year and nine months. And I never felt better in my life. Not in San Francisco, but until I came to Jonestown. I had a very good life. I had a beautiful life. And I don't see nothing that I could be sorry about. We should be happy. At least I am. That's all I'm gonna say.

Applause, music

WOMAN 11: (Weepy)—good to be alive today. I just like to thank Dad, 'cause he was the only one that stood up for me when I needed him. And thank you, Dad.

WOMAN 12: (Unintelligible word) I'm glad you're my brothers and sisters, and I'm glad to be here. Okay.

Voices

JONES: (Pleading) Please. For God's sake, let's get on with it. We've lived—we've lived as no other people have lived and loved. We've had as much of this world as you're gonna get. Let's just be done with it. Let's be done with the agony of it.

CROWD: (Applause)

Tape edit

JONES: It's far, far harder to have to walk through every day, die slowly—and from the time you're a child 'til the time you get gray, you're dying. (Pause) (Tape edit) Dishonest, and I'm sure that they'll—they'll pay for it. They—They'll pay for it. This is a revolutionary suicide. This is not a self-destructive suicide. So they'll pay for this. They brought this upon us. And they'll pay for that. I—I leave that destiny to them.

Voices

Tape edit

JONES: Who wants to go with their child has a right to go with their child. I think it's humane. I want to go—I want to see you go, though. I—They can take me and do what they want—whatever they want to do. I want to see you go. I don't want to see you go through this hell no more. No more, no more, no more. (Pause) We're trying. If everybody will relax. The best thing you do is to relax, and you will have no problem. You'll have no problem with this thing, if you just relax.

MAN 4: (Unintelligible phrase) A great deal because it's Jim Jones. And the way the children are laying there now, I'd rather see them lay like that than to see them have to die like the Jews did, which was pitiful anyhow. And I'd just like to—to thank Dad for giving us life and also death. And I appreciate the fact of the way our children are going. Because, like Dad said, when they come in, what they're gonna do to our children—they're gonna massacre our children. And also the ones that they take captured, they're gonna just let them grow up and be dummies like they want them to be. And not grow up to be a socialist like the one and only Jim Jones. So I'd like—I'd like to thank Dad for the opportunity for letting Jonestown be, not what it could be, (Emphatic) but what Jonestown is. Thank you, Dad.

CROWD: (Applause)

Tape edit

JONES: It's not to be afeared. It is not to be feared. It's a friend. It's a friend (Tape edit)—sitting there, show your love for one another. (Tape edit) Let's get gone. Let's get gone. Let's get gone.

Children crying

JONES: (Unintelligible word) We had nothing we could do. We can't—we can't separate ourselves from our own people. (Pause) For twenty years laying in some old rotten nursing home.

Music

Tape edit

JONES: Taking us through all these anguish years. They took us and put us in chains and that's nothing. This business—that—that business—there's no comparison to that, to this. They've robbed us of our land, and they've taken us and driven us and we tried to find ourselves. We tried to find a new beginning. But it's too late. You can't separate yourself from your brother and your sister. No way I'm going to do it. I wi—I refuse. I don't know who fired the shot. I don't know who killed the congressman. But as far as I am concerned, I killed him. You understand what I'm saying? I killed him. He had no business coming. I told him not to come.

WOMAN 13: Right, right.

Music and crying

Tape edit. Long pause follows

JONES: (Pleading) I, with respect, die with a degree of dignity. Lay down your life with dignity. Don't lay down with tears and agony. There's nothing to death. It's like Mac [Jim McElvane] said, it's just stepping over into another plane. Don't be—Don't be this way. Stop this hysterics. This is not the way for people who are Socialists or Communists to die. No way for us to die. We must die with some dignity. We must die with some dignity. (Pause) We will have no choice. Now we have some choice. (Tape edit) Do you think they're gonna stand—allow this to be done and allow us to get by with this? You must be insane. (Pause) Look children, it's just something to put you to rest. (Tape edit) (Despairing tone) Oh, God.

Children crying

JONES: Mother, Mother, Mother, Mother, Mother, please. Mother, please, please, please. Don't—don't do this. Don't do this. Lay down your life with your child. But don't do this.

WOMAN 14: We're doing all of this for you.

JONES: Free at last. Peace. Keep your emotions down. Keep your emotions down. Children, it will not hurt. If you'll be—if you'll be quiet. If you'll be quiet.

Music and crying

JONES: It's never been done before, you say. It's been done by every tribe in history. (Emphatic) Every tribe facing annihilation. All the Indians of the Amazon are doing it right now. They refuse to bring any babies into the world. They kill every child that comes into the world, because they don't want to live in this kind of a world. So be patient. Be patient. Death is—I tell you, I don't care how many screams you hear, I don't care how many anguished cries, death is a million times preferable to ten more days of this life. If you knew what was ahead of you—if you knew what was ahead of you, you'd be glad to be stepping over tonight. Death, death, death is common to people. And the Eskimos, they take death in their stride. Let's be digni—let's be dignified. (Reprimands) If you'll quit tell them they're dying—if you adults would stop some of this nonsense. Adults, adults, adults. I call on you to stop this nonsense. I call on you to quit exciting your children, when all they're doing is going to a quiet rest. I call on you to stop this now, if you have any respect at all. Are we black, proud, and Socialist, or what are we? Now stop this nonsense. Don't carry this on anymore. You're exciting your children. No, no sorrow that it's all over. I'm glad it's over. (Tape edit) Hurry, hurry, my children. Hurry. All I think (unintelligible) from the hands of the enemy. Hurry, my children. Hurry. There are seniors out here that I'm concerned about. Hurry. I don't want to leave my seniors to this mess. (Pause) Only quickly, quickly, quickly, quickly, quickly. (Tape edit) Good knowing you. (Pause) No more pain now. No more pain, I said (unintelligible). No more pain. Jim Cobb is laying on the airfield dead at this moment.

CROWD: (Applause)

Tape edit

JONES: Remember the—this—the Oli—Oliver woman said she—she'd come over and kill me if her son wouldn't stop her? These, these are the people—the peddlers of hate. All we're doing is laying down our life. We're not letting them take our life. We're laying down our life. Peace in their lives. We just want peace.

Music

Tape edit

MAN 5: All I would like to say is that my, uhm—my so-called parents are filled with so much hate—

JONES: (Clapping in reprimand) Stop this, stop this, stop this (unintelligible word). Stop this crying, all of you.

MAN 5: —hate and treachery. I think you—you people out here should think about how your relatives were and be glad about, that the children are being laid to rest. And all I'd like to say is that I thank Dad for making me strong to stand with it all and make me ready for it. Thank you.

JONES: All they're doing is—All they do is taking a drink. They take it to go to sleep. That's what death is, sleep. (Tape edit)—of it. I'm tired of it all.

WOMAN 15: Everything we could have ever done, most loving thing all of us could have done, and it's been a pleasure walking with all of you in this revolutionary struggle. No other way I would rather go to give my life for socialism, communism, and I thank Dad very, very much.

WOMAN 16: Right. Yes. Dad—Dad's love and nursing, goodness and kindness, and he bring us to this land of freedom. His love—his mother was the advance—the advance guard for socialism. And his love and his principles (unintelligible) will go on forever unto the fields of—

JONES: Where's the vat, the vat, the vat? Where's the vat with the Green C on it? Bring the vat with the Green C in. Please? Bring it here so the adults can begin.

WOMAN 16: Go on unto the Zion, and thank you, Dad.

Tape edit

JONES: (Unintelligible) Don't, don't fail to follow my advice. You'll be sorry. (Tape edit) You'll be sorry. (Tape edit)—if we do it, than that they do it. Have trust. You mu—You have to step across.

Music

JONES: We used to think this world was—this world was not our home—well, it sure isn't—We were saying—it sure wasn't. (Pause) He doesn't want to tell me. All he's doing—if they will tell 'em—assure these kids. Can't some people assure these children of the relaxation of stepping over to the next plane? They set an example for others. We said—one thousand people who said, we don't like the way the world is. (Tape edit) Take some. (Tape edit) Take our life from us. We laid it down. We got tired. (Tape edit) We didn't commit suicide, we committed an act of revolutionary suicide protesting the conditions of an inhumane world.

Music

INTERNAL DOCUMENTS
FROM THE BRANCH
DAVIDIAN SIEGE
1992–APRIL 19, 1993

The burning of the Branch Davidian headquarters in 1993 was the largest loss of life resulting from a law-enforcement action in US history. After a six-hour FBI tank and CS gas assault, the building went up in flames. A total of seventy-six Branch Davidians (of all ages, from babies to elderly) died in the fire from various causes, including smoke inhalation, burns, and gunshots. Eight adults and a teenager escaped the fire.[1] The event has been reviewed extensively by congressional committees, federal agencies, and religion scholars to identify the numerous mistakes that were made.

The Branch Davidians splintered off from an earlier group in Waco, Texas, known as the Davidians, which was an offshoot of the Seventh-day Adventist Church. In 1935 a Bulgarian immigrant named Victor Houteff (1885–1955) founded a group called the General Association of Davidian Seventh-day Adventists (the Davidians), headquartered on a property called Mount Carmel Center, next to Lake Waco. After Houteff's death, the general association sold that property and purchased new property outside of Waco that the Davidians called New Mount Carmel Center. After an apocalyptic prophecy failed on April 22, 1959, eventually the General Association of Davidian Seventh-day Adventists sold off most of the property, leaving seventy-seven acres of what became known simply as Mount Carmel Center. The General Association of Branch Davidian Seventh-day Adventists was founded by Ben Roden (1902–1978) in 1955 and eventually bought the remaining Mount Carmel Center property. The next Branch

Davidian prophet was Ben's wife, Lois Roden (1916–1986).[2] In 1981 a newcomer arrived named Vernon Howell (1959–1993). Howell had an extensive knowledge of the Bible and eventually became the group's leader.

In 1985 Howell visited Israel, where he reported he had a spiritual experience that led him to believe he had a special role to play in the Last Days. He considered himself an anointed one (messiah, Christ) who was chosen by God for a special purpose. He legally changed his name to David Koresh in 1990. "David" is a reference to the king of Israel from whose line the messiah is prophesied to be born. "Koresh" is the Hebrew name for Cyrus the Great of Persia, who conquered Babylon and allowed captured Jews to return home. Koresh believed that he and his followers would have to participate in a battle in which they would be killed by the forces of "Babylon," meaning "the world," specifically the United States. Koresh's followers tore down the little houses at Mount Carmel Center and built one fortified large residence, with dorm rooms, kitchen and cafeteria, three towers, a chapel, and a gymnasium. They stockpiled weapons, some of which they sold to generate income, but they also kept some ready to fight the forces of Babylon when they attacked the group. Koresh traveled to California, Hawaii, Australia, and the United Kingdom to spread his message.

Psalm 45 appears to describe princesses marrying a king and giving birth to princes who will rule throughout the land. Koresh interpreted this passage as a prophecy about himself. In 1986 he began taking additional "wives," some of whom were minors. In Texas it was legal for girls as young as fourteen to marry with the consent of their parents. However, Michele Jones, the younger sister of Koresh's legal wife, Rachel, was only twelve when Koresh took her as a "wife." In 1989 Koresh announced a revelation that all his female followers, including women already married, were his wives, but his male followers were to remain celibate.

Following this revelation, Marc Breault and his wife left

Mount Carmel Center, moved to Australia, and began to denounce Koresh as a cult leader who was abusing children. The mass suicide/murders of the Peoples Temple at Jonestown, Guyana, became the lens through which the media and law-enforcement agents frequently interpreted the Branch Davidians. Breault and other former members warned law-enforcement personnel that the Branch Davidians might commit mass suicide during Passover of 1992. There is little evidence that the Branch Davidians were planning a mass suicide; however, these predictions of violence ultimately became a self-fulfilling prophecy.

On February 28, 1993, agents with the Bureau of Alcohol, Tobacco, and Firearms (ATF) conducted an armed raid on the large mixed-use building on the Mount Carmel property. Ostensibly, they were there to execute a "no knock" entry to serve warrants to arrest Koresh and search the building for possible illegally modified weapons. But in their black uniforms and combat gear they resembled the army of Babylon that Koresh had long predicted would attack. Furthermore, surviving Branch Davidians have reported that one of the ATF agents' first actions was to shoot the five Alaskan malamutes that were kenneled outside the front door to the residence.[3] While one ATF team approached the front door, two more teams went up on the roof, broke windows, and attempted to go inside. A shootout ensued in which four ATF agents and five Branch Davidians were killed. A sixth Branch Davidian, Michael Schroeder (1963–1993), was shot and killed later that afternoon by ATF agents stationed behind the building as he attempted to walk back to the residence. In addition, twenty agents and four Branch Davidians, including Koresh, were wounded.

On March 1, 1993, FBI agents took control of the situation and began a siege that lasted fifty-one days. Koresh and most of his followers refused to leave the building. The FBI was reluctant to use force, knowing that children and two pregnant women were inside. Between February 28 and March 5, twenty-one children were sent out. Then, be-

tween March 2 and March 23, fourteen adults came out and were taken into custody as a result of negotiations.[4] *Negotiations continued with Koresh for weeks, and FBI officials and agents grew increasingly frustrated, both with his noncompliance and his attempts to explain his understanding of biblical prophecy to negotiators, which they dismissed as "Bible babble." They used a variety of "stress escalation tactics" on the Branch Davidians, such as shining floodlights and using speakers to project loud music and disturbing noises all night.*

On April 14, 1993, the day after Passover week concluded, Koresh proposed an exit plan: He would write his interpretation of the Seven Seals in the book of Revelation and deliver it to Bible scholars he trusted, and then he would surrender. On April 16 Koresh reported that he had completed his commentary on the First Seal, and the Branch Davidians began asking for supplies to use with a battery-operated word processor (the building's electricity had been turned off by the FBI). On the evening of April 18, Jeffrey Jamar, the FBI special agent in charge, permitted these supplies to be sent inside. But at 6:00 a.m. (Central Standard Time) on April 19, the FBI's Hostage Rescue Team (HRT) carried out a tank and CS gas assault. Tanks called combat engineering vehicles (CEVs) were used to tear open the walls and insert booms with spray devices attached that dispersed CS gas. This tear gas is actually a talcum-like powder suspended in methylene chloride that accumulates and sticks to surfaces. It is an outdoor crowd-control agent and is not intended for use in enclosed spaces. By 12:07 p.m. (Central Standard Time), the first fire was visible. The fire spread rapidly, killing seventy-six Davidians of all ages.[5]

The cause of the fire has been heavily debated. One theory is that the Branch Davidians set the fire themselves as an act of mass suicide rather than yield to federal agents. Another is that the Branch Davidians set the fire as a last-ditch effort to stop the tanks but were unable to control it. Yet another is that the Branch Davidians were not responsible for the fire at all and that it resulted from the CS gas igniting. After the fire, the FBI told the press that it had used "non-lethal and non-flammable chemical agents." But in a lawsuit against the federal government, chemist Eric R. Larsen testified that the accumulated CS dust would pose the risk of a flash fire.[6] In addition to spraying CS gas from containers on the CEVs, the FBI's HRT used army-issue grenade launchers to fire four hundred "ferret rounds" at the building. On impact, these rounds disperse CS dust using methylene chloride, which is flammable in high concentrations. Prior to 1993, there had been at least two incidents in which the FBI fired ferret rounds releasing CS into a building, after which the structure rapidly burned down.[7] The FBI claimed no pyrotechnic devices were used to release CS gas at Mount Carmel and testified as much before House of Representatives committees in 1995. But in 1999 it was revealed by journalist Lee Hancock that at least two such devices were used: A tunnel leading out of the building could not be penetrated with ferret rounds, so agents fired two M-651 tear gas grenades, which use a burning explosive capable of starting fires.[8]

At best, federal agencies demonstrated recklessness and treated the Branch Davidians more like a foreign army than civilians defending their home. After learning of the fire at Mount Carmel Center, the response of ATF agent Chuck Hustmyre was allegedly: "Holy shit, this is great. All those assholes are going to die."[9] Catherine Wessinger, an expert on this event, has suggested that referring to the Branch Davidians as "cultists" throughout the fifty-one-day siege caused agents to lose sight of the fact that these were ordinary people with strongly held religious beliefs:

> It is important that people become aware of the bigotry convened by cult. The word cult dehumanizes the religion's members and their children. It strongly implies that these people are deviants; they are seen as crazy, brainwashed, duped by their leader. When we label people as subhuman, we create a context in which it is considered virtuous to kill them.[10]

After the fire, public opinion changed rapidly, and many felt that the Branch Davidians had been murdered by federal agents. On April 19, 1995, domestic terrorist Timothy McVeigh (1968–2001) bombed the Alfred P. Murrah Federal Building in Oklahoma City in retaliation for the events at Mount Carmel Center in 1993. McVeigh only compounded the violence, killing 168 people, including 19 children.

In 1993 FBI agents had never faced a situation quite like the Branch Davidian standoff. They believed that Koresh's followers were "brainwashed," so they could not decide whether to treat them as hostages or hostiles. The following primary documents provide some insight into what happened in 1993 and why.

The first document is a 1992 letter from David Jewell to his congressman, warning about the Branch Davidians, which he describes as a cult. Jewell's ex-wife, Sherri Jewell (1950–1993), was a Branch Davidian, and David Jewell had recently won full custody of their daughter, Kiri.

David Jewell's letter is accompanied by an affidavit by ex-member Marc Breault alleging, among other things, that Koresh was obsessed with sex and had impregnated a minor, and that his followers were becoming a dangerous paramilitary group. The affidavit offers an interesting portrayal of how Koresh's group was developing in the 1980s. However, much had changed since Breault left the group. By 1993, for example, the Branch Davidians had created a larger residence at Mount Carmel. More importantly, Breault's account must be read critically because he was engaged in a vigorous campaign to mobilize media, anticult groups, and law-enforcement against the Branch Davidians. He was also a key figure in the ATF's decision to conduct a raid. Branch Davidian survivor Catherine Matteson (1916–2009) said of Breault, "Well, that man started it all. He started all our problems. He started them about three years before we had any contact with the government in any way. And I personally hold him totally responsible, because without him then we never would have had any problems."[11]

Sociologist Stuart Wright has raised several objections to Breault's account. One concerns the movies mentioned in this affidavit. In Wright's view, Full Metal Jacket *(1987),* Hamburger Hill *(1987), and* Platoon *(1986) are antiwar films that critique the absurdity of the Vietnam War.*[12] *On the other hand, Koresh showed these films to both adults and children following Bible study, and he was preparing his followers for a war in which he believed many would die. A bigger objection concerns Breault's claim that Wally Kennett nearly shot a newspaper deliveryman while standing guard at the front entrance to the Mount Carmel property. First, despite the alleged paranoia of the group, in Breault's account no one got up to investigate a gunshot at 5:00 a.m. Second, Breault reports that he saw this event at a distance while it was still dark, but Breault is legally blind. According to surviving Branch Davidians, he had trouble recognizing people even from a short distance away. ATF agents met with Breault and must have known about his disability, but there is no mention of it in the ATF affidavit filed to obtain a warrant. Third, Kennett denied that this event ever happened and claimed that Breault had "a tendency to tell tall tales." Either Breault or Kennett was telling the truth.*

Breault does not mention it, but Koresh was likely posting sentries because he feared a man named George Roden (1938–1998). George was the son of Lois Roden, the group's leader before Koresh. After Koresh arrived in 1981, he began a sexual relationship with Lois Roden, who was in her late sixties. Fearing Koresh's growing influence, George Roden drove Koresh and most of his followers off the property. In 1985 he filed a federal lawsuit accusing Koresh of brainwashing and raping his mother. In 1987 George Roden allegedly proposed to Koresh a strange challenge to determine the group's rightful leader: He had exhumed the twenty-year-old skeleton of a woman named Anna Hughes, and whoever could resurrect the corpse would be the true leader. Koresh simply called the sheriff's office and reported Roden for abuse of a corpse. The sher-

iff's office responded that it needed evidence, so Koresh led an armed group of his followers onto the property, ostensibly to find evidence. Roden was waiting for them with an Uzi submachine gun, and a shoot-out ensued between Roden and Koresh. Somehow, no one was killed. Koresh and his followers were charged with attempted murder. A jury found Koresh's seven men not guilty and was divided (hung) on Koresh, after which the prosecution dropped the case.[13] Koresh paid back taxes on Mount Carmel and took control of the property. In 1989 Roden murdered his roommate, whom he claimed was a hitman working for Koresh. Roden was found not guilty by reason of insanity and was sent to a mental institution, which he repeatedly escaped from before finally dying of a heart attack in 1998. Koresh likely feared a visit from an unstable and armed George Roden rather than from law enforcement.

Many of the Breault affidavit's claims about Koresh's sexual improprieties can be corroborated. Following Jewell's 1992 complaint, Texas Child Protective Services investigated the Branch Davidians but closed the case because of a lack of evidence. Kiri Jewell refused to press any charges against Koresh because she did not want to press charges against her mother. However, in a congressional hearing held in 1995, Kiri testified that Koresh had sex with her when she was ten years old. The encounter occurred in a motel room where her mother had left her. It should be noted that the Bureau of Alcohol, Tobacco, and Firearms has no jurisdiction over child abuse.

This letter and the affidavit offer important insights into the mindset that led to the ATF carrying out the raid. Both Jewell and Breault call the Branch Davidians a cult. Jewell warns of a "holocaust" and urges the government to "do whatever is necessary to avert another Jonestown massacre." Most importantly, Breault's story about armed guards led directly to the ATF's decision to serve arrest and search warrants in the form of a paramilitary raid.[14] In an affidavit used to obtain the warrants, ATF agent Davy Aguilera wrote that he had interviewed Breault, who said that the guards had been given "shoot-to-kill" orders if anyone attempted to come through the gate onto the property.[15]

Finally, it must be noted how many people referenced in Breault's affidavit died on either February 28 or April 19, 1993. These include Asian American Sherri Jewell, 43; Samoan American Neil Vaega, 38; Chinese American Margarida Vaega, 47; white American Rachel Sylvia, 12; Mexican American Audrey Martinez, 13; white Australian Nicole Gent, 24, and her unborn child; white American Lisa Marie Farris, 24; white American Rachel Koresh, 24; white American Michele Jones, 18; white American Serenity Sea Jones, 4; white American Cyrus Koresh, 8; white American Steve Schneider, 43; white Australian Aisha Gyarfas Summers, 17, and her unborn child; white American Jaydean Wendell, 34; and white American James Riddle, 32.

The second set of documents are memos from the FBI siege discussing strategies for negotiating with Koresh. The first memo, dated March 7, 1993, written by FBI Supervisory Special Agent Peter Smerick and Special Agent Mark C. Young, proposes a list of psychological tactics for putting stress on the Branch Davidians. Many of these tactics were used during the siege. Clive Doyle, a Branch Davidian who survived the siege, questioned the purpose of these tactics, asking, "If they thought we were all brainwashed and such a bunch of crazies, why would the FBI push David or the rest of us to the limit?"[16] *After the tragedy at Mount Carmel, Smerick was interviewed by Susan DeBusk of the Department of Justice. She wrote:*

> The reason he put all these ideas on paper is that he was concerned the Bureau commanders were moving forward too rapidly toward a military resolution of the situation and he thought it was totally wrong. Basically, Smerick says the list of tactical activities in his memos was a "shopping list" to try to "buy time" from the tactical people [the Hostage Rescue Team] by giving them ideas of things they could do to make them feel they were taking some action, while giving the negotiators time to do their work.[17]

The Smerick-Young memo also references a similar event that occurred in 1985 in Philadelphia, where police engaged in an armed standoff with a Black movement called MOVE. This incident concluded when police dropped a bomb on the residence, burning it up, killing six adult MOVE members and five of their children, and destroying a total of sixty-five houses. In their memo, Smerick and Young urge the FBI not to repeat the mistakes of the 1985 scenario and to consider the public outcry if FBI agents were responsible for the death of children. Chillingly, this warning is exactly what came to pass.

The second memo, dated March 3, 1993, is by Smerick and forensic psychiatrist Park Dietz. It discusses various talking points that could be used to appeal to Koresh's religious beliefs and his desire to spread his message. Ultimately, the FBI abandoned negotiations in favor of the tank and CS gas assault on April 19, 1993. This memo mentions "Robert Gonzales." This was the undercover name for Robert Rodriguez, an ATF agent who had moved into a house across the street from Mount Carmel Center and tried to befriend Koresh and the Branch Davidians to gain information about possible illegal weapons, which he reported to ATF that he did not see. Koresh shot an AR-15 rifle with Rodriguez and gave him Bible studies, the Branch Davidian method used to try to convert people. Koresh later stated that he suspected Gonzales/Rodriguez was an undercover agent but that he hoped he could explain to him that they were living out an apocalyptic prophecy so that "they would realize what they're dealing with."[18] The morning of the ATF raid, Rodriguez discovered that Koresh knew a raid was coming. Rodriguez reported this to his immediate supervisors, demanding that the raid be called off. Instead, the decision was made to conduct the raid as quickly as possible. In hindsight, this was yet another reason why the raid was poorly planned and executed. The Branch Davidians knew a raid was imminent, and they had time to get their weapons.

The final document is the "event log" for April 19, 1993,

*as recorded by FBI officials in the Strategic Operations In-
formation Center (SOIC) in the J. Edgar Hoover Building
in Washington, DC. It describes the FBI's assault on the
Branch Davidians' residence using tanks and CS gas in
grim, detached terms. It also provides some clues about
what actually happened and who was to blame for the disastrous outcome. The log describes the building not as a
church or residence but in terms of military "tactical cod-
ing": The "white" side of the building refers to the front of
the building, which was visible to television cameras placed
miles away and was the direction from which the main assault by tanks approached from the front driveway; the
"black" side refers to the rear of the building, not visible to
television cameras; the "green" side refers to the southeast
side of the building to the right of the main assault direction; and the "red" side refers to the northwest side, to the
left when looking toward the front of the building. All the
windows are referenced in terms of alpha, bravo, etc.*

*The events described in the SIOC April 19, 1993, log are
subject to "the fog of war" and should not be regarded as
completely reliable. For example, the telephone line to negotiators, lying on the ground, was severed by a CEV at the
start of the raid. The log reports that someone threw the
telephone out the front door. Survivor Graeme Craddock
testified that this never happened, but even if it had there
were multiple phones in the building: The problem was that
the line had been cut.[19] The report repeatedly says that the
HRT never returned fire; however, this may not be entirely
true. The FBI had an aircraft circling the scene using
forward-looking infrared (FLIR) to record heat signatures.
Congress asked infrared expert Carlos Ghigliotti to examine the footage. Ghigliotti's report stated that at 11:24
a.m., "two subjects" emerged from under a tank that had
just torn a hole in the gym and then fired into the hole, resulting in a brief firefight. Ghigliotti died of a heart attack
shortly after completing his report, and Congress stated
that it never received this report.[20]*

The report also omits that the FBI gassed an old concrete vault where the young children, mothers, and two pregnant women were sheltering. At 11:31 a.m. (Central Standard Time), the driver of CEV-1 was ordered to spray the former vault, which required driving into the building. Two bottles of CS gas were then sprayed through the open entrance of the shelter.[21]

A striking feature of this log is the massive amount of CS gas that was used. It describes the CEVs returning to re-fill containers with even more gas. By one estimate. the concentration of gas inside the headquarters reached as high as thirty to ninety times the level required to deter able-bodied soldiers. Some of the adult Branch Davidians had gas masks, but the children did not. Chemist Eric R. Larsen testified that many of the deaths at Mount Carmel, particularly of the children, were caused directly or indirectly by the gas. He concluded that the FBI was not famil-iar with chemical weapons and that although the FBI "understands guns," "they don't understand an equal op-portunity killer like gas that turns corners and permeates things and kills or injures anyone it comes in contact with."[22]

Representative Fred Upton
421 Main Street
St. Joseph, Michigan 49085

17 March, 1992

Dear Congressman,

I write to call your attention to an extremely grave situation which begs for action. It involves a religious cult known as the Branch Davidian Seventh Day Adventists centered at Mt. Carmel, near Waco, Texas with additional property holdings and group membership in Southern California.

I recently won a child custody battle in Judge Ronald Taylor's court, Berrien County, Michigan against my former wife, Sherri L. Jewell, based on her exposing our eleven year old daughter to the practices of this group. Rather than elaborating herein on the specifics of these activities, I am forwarding a copy of an affidavit provided in the case by Marc Breault. Breault is a former member of this cult and it was he who called my attention to the dangerous situation that my daughter faced. I have enclosed only this one affidavit but am in possession of several more from people who corroborate Breault's testimony.

While the charges raised in these affidavits are absurdly fascinating they are not the matters of greatest concern to me at this time. During the process of the trial last month it was learned outside the courtroom that the group leader, Vernon W. Howell, a.k.a., David Koresh, has announced a plan for mass self-destruction if this case went against them.

One group member, Steven Schneider, who accompanied my former wife from California to face the court, told his family (non-members of the cult) that he expected to do something soon that would result in his own death and that he would probably never speak to them again.

We have since heard the same ominous expectations voiced by other sources. One young mother recently fled the group with her babies (fathered by Howell/Koresh) to avoid the holocaust.

My former wife returned to California where she gave virtually the same suicidal message to her close friend. This friend is adamant in her belief that Sherri intends to participate in an act of mass self-destruction within the next few weeks.

Though my daughter is safe with me we are very fearful for the safety of the children of those still under the influence of Howell/Koresh, who may be sacrificed at his command.

Those who know the mind of this man better than I are convinced that he will activate his plan during Passover (sometime between now and Easter), and further, that it may involve homicidal actions against "Babylon" (all those outside his fold) prior to turning to self-destruction.

I understand any immediate reaction of skepticism, but in the interest of the children's safety, perhaps this is the time to err on the side of caution. I am convinced that a sincere scrutiny of this group and its leadership will persuade those in authority to do whatever is necessary to avert another Jonestown massacre. I have presented this information to the FBI. They have offered no confirmation of action.

A great deal of background information was given February 25–28 of this year in Judge Taylor's court. I would encourage you to avail yourself of those transcripts and/or to contact Judge Taylor personally. I believe you will find him most willing to share information with you.

Please enlist the support of Congressional officials in Texas and California toward a full investigation.

I have tried to encapsulate this matter and, as a result, have undoubtedly left several aspects unclear. Please do not hesitate to contact me for clarification. It is the sincerest hope of myself and my friends and family that immediate action will save at least the children.

Thank you,

David S. Jewell

I, Marc Breault, a Computer Analyst/Programmer reside at . . . Australia.

I was a member of the cult known as the Branch Davidian Seventh-day Adventists from January 1986 to August 1989. At first Vernon Howell (n.k.a. David Koresh) appeared to be a conservative person whose only wish was to reform the Seventh-day Adventist Church. As time progressed however, Howell became power hungry and abusive, bent on obtaining and exercising absolute power and authority over the group. I lived separate from the group from January 1986 to January 1988. From January 1988, I lived with the other group members in either Mount Carmel Texas or Pomona California. During my involvement with the group I witnessed the following.

In April of 1986, Vernon admitted in front of the entire group membership that he had sexual relations with one Karen Doyle a girl who was only 13 or 14 years old at the time. Howell taught that this act was according to Bible Prophecy. Howell related that God had said to him "Give seed to Karen." Upon hearing this Vernon approached Karen Doyle and informed her what God had told him. Karen responded by saying that she would do whatever God told her to do. This is how Howell related the story. The girl's father Clive Doyle was in Australia at the time, and he did not know this had happened. In April of 1986 I assumed that Clive Doyle had been informed. I have since discovered my error in this regard. Clive's ex-wife, Karen's mother, was not a member of this group and she also had no idea of what had taken place.

Once, during the Summer of 1987 (I think it was late May or early June), I was visiting the group's California residence in San Bernardino California. At approximately 5:30 a.m., Howell's father-in-law Perry Jones called from Texas. I took the call and Perry informed me that it was urgent he speak to Howell. I put the phone down and proceeded to Howell's room. I knocked but learned that he was not there. I went outside to look for him. Since Perry had informed me the matter was urgent I called out for Vernon. There were three little shacks positioned at the side of the San Bernardino house. Karen Doyle was staying in one and Michele Jones (then aged 12) was staying in another. When I called out, Michele Jones called out from her shack asking if I was looking for Vernon. I said that I was and that Perry (Michele's father) said it was urgent he speak to Vernon. Michele said for me to hold on and she would get him. A moment later, I saw Vernon exit Michele Jones' shack (where she was supposedly staying alone).

Vernon was not wearing a shirt, but pants only. He went inside and took the call.

In October of 1987, Sherri Jewell, mother of Kiri Jewell took me aside (we were good friends) and told me she was in love with Howell, and that she had become one of his "wives." She said she wanted me to know because she felt she could trust me with that knowledge. At the time, Sherri Jewell and Dana Okimoto were sharing the same shack. Sherri said that she and Dana had become very good friends now that they were both in the "House of David" i.e. one of Vernon's "wives." Some time before this incident, Howell had given Bible studies from the Song of Solomon saying that he was entitled to 140 wives. Howell further broke the number 140 down to 60 proper wives and 80 concubines. A concubine is a slave who acts as a mistress to her master.

At about the same time as the incident with Sherri mentioned above, Dana confided to me that Vernon and her were having sexual relations as well. Dana even told me that her first night with him was 31 August 1987. Both Sherri and Dana felt I was going to be one of the group's evangelists and that I should know what was happening. Howell did not mind my knowing.

Two of the cult members; Neil and Margarida Vaega owned a bakery in Honolulu. When they joined the group they gave it to Vernon. This was done via a verbal agreement. While the bakery was operational, under Howell's control, Howell sent a number of group members to Hawaii to work. These were Bonnie Haldeman (Vernon's mother), Jimmy Riddle, Peter Hipsman and Clive Doyle. These were the core workers. Howell also started up a bakery in San Bernardino California. This bakery was operated without a license.

Several group members worked for that bakery. At no time were any W4 forms filled out or filed. To my knowledge, little and, in some cases, no wages were given for the work done. At no time were the profits registered with the proper government agencies. Both Douglas Wayne Martin and myself strenuously urged Howell to discontinue this practice. Eventually, both bakeries were closed down. The one in Honolulu was sold (and I do not think that was legally recorded), while the one in San Bernardino was just shut down.

From January to May 1988, I lived on 19th Street in Waco Texas. This is where we had the musical equipment. During this time, I personally witnessed Dana Okimoto, Robyn Bunds, Sherri Jewell, and Rachel Howell (his legal wife) spend the night in Howell's room on various occasions.

Later, in 1988/1989, we would occasionally stay at the Pomona House in California. Vernon would have his own room and he would usually sleep in that room with a number of his "wives." Sherri Jewell was one of those "wives." Kiri Jewell would also sleep in the same room as Vernon and his women. I know this because I used to sleep in the living room and I often saw Sherri and Kiri enter Vernon's room to go to sleep for the night.

Eventually, Howell moved into the garage of the Pomona house. He would pick his "wife" for the night and she would come out to him in the garage. The wives all slept in Howell's former room in the house and Kiri continued to sleep in that room as well. On one occasion, Howell related the following story to me.

Howell told me that one of his "wives," Nicole Gent (n.k.a. Nicole Little) was very depressed. Howell was sleeping on the floor in his room (before he moved out to the garage). He was positioned near Sherri Jewell, Lisa Farris, and Kiri Jewell. Both Sherri Jewell and Lisa Farris knew that Nicole was depressed and they encouraged Howell to move from the floor to the bed where Nicole was sleeping so he could be with her. So Howell complied. Howell related this story to me saying that he was amazed that women (wives) would be willing to encourage him to go and "make love" to another woman in their presence. Howell told me this story in an effort to convince me that the Holy Spirit was with his "wives."

I can say for certain that Kiri Jewell knew about Sherri's sexual involvement with Howell. Sherri would often employ Kiri in covering for her when outsiders were involved. Sherri told me that she was drilling Kiri in case she was questioned by outsiders about her (Sherri's) involvement.

During the Fall of 1988 I saw Howell put Kiri Jewell on his lap. Sherri Jewell was also present. Howell told Kiri that she (Kiri) was his (Howell's) daughter and he asked her if she (Kiri) would behave herself. From then on, Sherri Jewell emphasized to Kiri that she was Howell's daughter. By early to mid 1989, Sherri was beginning to prepare her daughter Kiri, to become one of Vernon's "wives." By this time, I had become quite disenchanted with Howell but I had no place to go. When I saw Sherri was doing this to Kiri I often took Kiri aside and explained to her that she was very young and that she should wait before she decided whom she should marry. I saw Kiri and her girl friends Rachel Sylvia and Audrie [Audrey Martinez] (about her age) were intensely interested in marriage and were primed to look forward to it. Sherri would often teach Kiri Howell's doctrine and even take pride in the fact that Kiri knew and memorized scriptures Howell used to teach his "wives" doctrines.

In about April of 1988 I was breaking up with a girlfriend of mine.

Howell took me aside and confided in me that he was having girl troubles of his own. He said it wasn't easy having all these women. He asked me to guess who his favorite "wife" was. I guessed Rachel Howell or Sherri Jewell. Howell said I was wrong—He said that his favorite "wife" was Michele Jones and that he had been with her since she was 12 years old. "Can you believe it, Marc, she's [Michele] been with me since she was 12 years old." Those were his exact words. That was the first time I actually knew for certain that Howell had slept with Michele Jones. Previous to this incident, I had been suspicious, but I did not wish to believe Howell could do such a thing.

In April of 1988 I saw Michele Jones' baby Serenity Sea. The baby was being looked after by its grandmother Mary Bell[e] Jones [1932–2014]. I went into the house to use their phone (as I did not have one myself) and Mary Bell[e] was telling me how quiet the baby was etc. The baby was only a month or two old. Mary Bell[e] told me specifically that Howell had instructed her to hide the baby in case any outsider or fringe member happened to see it. This was because Howell did not want anyone to know he (Howell) had been sleeping with Michele Jones. In June of 1991, I discussed the matter with Michele Jones' brother Joel, a very good friend of mine. He informed me that Michele Jones (his younger sister) was born on July 4, 1974. I saw baby Serenity Sea in April of 1989. Thus, Michele Jones would have only been 14 years of age when she gave birth to the baby.

On one occasion Howell's right hand man Steve Schneider told me that Howell had told him that he (Howell) would have to undergo a test greater than that which Abraham had to endure when God told Abraham to slay his son Isaac. Steve went on to say that Howell told him people would think he was crazy for doing what he was required to do.

On one occasion, Howell's son Cyrus had misbehaved. As punishment, Howell forced his son Cyrus to sleep on the hard kitchen floor with only a thin blanket for covering. Howell had asked Cyrus to call Nicole Gent (n.k.a. Nicole Little) mommy. The child's real mother is Rachel Howell. Cyrus would not call Nicole mommy. Thus, Howell instituted that punishment. On the following day, Howell ordered James Tom to prepare a place in the garage (Pomona house) for his son Cyrus to sleep in that night. Howell emphasized to the little child (about three years old) that there were large rats in the garage and they would eat him because he had been naughty. The child was absolutely terrified and began begging to be allowed to stay in the house. Howell then tried once again to force Cyrus to call Nicole mommy but the child would not. James Tom also objected strenuously but his objections were silenced by Howell.

On one occasion, shortly after this incident, Howell asked his son Cyrus whether he liked him (Howell). The child replied that he did not like his father Vernon. Vernon was enraged and beat his son severely. He then asked the child again if he liked him (Vernon). Once again the child replied that he did not. Vernon continued to beat the child until Cyrus finally said he loved his daddy. These and other incidents prompted me to begin planning my escape. I took Cyrus in hand, so to speak and used to sneak out with him and some of the other guys and we would play ball in the park. Cyrus enjoyed those times very much.

In March of 1989 Howell told me that the Gyarfas family was scheduled to visit the group in the US. Howell asked me if I thought he should pay for Aisha Gyarfas's way over. Aisha was only 13 years old at the time. Howell said that since he wanted Aisha as one of his wives, he should be responsible for her upkeep. He also said that the Gyarfas family were not well off financially. I objected strenuously to Howell's intention.

I was seriously considering leaving the cult in the Summer of 1989 because of what Howell was doing to young girls. But I wanted to make sure. I saw Aisha Gyarfas (Now Sommers)

[Summers] enter Vernon's room on a number of evenings. She entered alone. The next morning, she would emerge.

To make sure of this, I stayed in the office downstairs the entire night, under the pretext that I had some work to do. My PC was in the office and I did write a few unimportant letters. In reality, I was playing a Star Trek simulation game. The point is, however, for Aisha to exit, she would have had to come through that office and she did not. The next morning, Aisha emerged from Koresh's room and was somewhat surprised to find me in the office so "early" in the morning. But by that time, it was feasible for me to be there so I did not have to give her any story.

On another occasion, Howell gave me permission to practice in his room. While I was practicing, Aisha came up to retrieve some clothes which she had forgotten the night before. There might have been a couple of other belongings she forgot, but I do not remember. When she saw me in the room, I explained that Koresh (then Vernon Howell) had allowed me to practice in the room. Indeed, I practiced in that room regularly, almost on a daily basis.

On another occasion, around this time, Howell told me that a lot of people thought that 12 and 13 year old girls were not ready for sex. Howell assured me this was incorrect. He said that girls that age were extremely ready for sex and that they were very good in bed. He said they were fast and eager at that age. He used Aisha Gyarfas as an example.

During the summer of 1989 I was staying at Mount Carmel Texas. Kiri and I were walking together up to our respective houses. Sherri Jewell and Kiri were staying next door to where I was staying. Howell walked up and said hello. He asked Kiri whether she had been behaving lately. Kiri responded that she had been behaving. Howell said this was good because if she wanted to be in the "house of David" (one of his wives) she would have to be a good girl.

In general, I have seen Howell order the deprivation of basic human rights. I have seen this primarily with food. On many occasions, he has commanded that no food be eaten during an interval of from one to two days. He has assigned various juice fasts to a number of people. He would often declare starch free diets. During April of 1989, Howell forbade all fruit except for bananas. Howell also forbade anyone buying food for themselves for any reason whatsoever. All meals had to be eaten in the dining area and only the association could purchase food, and that only by Howell's direction. Howell maintained strict and meaningless dietary rules.

For instance, Howell forbade anyone to eat oranges and grapes the same meal, but they could eat oranges and raisins at the same meal.

During 1988, many children were not going to school. And even when Vernon allowed children to go to school during the 1988/1989 school year, he would often call studies during the afternoons and evenings, preventing the children from completing homework assignments.

On 5 August 1989, Vernon gave a Bible study in which he stated that he was the Lamb of God. As the Lamb of God he was entitled to have all women and girls sexually. Only he had the right to procreate. Howell stated that he would give some married couples time to adjust to this new "revelation" as he called it. At one point during this study, Howell saw that the married couples were very upset. Howell commanded everyone to look at Sherri Jewell. Sherri was actually quite taken with the study and Howell pointed this out and said Sherri liked this doctrine because she had been sacrificing for years and now it was the married couples' turn to sacrifice. In fact, Sherri Jewell was quite enjoying this study. Howell commanded that no one tell anyone of this "new light" as he called it.

Shortly after this study, Sherri Jewell wrote a letter to the group members in Texas. She stated that people were having difficulty coping with some "new light" Howell had given. The letter was quite condemning of those who would not go along with Howell's doctrines. A copy of the letter was read to me.

When Howell discovered I had left the group and joined my wife Elizabeth in Australia, he forbade anyone to communicate with Elizabeth and I without his permission. When Howell arrived in Australia he had Steve Schneider call me up. Howell was prompting Steve what to say. At one point, I heard Howell tell

Schneider to tell me that he would kill my wife Elizabeth because she was his enemy.

Later on I was told three things by former Australian members. One was that Vernon had created a hit list and that I was on top of that list. This was because I had been instrumental in causing Australian members to break away from Howell. I was also told that during the time the Australians were following Howell, Howell had told them that if I came to visit them at their home, they were to open the door, kick me in the balls, and slam the door in my face. Finally, we were told that Howell had sent some of his followers to spy on us, driving by our house at about 2:00 in the morning to see if any Australians who were considering breaking away were, in fact, visiting us.

In June of 1991 I confronted Sherri Jewell regarding Howell's sexual activities with young girls. I verbally backed Sherri Jewell into a corner and she admitted, in front of her mother Ruth Mosher, that Michele Jones had been pregnant and had given birth to a child by Howell, when she was only 14 years of age. I forwarded the details of this confrontation to Barbara Wiggins of the La Verne Police Department.

Included in my statement to Barbara Wiggins was the pertinent portion of the conversation between Ruth Mosher (Sherri's mother and Kiri's grandmother), Sherri and myself. The exact wording of my recollection of that conversation follows.

MARC: One of the reasons I'm doing this is that I'm afraid that children will suffer for the rest of their lives. After all, they don't have the power to choose. One of the things I don't agree with is that they're pulled out of school.

SHERRI: The kids aren't pulled out of school. They went while you were there.

RUTH: Yes, I know Kiri was going to school while she was living in Waco.

MARC: That's true she was. Many of the kids were bussed to school like Shari Doyle, Brad (I name others). But they were pulled out of school.

SHERRI: Yes but we taught them ourselves. I taught Kiri myself. She was so much more advanced than the other kids who went to normal school that she skipped a grade.

MARC: It helps being a school teacher Sherri. That is good. But my point is that Michele Jones didn't go to school. I believe Michele stopped going to school after the sixth grade or somewhere around there. My point is, she did not go to school while the other kids were.

RUTH: How old is Michele?

SHERRI: (by this time she is very wary) I don't know.

MARC: Michele Jones was born on July 4, 1974.

(When Sherri was teaching Kiri, that was in 1989. Ruth knew that so she would have known that at the time in question, Michele was only 14 years of age.)

RUTH: And she was pulled out of school?

MARC: Yes she was. She was pulled out of school because she was pregnant. I know because I was there. Michele Jones did not go to school with the other kids because she was pregnant.

RUTH: (indignant) Were her parents there?

MARC: Yes they were. Michele was definitely pregnant and I saw the child myself.

RUTH: And they condoned it?

MARC: Yes they did.

RUTH: Who was the father of the child?

MARC: Vernon was. People were not supposed to know about it.

RUTH: (To Sherri) Did you know she was pregnant?

SHERRI: Well I noticed her tummy was a bit pouchy.

RUTH: (To Sherri) Oh come on. You knew she was pregnant.

SHERRI: Yes she was.

Ruth Mosher also told Elizabeth and I that Kiri had gone to Mount Carmel Texas in around April of 1991 to see a baby being born, that is, to physically witness a baby being born. We have since received confirmation of this story from an ex-member, one Doreen Saipaia. Doreen related that Kiri was with the woman delivering the baby of one Dana Okimoto. Doreen informed us that Kiri was said to inform Howell that he (Howell) had a new son. Doreen also indicated that Kiri's participation was in preparation for her (Kiri) becoming one of Howell's "wives."

During my involvement with the group, Sherri would often take on a maternal role with regard to the women in Howell's harem. To my knowledge, Sherri was the oldest member of that harem and girls would sometimes confide in her for advice. Rachel Howell, being Vernon Howell's legal wife would also sometimes assume this role. Lisa Farris, another of Howell's women would often seek Sherri out for advice. Because Sherri and I were good friends, I often saw this take place. During 1986, Sherri would also console Robyn Bunds, Dana Okimoto and Lisa Farris. Both Dana and Robyn were pregnant and were often upset at Howell's various actions toward them. Sherri also drove a number of Vernon's women from Texas to California, or vice versa. Once Sherri had "repented" from her "adultery" (early 1988), Howell felt he could trust Sherri with many responsibilities regarding the harem.

On one occasion, Sherri and a few other young women made what was to become the Branch Davidian flag. It depicted a white unicorn surrounded by both visual and textual references to scriptures Howell used to formulate his harem theology. Sherri led out in this activity.

During the month of May through July of 1989, Howell conceived the idea of heavy physical training. He had shown the entire group movies such as Platoon and Full Metal Jacket, movies about the Viet Nam war. He required little children to attend these violent R rated movies. Kiri was also required to attend and watch. In some of the war movies, Hamburger Hill was another such movie, Marine training exercises were shown in great length. Among these scenes were marching songs, the type one sings during forced marches and runs during boot camp. Many such "songs" were very sexual, as one might expect from Marines.

When Howell decided everyone needed physical training, the women and girls did their own training. Jaydeen [Jaydean] Wendel and Sherri Jewell were inspired by the Marine songs in the above mentioned movies, and they created songs about Branch Davidian doctrines. These songs, as I recall, included references to killing "Babylonians" i.e. Howell's enemies. Sherri and Jaydeen [Jaydean] would lead both women and girls on marches and runs, acting as drill sergeants, even to the extent of "left, left, left right left" chants, followed by these various songs. Sherri or Jaydeen [Jaydean] would call out one line, and the rest would answer, just as a drill sergeant does in military boot camp. Even Kiri was obliged to participate in these "exercises." They usually began at 5:30 in the morning.

Howell also had a theory that people should not hydrate themselves in hot weather. He felt that not drinking during exercises in hot weather was a sign of toughness. The women would exercise two or three times a day, each exercise period consisting of the above mentioned marches. During that summer, the weather would consistently exceed 100 degrees and no one was allowed to hydrate themselves during those exercises in the heat.

The men, only exercised once in the early morning and there were no Marine-style chants. The rest of the day was spent in building the new church which now stands on the Mount Carmel property.

Howell was increasingly obsessed with guns and the need to use them. Howell mounted a 24 hours a day, seven days a week, armed guard at the front gate of Mount Carmel. Some of the women stood guard duty, including Sherri Jewell and Jaydeen [Jaydean] Wendel. Even Dana Okimoto stood guard duty, a loaded gun at the ready. Very few, if any had adequate fire arm training and little children would often come to visit their parents despite the fact there were loaded guns in the vicinity.

One summer night (I think it was in 1988), I had just arrived at Mount Carmel. It was very late and I was just preparing to go to sleep. I heard a noise and when I looked out I saw Wally Kennett, who was standing guard duty at the front gate, fire his gun at an intruder. It was about 5:00 in the morning. The intruder was the newspaper delivery man. He had surprised Wally and Wally had panicked. Those in charge had forgotten to tell Wally about the newspaper delivery man, who delivered papers to the Chuns, an elderly couple. When Kennett panicked he cried halt, and then fired his gun. He said later it was in the ground but I have no way of verifying that. All I saw was the shadow of a figure, Wally cry out halt, and then the gun being fired. The poor newspaper man cried out something like "Holy Shit, don't shoot, please don't shoot." I saw him run away in panic. Wally was badly shaken up. That very morning, the newspaper called and refused to deliver any more papers to that property. My point is that the firearm situation within the group is a very serious accident waiting to happen.

In the above-mentioned case, someone was literally nearly killed or seriously hurt. In fact, I was so frightened for the poor newspaper man that without thinking, I ran out and yelled to Wally to take it easy. I explained who the man was.

Howell is very paranoid and he instills that paranoia to his members. Howell would often walk around the property late at night and shoot his AK-47 rifle and various objects.

During my time at Mount Carmel, the sanitation conditions were appalling. Howell had promised both his members and the media to put running water on the property. Because there was no real toilet facilities, raw sewage was simply buried in the ground wherever there was room. Some people in that area get their water from wells. Mount Carmel also has a well but it was never restored. Water would be brought in on a large yellow container, situated on a flat bed truck. Drinking, cooking, and bathing water was obtained from this yellow container. It was rarely, if ever cleaned. Thus, this container was literally crusted with algae and Howell eventually forbade anyone from obtaining their own water. Compounding this sanitation problem was the fact that one of Howell's followers is a carrier of Hepatitis B, a highly contagious condition. When people carried their excrement to be buried, it would sometimes spill out of the bucket and fall unburied on the ground.

When food was prepared in the dining hall, no hair nets or gloves were used. Someone on the property was always sick. During the winter, there was virtually no real heating and there was no way to get firewood. At one stage Howell forbade any store bought firewood. In fact, I cannot recall one instance in which firewood was brought in for anyone.

I have been told by several persons that health and sanitation conditions are far worse now than they were when I was at Mount Carmel. In my opinion, anyone, especially children, who lives on Mount Carmel for any length of time is in extreme danger of disease and infection. Compounding this is Howell's belief that he is sufficiently capable of handling most medical situations.

On one occasion, the children brought lice back to Mount Carmel from school. Sherri and Kiri were both affected, Kiri severely so.

The lack of running water made it virtually impossible to alleviate the lice plague. Poor Kiri had lice for months and I am not even certain she was rid of them by the time I left the group in August of 1989.

Finally, Howell is obsessed with sex. I have often witnessed Howell give Bible studies, if you can call them that, in which literally hours of time was spent describing sex, sexual acts, and sexual preferences in graphic detail. Little children were also forced to listen. During a number of studies, for example, Howell would describe what he felt to be the differences between male and female genitalia of different races. In Kiri's presence, Howell would describe Sherri's sexual habits with him, as well as her genitalia. These studies were especially sexual in nature in 1989, but sex was always part of Howell's studies. I could even say that when I first met Howell, he was mindful of children's sensitivities in that area but by 1989, he had lost all restraint.

I affirm under penalties of perjury that the foregoing is true to the best of my knowledge and belief.

Signed,
Marc A. Breault

MEMORANDUM

To: SAC's WAC MUR (89B-SA-38851) (MC 80)

Date: 3/7/93

From: SSA PETER A SMERICK & SA MARK C. YOUNG

PSYCHOLOGICAL PROFILERS

Subject: NEGOTIATION STRATEGY CONSIDERATIONS

The following ideas and suggestions are offered for consideration, in no particular order of preference:

1. FLOODLIGHTS AT NIGHT

2. NOISES, SIRENS, ETC.

3. LOUDSPEAKERS WITH IDEOLOGY & BIBLICAL REFERENCES DISCREDITING KORESH

4. CHEMICAL LIGHTS AROUND THE COMPOUND

5. FLARES AT NIGHT

6. AIRCRAFT FLY-OVERS

7. SCENT OF FOOD COOKING

8. START MILITARY ARMORED VEHICLES ENGINES PERIODICALLY (OUT OF SIGHT OF THE COMPOUND)

9. HAVE ARMORED VEHICLES DRIVE BACK AND FORTH PERIODICALLY

10. PULL ALL PERSONNEL BACK, THEN MOVE THEM FORWARD AGAIN

11. SHUT OFF UTILITIES

12. JAM TELEVISION/RADIO RECEPTION

13. CONTAMINATE WATER SUPPLY, FOR TASTE ONLY, NOT TO CAUSE ILLNESS

14. CONTINUE MOVING THE PERIMETER CLOSER TO THE COMPOUND

15. VIDEO TAPE KORESH'S FORMER ATTORNEY TELLING KORESH HE CAN BEAT THE CHARGES, NOT GO TO JAIL, SPREAD HIS MESSAGE TO THE WORLD, & HAVE MOVIES MADE ABOUT HIM

16. DISCONTINUE NEGOTIATIONS FOR AWHILE

17. DURING NEWS CONFERENCES, DESCRIBE DAVID AS A MAN HIDING BEHIND INNOCENT CHILDREN

18. UTILIZE A THIRD PARTY NEGOTIATOR (SUCH AS MC CLENNAN COUNTY SHERIFF, JACK HARWELL, WHO HAS HAD A HISTORY WITH THESE SUBJECTS, INCLUDING THE ARREST OF KORESH, IN THE PAST)

19. TELL DAVID ALL NEGOTIATIONS ARE OFF AND A FENCE WILL BE BUILT AROUND HIS COMPOUND; COMPLETELY ISOLATING HIM FROM THE WORLD. ONLY MILK WILL BE SENT IN TO HIS CHILDREN. HIS MESSAGE WILL NOT GET OUT AND FOR ALL PRACTICAL PURPOSES, HE WILL BECOME A PRISONER, WITHOUT HIS DAY IN COURT.

20. CALL DAVID, TELL HIM FROM NOW ON HE WILL BE PORTRAYED ON THE NEWS MEDIA AS A COMMON CRIMINAL KNOWN AS VERNON HOWELL.

We certainly have a number of options to consider which could increase the stress and anxiety on DAVID KORESH and his followers. Many of these options however, would also succeed in shutting down negotiations and convince KORESH and his followers that the end is near.

If trust between DAVID KORESH and negotiators is broken, we are then faced with the prospect of eventually taking physical action against the compound, to destroy it, thus forcing people out. If the compound is attacked, in all probability, DAVID KORESH and his followers will fight back to the death, to defend their property and their faith, as they believe they did on February 28, 1993. If that occurs, there will have to be a HRT response and the possibility of a tremendous loss of life, both within the compound, and of Bureau personnel.

Commanders are thus faced with the prospect of defending their actions and justifying the taking of the lives of <u>children</u>, who are with their families in a <u>"defensive position,"</u> defending their religion, regardless of how bizarre and cult-like we believe it is manifested.

If we physically attack the compound, and <u>children are killed</u>, (even by [Branch] Davidians), we, in the FBI, will be placed in a difficult position. The news media, Congress, and the American people, (who are currently applauding our negotiating efforts), will ask questions:

Why couldn't you just wait them out?

What threat did they pose to anyone, except themselves?

Why did you cause children to be killed?

Attached to this report is a news article (one of many) relating to the actions of the Philadelphia Police Dept. against the "MOVE" sect, a "back to nature" cult, in 1985. Their house was deluged with over one million gallons of water, over 10,000 rounds were fired, during the initial assault, and a bomb was dropped on the roof of the house. As a result, eleven people, including **5 children**, died.

The public outcry, against the tactics employed by the Philadelphia PD continues to this day.

It is imperative that the FBI learn from the mistakes made in Philadelphia.

RECOMMENDATIONS

1. We recommend a continued effort to negotiate the release of all persons inside the compound, with assistance of Sheriff JACK HARWELL. His participation is necessary because of KORESH'S hatred and distrust of the Federal Government.

MEMORANDUM

To: SACs, Waco Situation

Date: 3/3/93, 12:51 p.m.

From: Pete Smerick and Park Dietz

Subject: Negotiation Strategy Ideas

Overall Strategy:

(1) Acknowledge part of David's world view re. conspiracy against his organization and right to defend themselves from what they perceived as an illegitimate attack on Sunday.

(2) Create illusion that he can win in court and in the press, not go to prison, and emerge with more followers than he has now.

Specific points to Make with Koresh:

—Enemies of your religion have provided information to ATF and other organizations about you. This information has been fed in from around the world.

—These allegations have included suspected child abuse (leading to a social service investigation) and claims that the Branch Davidians have been involved in drug smuggling operations for drug cartels and illegal arms trading (leading to greater scrutiny of your weapons purchases than of most gun purchases).

—To David's credit, when he found a methamphetamine lab on the premises, he turned it over to the Sheriff, but this did not halt the development of rumors about drug operation.

—The ATF continued to receive information, some anonymously, from people who painted the Branch Davidians in an unflattering light and portrayed them as a threat to the community. Acting on the information they received, ATF was attempting to protect society from what they thought was a dangerous organization. To try to obtain more reliable information, ATF even resorted to deception, having Robert Gonzales cultivate your acquaintance, as you suspected.

—As a result of numerous miscalculations, this tragedy at your Temple occurred on Sunday.

—Sitting as a Monday morning quarterback, it looks like your organization may have been the victim of a conspiracy by your enemies, who were attempting to paint you as evil.

—David, we can understand why your people acted as they did Sunday morning because of your fervent beliefs in self defense, defense of your religious beliefs, defense of your family, and in the Word of Revelations [sic].

—You must know that in their zeal to seize weapons from drug dealers, criminals, organized crime, and gangs, ATF always runs the risk of seizing weapons from people who are not criminals.

—David, mistakes have been made but you have an obligation to your God and your family to expose the conspiracy that has been perpetrated against you and your beliefs. You must come forward now to expose this conspiracy and to let both Christians and those who have not yet accepted God's Word know the truth.

—Others who have been in a similar situation have stood up against ATF, sometimes with the help of the Gun Owner's [sic] of America, the Second Amendment Foundation, or the friends of their churches, and victories have been won by _____
_____.

—You must emerge now to air your side of the story in the press and in court, as this is your opportunity to reach people the world over both to expose them to the conspiracy and to the knowledge God has given you.

—Taking your story and your message to the people will no doubt test your faith, but this is the only way your flock can grow. Even now, there are people responding to news reports by traveling to

Waco to join you, but they cannot in this situation. Ask yourself, David, whether this is God's way of testing your resolve to spread His Word beyond the walls of your Temple.

EVENT LOG 4/19/93
OF CONVERSATIONS BETWEEN
SIOC AND WACO NEGOTIATORS

[The times are given in Eastern Standard Time, which reflects the time zone where SIOC and the Hoover Building are located in Washington, DC. Waco, Texas, is in the Central Standard Time zone, which is one hour behind Eastern Standard Time. Therefore, in Waco, the tank and gas assault began at 6:00 a.m., and the first flames were seen in the building at 12:07 and 12:11 p.m.]

7:06am—Command Post (CP) advises Schneider of actions being taken by the FBI and that this is not an "assault"; however, Schneider hangs up phone. Schneider was read prepared statement.

7:10am—CP advises tanks are being fired at from compound.

7:12am—CP advises announcements continue to be made over loud speaker for everyone to come out and surrender. Prepared statement is read.

7:15am—Gas is being put into the tower according to CP.

7:19am—There is an attempt to telephonically contact the compound, no answer.

7:20am—Technical coverage indicates one is operational and second one is receiving nothing, according to the CP.

7:21am—There is an attempt to telephonically contact the compound. No answer. Individuals in the compound are firing weapons, however FBI is not returning fire.

7:24am—CP asked if any information intercepted regarding subjects being told to put on gas masks. Negative.

7:25am—CP reports subjects have masks on and others are attempting to locate masks.

7:26am—CP reports gas being inserted into black side by farret [*sic*] round.

7:27am—CP reports gym building has been gassed.

7:28am—Red/White and black sides have all been inserted with gas. Gun fire continues to be taken from inside the compound.

7:29am—Green side is being gassed. CP reports that telephone lines are believed to have been cut by the tanks.

7:34am—CP reports a white flag or object has been seen at the door.

7:37am—CP reports there is continual reading of prepared statement to "Come out" being given over the loudspeaker.

7:40am—CP advises a white flag is hanging out the compound door.

7:41am—CP advises the front door is opening and a red flag is seen, and subjects have thrown the telephone out the door and tanks ran over the lines.

7:45am—Advised compound to have everyone come out or more gas would be inserted.

7:47am—CP advises more gas being inserted.

7:49am—CP advises continual announcement being made over loudspeaker that FBI in [*sic*] not assaulting the compound and that everyone should surrender. Technical coverage revealed subjects re-assuring each other. Koresh tells everyone to put gas masks back on.

7:50am—CP advises HRT is taking gun fire from two sides of the complex simultaneously.

7:55am—CP reports gun fire at tank stops. FBI HRT, according to CP, has not returned any gun fire, nor has any other law enforcement personnel.

7:58am—CP advises CEV is empty and going to re-load with gas. This will take about one hour. Gun fire from inside the compound is sparatic [*sic*].

8:00am—CP reports gun fire from compound continues (M-16 and hand guns) however FBI is not returning gun fire.

8:04am—All gas has been put in the Red/White/Green sides of compound and it is still being put in the black side.

8:05am—CP based on technical coverage is aware that all loudspeaker announcements being made for the surrender of subjects is being heard loud and clear in the compound.

8:12am—CP advises muffled voices on the technical coverage is indicative of the fact that subjects are wearing masks.

8:18am—CP reports winds of approximately 25 mph.

8:20am—CP reports still hearing muffled voices indicative of subjects using masks.

8:22am—CP reports FBI taking gun fire from white side tower (front) and that gas is being inserted in the red side.

8:28am—CP reports that technical coverage indicates that Steve Schneider and Koresh are together and are believed to have said "all we can do is just wait."

8:30am—CP advises that tanks physically breached the white side of the building on initial insertion of gas.

8:31am—CP reports gun fire from red side which precipitates insertion of gas on red side.

8:36am—CP advises attempts to put gas in the bus on green side has failed due to required angle.

8:40am—CP reports technical over hear of Koresh stating "Don't fire until the last minute" in anticipation that FBI would assault.

8:53am—CP reports on technical coverage of unknown stating "stay low, stay ready."

8:58am—CP reports hole put in 2nd floor and gas is being inserted by tank.

9:00am—CP reports that parts of the building may not have been penetrated by gas.

9:25am—Kahoe requests per DD Clarke that arrangements be made to have remote camera put on tank boom which can be used to look inside rooms for subjects before building is gassed or torn open in order to prevent injuries.

9:30am—CP advises that CEV's are still re-loading with gas. In addition an AM/FM radio and hammering noise was heard in the compound.

9:35am—CP advises that PA system announcement re surrender is given every ten minutes.

9:40am—Nothing to report from CP.

10:04am—CP reports an unknown individual was seen walking in from a mile out and will be intercepted.

10:05am—CP reports hearing David or other male saying "Its worship time."[23]

10:06am—CP advises gas will be inserted in Alpha windows 1, 2, 3, 4 and then into main door on white side—10.

10:10am—CP reports banner has been hung out of compound stating "We want our phone fixed." FBI responds over loudspeaker "If you want to talk come out of compound."

10:13am—CP reports ATF found an abandoned rental car, possibly used by individual reported at 10:04am.

10:35am—CP attempting to re-establish telephonic contact with compound.

10:45am—CP advises a white male wearing camouflage clothing signals lines of telephone were cut indicating the phone is inoperable. The individual was standing at front door of compound.

10:51am—CP reports that Gram Summers (ph) [Graeme Craddock] is trying to pull the phone [line] back into the compound. Technical coverage indicates that "David's transcript is almost complete."

10:53am—CP advises Graham [Graeme] has picked up phone outside compound and is pointing to where it is cut.[24] (Graham [Graeme] has repaired phone in the past). He took phone and line into compound.

11:03am—When Graham [Graeme] came out he did not have on gas mask.

11:25am—CP reports that SAC Ricks [Special Agent in Charge Bob Ricks] News conference will take place in 10 minutes.

11:58am—CP reports that there is no information to report other than news conference is ended.

12:10pm—CP reports gas was inserted in Red side windows 1–6 as people were gathering in this location.

12:30pm—Attempts were made to call into the compound.

12:39pm—CP advises CEV has hit the back of the "Dog House" causing outer sheet of siding to fall down.

12:45pm—CP advises Bravo 1 green side wall is down and FBI can see inside entire building as wall collapsed.

12:49pm—CP reports sounds of running feet and people saying "Look out . . ." when CEV hits wall. CP reports that when Graham [Graeme] came out to get the telephone he was told by someone inside the compound to "Take off the mask before you go out."

12:54pm—CP reports gas being inserted in white side and FBI continues to advise subjects to surrender.

12:59pm—CP reports that negotiations phone is not operational, however efforts are continuing to locate problem.

1:01pm—CP reports no technical coverage at this time.

1:06pm—CP reports a white male wearing a gas mask was observed at Alpha 10, white side.

1:09pm—CP advises roof on Black Alpha 1 thru 12 is on the ground and the roof is gone.

1:11pm—Fire is reported to have started at the compound. CP reports fire started on inside by subjects.

1:15pm—CP advises subjects being told to get out of compound.

1:16pm—CP advises male on roof of building refused to get off roof to take assistance from a tank.

1:20pm—CP advises five people were observed coming out of the compound on the green and white side.

1:25pm—CP advises fire started from a number of locations simultaneously.

1:26pm—CP advises that some people were picked up and taken to a rally point.

1:28pm—CP reports multiple helicopters were moving onto the site.

1:32pm—CP reports people on roof being taken off building by the tank.

1:40pm—CP confirms that five males and one female (badly burned) have been rescued.

1:44pm—CP advises there are reports of individuals shooting at HRT on green side.

1:49pm—CP reminded of possible danger to HRT and other law enforcement from sympathizers in the area.

2:08pm—CP reports two women taken to a hospital.[25]

2:31pm—CP reports that HRT using spotting scopes observed the fire being started inside the compound buildings by subjects.

2:52pm—CP reports five women and 3 men is total number confirmed as rescued. CP states woman stated subjects started the fire and search of bus was negative for survivors.

3:30pm—CP instructed to ensure that clothing of victims is placed in 1 gallon cans as soon as possible for preservation for laboratory.

3:53pm—CP provides list of names of those rescued:

> 1. Jamie [Jaime] Castillo 6/4/68
> 2. Clive Doyle 2/24/41
> 3. Misty Ferguson 16
> 4. Derek Lovelock 8/13/55
> 5. David Thibodeau 2/13/69
> 6. Renos Avraam 2/26/64
> 7. Ruth Riddle 10/24/63
> 8. Graham Craddock 11/29/61
> 9. Unknown Black Female[26]

3:57pm—CP advises Renos Avraam heard other people in the compound state "the fire is lite [sic], its [sic] lite" just prior to the compound burning. He also saw people putting fuel oil around the compound.

3:58pm—CP advises bunkers[27] on the east and west side of the compound may have people in them due to ventilation shafts, however they are too hot to enter.

4:05pm—CP advises technical information indicates fire started in three separate locations simultaneously.

4:20pm—CP reports that individual Graham Craddock had come out of a tunnel near the water tower.

THE SENTENCING OF SHOKO ASAHARA FOR THE AUM SHINRIKYO ATTACK

MARCH 20, 1995[1]

On March 20, 1995, five members of a group called Aum Shinrikyo (Aum) boarded five subway trains at different stations in Tokyo just before the morning rush hour. Each member left a plastic bag of sarin nerve gas on the floor of the subway and punctured it, using the sharpened tip of an umbrella, before exiting the train. The gas spread through the subway, killing twelve and injuring more than five thousand. The attack was intended to trigger an apocalyptic war that would pave the way for a new world.

Aum's founder was born Chizuo Matsumoto (1955–2018). From childhood, Matsumoto was almost totally blind. He became interested in comparative religion after a failed career in holistic medicine. In 1987 he changed his name to Shoko Asahara and founded Aum Shinrikyo. By 1995 the movement had attracted about ten thousand followers in Japan and another thirty thousand in Russia. Asahara's teachings were a mishmash of apocalyptic ideas borrowed from Buddhism, Hinduism, the Book of Revelation, the prophecies of Nostradamus, conspiracy theories, and even Japanese anime. He claimed to be an incarnation of Shiva, an enlightened Buddha capable of perfectly predicting the future, and a messiah appointed to transform the world. Asahara envisioned a Buddhist kingdom called "Shambhala" that would last one thousand years and be inhabited by spiritual adepts with advanced psychic abilities. Aum's goal was to create this enlightened paradise by transforming Japan, and then the entire world, into Shambhala.

Initially, Asahara taught that Shambhala could be achieved peacefully. He described a race to prevent Harumagedon (Armageddon) by establishing Shambhala first. In 1987 he predicted there would be a nuclear war between 1999 and 2003. This war could be prevented if Aum centers (called Lotus Villages) were established around the world and if the movement gained three thousand shukkesha *(renunciants). The* shukkesha *would be trained to have psychic powers and could prevent Harumagedon by transforming the world's negative karma.*

As Asahara's movement met with mounting setbacks, his vision of the future became increasingly catastrophic. Aum was making nowhere near the progress that Asahara said was necessary to prevent Harumagedon. Families of converts who had become shukkesha *organized a public campaign against Aum. Asahara interpreted any criticism of his movement as part of a massive conspiracy perpetrated by Jews, Freemasons, and the governments of the United States and Japan. In 1988 a member wanted to leave and was submitted to a purification ritual in which he was forcibly immersed in frigid water until he died. Another member who wished to leave was strangled to death. As Aum's inner circle became accustomed to killing, more murders were conducted to prevent dissent and silence critics. It is estimated that Aum members killed thirty-one people between October 1988 and March 1995.*

As described below, Asahara justified these killings through his interpretation of an obscure Buddhist doctrine called phowa *(Aum spelled this as* poa*). Buddhism is often described as having three branches. The oldest is sometimes pejoratively called Hinayana, meaning "the lesser vehicle." Mahayana ("greater vehicle") Buddhism incorporates ideas and practices that do not appear in the oldest Buddhist texts. These innovations were justified by claiming that the Buddha kept these teachings secret, believing they were too profound for Hinayana Buddhists to understand. Finally, Vajrayana Buddhism is found in Tibet and surrounding regions. It is a form of Mahayana Buddhism that emphasizes esoteric teachings known as tantra. It is from Vajrayana*

Buddhism that the idea of phowa *originates. Essentially, Asahara claimed that if people are engaged in bad actions, then killing them before they can acquire more negative karma is actually an act of compassion. Furthermore, Asahara claimed that because he was an enlightened Buddha he knew everyone's karma and when killing was justified.*

In 1990 Aum members, including Asahara, entered national elections. This resulted in public humiliation as Asahara's ideas were widely ridiculed. This defeat, combined with other setbacks, convinced him that the world could not be saved: Harumagedon was inevitable, and those few who survived would create Shambhala.

The movement's Lotus Villages were now equipped as bases to survive nuclear, biological, and chemical weapons. Aum technicians began researching a variety of chemical and biological agents as well as lasers, rail guns, and other high-tech weapons. When the Soviet Union collapsed, in 1991, Aum was able to purchase help from former Soviet scientists and KGB agents. This is likely how Aum learned to manufacture sarin gas. As Aum began experimenting with these weapons, Japanese police began closing in. In 1995 the movement learned that a police raid was impending and hastily carried out the attack on the Tokyo subway. In the immediate aftermath, Asahara denied responsibility and claimed that Aum members were being sprayed with nerve gas by US troops. On March 22, 1995, Tokyo police deployed 2,500 officers who raided 25 Aum centers simultaneously. Asahara was finally apprehended on May 16. He was sentenced on February 27, 2004, and was executed by hanging on July 6, 2018.

SENTENCING STATEMENT

The defendant, Asahara Shoko, claimed to have attained enlightenment and thereby recruited many disciples and founded the Aum Shinrikyo cult.[2] In order to expand the cult's influence, he planned to run in the election to make his debut on the national stage but failed utterly. Shortly after, he schemed to increase the cult's power through weaponization and the pursuit of arms. In the end, he fantasized about ruling Japan as its king in the name of salvation. He recruited many ordained adherents and completely siphoned off their assets under the pretext of collecting alms. Much of these funds were used to advance the weaponization of the cult: large quantities of the chemical weapon sarin gas were manufactured with the intention of indiscriminate mass murder across the city of Tokyo; amidst the chaos, Asahara intended for cult devotees to take control of the capital with automatic rifles and other firearms. In preparation for these murders, the cult nearly completed a functioning plant for the large-scale production of sarin. They also produced parts for approximately 1,000 automatic rifles but were successful in manufacturing only a single weapon.

Thus, the defendant regarded as an enemy any person who was an obstacle to his imagined vision, regardless of whether they were members of the cult. The act of *poa*—that is to say, murder—was the name of the egotistical doctrinal explanation, under which even the taking of life to expel these enemies was thought to be justified in order to prevent the accumulation of evil karma. Moreover, the defendant considered some of these victims to be test subjects for measuring the lethality of chemical weapons, including sarin gas, which was manufactured for the purpose of indiscriminate mass murder, and VX, a most potent chemical weapon used in assassination. He instructed his disciples to undertake a series of murders and attempted murders.

———

In a sermon on Buddhist doctrine delivered at the Setagaya Dojo on September 24, 1989, the defendant stated the following:

"Suppose there is a person—Mr. A—who begins on a righteous course after birth and begins accumulating Buddhist merit; however, he becomes prideful and his evil deeds begin to accumulate, such that at the end of his life he will have committed so many evil deeds that he would fall to hell.

"If an enlightened person were to kill Mr. A at this crucial moment, Mr. A would be reborn in the heavenly realm. Yet, when other people—people of the human world—witness the killing, they would understand it as murder. And if at this time Mr. A dies and goes to heaven, where a great savior of the heavenly realm reveals the truth to him and enables Mr. A to attain eternal life, what karma has the enlightened person who killed Mr. A accumulated? If the enlightened person was all-knowing and had allowed Mr. A to live, we would accrue evil karma and fall to hell; however, in this case, he thought it would be better to end his life and committed *poa*. What kind of karma would the killer have accumulated? Was this murder, or was it a good deed that allowed Mr. A to be reborn in a higher state of existence? When viewed from a human, objective point of view, this is mere killing. But if we consider the Vajrayana way of thinking, this is a fine *poa*.

"And if a wise person—wisdom is the important thing here—if a wise person were to see this phenomenon, this murdered person, this murderer, he would understand that both parties benefitted. However, if a person without wisdom, an ordinary unenlightened person, were to see this situation, they would think 'that person is a murderer.' . . . If we elevate a person, here now, from the human world to the heavenly realm, and if there is a great savior for them there, and they are linked by fate, and the person that ascended to heaven enters the eternal life of Maha Nirvana, since we have sent someone there, would that not amount to a vast accumulation of Buddhist merit? And so, please think of Vajrayana or Tantrayana as able to accrue great merit. However, this is the final training you will undertake. For now, you must practice Hinayana before you are able to understand the truth of the next stage, Mahayana."

Asahara explained that according to Vajrayana teachings, if an enlightened person kills a person who is bound for hell due to the accumulation of evil deeds and consequently sends that person to heaven, it is a fine *poa* and a great deed of Buddhist merit. He called acts of murder *poa* and used Vajrayana teachings as a way of justifying it.

THE DEPARTURE OF THE HEAVEN'S GATE GROUP

MARCH 26, 1997

On March 26, 1997, thirty-nine members of the Heaven's Gate group were discovered dead in a San Diego house they had rented. They had taken the sedative phenobarbital mixed with either applesauce or pudding and then gone to sleep with plastic bags over their heads. The bodies were found draped in purple shrouds. They wore identical uniforms: black shirts, black sweatpants, and Nike shoes. In each corpse's pocket were quarters and a five-dollar bill. (This last detail appears to have been an inside joke, for members of the group were instructed to always carry money for pay phones and cab rides when traveling.)

Most people who know this story remember Heaven's Gate as a loony cult whose members killed themselves while believing that they would board a UFO traveling behind the Hale-Bopp comet as it passed the Earth. Few know much about the group's nearly thirty-year history. Scholars still debate exactly why the members of Heaven's Gate died by suicide. Unlike Jim Jones, Heaven's Gate did not fear angry relatives or the media exposing its scandals. Nor was Heaven's Gate in any sort of conflict with law enforcement like the Branch Davidians. On the contrary, in 1997 most people had never heard of this group, and no outside force was pressuring them to do anything. Of the group's two founders, Bonnie Lu Nettles (1927–1985) had died and Marshall Herff Applewhite (1931–1997) was entering old age. It is possible that the members understood that their community was not sustainable and wanted to end their story on their own terms. However, Heaven's Gate scholar Ben Zeller points out that, to them, this was not a suicide at all: They were exiting their human bodies and "graduating" to "The Level Above Human." At any rate, the documents below offer some context to this strange case.

Applewhite was born in Spur, Texas, the son of a Presbyterian preacher. He graduated from Austin College in 1952. After exploring seminary and a stint in the military, he received a master's degree in music and voice from the University of Colorado. He directed choirs at several churches, sang in the Houston Grand Opera, and joined the music faculty at the University of St. Thomas in Houston in 1966. He married Anne Pearce and had two children with her, but the couple divorced in 1968. In 1970 the university granted him a leave of absence because of "health problems of an emotional nature."[1] He spent a year of study in New York and then returned to Houston, but he never resumed his teaching position. Applewhite was a semi-closeted bisexual man in 1970s Texas. He found his relationships unsatisfying until he formed a platonic relationship with Nettles.

Nettles was a registered nurse, a mother of four children, and in a failing marriage. Though raised a Baptist, she was interested in astrology and other occult subjects. She had been part of the Houston Theosophical Society and ran a séance group where people would "channel" spirits from higher realms of existence. She divorced her husband in 1972—around the same time that Applewhite was also going through a period of change.

The two met in 1972 in Houston at the Bellaire General Hospital, where Nettles worked. After the 1997 suicides, Newsweek reported that Applewhite was a patient in the hospital, that he was hearing voices and sought to be "cured" of his homosexual desires. Although this is possible, no previous source ever claimed it, and Newsweek does not state the source for this information.[2] Earlier newspaper articles about Applewhite state that he met Nettles at the hospital while visiting a friend. However they met, they formed an instant bond and soon came to identify themselves with the two witnesses described in Revelation 11:1–14. They would refer to themselves variously as "Bo and Peep," "Ti and Do," "Guinea and Pig," or just "The Two."

Initially they announced that they were creating a "Christian Arts Center" to study mysticism. Their group was briefly called "Anonymous Sexaholics Celibate Church" and then "Human Individual Metamorphosis." Their belief system combined elements of "UFO religion" with biblical prophecy. They believed that the Bible described contact with alien beings who live on "The Level Above Human," or TELAH. TELAH is synonymous with "the kingdom of heaven" promised in the New Testament. The purpose of life on Earth is to transcend our base human "mammalian" drives—especially sexual desires—in preparation for joining TELAH. "Graduation" would result in a new body, free from human desires and departing Earth in a UFO. As their group continued to change names, it was often referred to as just "The Class."

The Two began traveling the country, holding meetings and spreading their message. By 1975, they had attracted several dozen followers. On October 7, 1975, they held a meeting in Waldport, Oregon, that made national news. By some accounts, more than 250 people attended the meeting. Of these, between 20 and 33 people decided to renounce their lives and material possessions and become followers of the Two.[3] (This event inspired a 1982 made-for-TV movie called The Mysterious Two.) At the time, members were organized into "cells" scattered across the country, and the group had almost no organization. In 1976 the Two called the members together and imposed a rigid social system with matching uniforms and strict codes of conduct to prepare the class for TELAH.

The group was fascinated by science fiction, especially the television show Star Trek, and their uniforms and protocols emulated the space-age naval traditions of the show. They sometimes referred to themselves, as well as Jesus, as

"captains" and their followers as "crew." In the texts below, the phrases "Enterprise," "away team," and "prime
directive" are borrowed from the show. In fact, the brother
of Nichelle Nichols, who played Lieutenant Uhura in the
original series, was a member of the group and one of those
found dead in 1997. As Nichols stated, "My brother was a
highly intelligent and beautifully gentle man. He made his
choices and we respect those choices."[4]

In the 1980s Nettles's health began to deteriorate. She
was diagnosed with cancer, and in 1983 one of her eyes had
to be surgically removed. She died of liver cancer in 1985.
Her death presented the group with a leadership problem,
but it was also a problem for their belief system, which had
taught that their bodies would be physically transformed
and that they would enter a spaceship. Previously, when
journalists asked the Two's followers whether you had to
die to get into the Two's version of heaven, the response
was "Absolutely not."[5] With Nettles dead, this was no longer clear.

The group's beliefs began to shift. There was increased
discussion of evil aliens called "Luciferians" who were trying to suppress the truth about TELAH. The Luciferians
were said to have made secret treaties with the government
so they could experiment with genetic hybridization programs. Applewhite also announced that the world had
neared the end of its usefulness as far as producing new
graduates to TELAH and that it was about to be "spaded
under." There was little time left to join the class before the
end of the world. In 1991 the group changed its name to
"Total Overcomers Anonymous" and reemerged from obscurity. In 1993 it took out a one-third-page advertisement
in USA Today announcing its "Final Offer." The ad was
also printed in alternative newspapers around the United
States as well as in the United Kingdom, Australia, and
New Zealand. It received about twenty respondents. Around
this time, the group changed its name a final time, to Heav-
en's Gate.

The increased sense of urgency put even more pressure

on the class members to control their "mammalian" urges. Between 1994 and 1995, some members received medical castration, including Applewhite. The group began to discuss the possibility of "leaving their vehicles" (i.e., their bodies). Several members departed when this topic was considered, and no one attempted to stop them.

In 1995 astronomers Alan Hale and Thomas Bopp discovered a comet headed toward Earth. Excitement began to build for the Hale-Bopp comet, which was projected to pass Earth in 1997. On November 14, 1996, an amateur astronomer named Chuck Shramek called the late-night paranormal talk show Coast to Coast AM and announced that he had photographed a "companion" following Hale-Bopp. The following night, political scientist and paranormal writer Courtney Brown called the show. Brown ran something called the Farsight Institute, which claimed to train individuals to use a psychic power called "remote viewing." He said that his remote viewers had determined that the companion following Hale-Bopp was "larger than Earth, hollow, and under intelligent control."[6] Soon the internet was abuzz with rumors of an alien spaceship and doctored photos claiming to show the "companion." The members of Heaven's Gate were uncertain whether the rumors of a spaceship were true, but they did take the arrival of the comet as a sign. When Nettles and Applewhite began their group in 1973, religious groups were ascribing significance to a different comet—Comet Kohoutec. In the story that Heaven's Gate was telling about itself, the two comets formed cosmic bookends to their mission on Earth.

On Friday, March 21, 1997, the group went to a restaurant for a final meal of salad, pot pies, and cheesecake. On Saturday, when Hale-Bopp was expected to be closest to Earth, they began a carefully orchestrated suicide that unfolded using three "teams." The first team of fifteen were poisoned, and the rest of the group covered their bodies in purple shrouds. On Sunday another fifteen were poisoned, followed by seven more on Monday. The final two people *to take poison were found without shrouds covering their bodies.*

The first document presented here is the "Final Offer" published in newspapers around the world. Note that Heaven's Gate describes so-called normal society as a "cult" under Luciferian control. There is also a reference to "cults" that "have weapons or break laws in general." This is likely a reference to the Branch Davidians, whose tragic conflict with the FBI ended just over a month before "Final Offer" went to press.

"Final Offer" also gives some context to the group's suicide. It states, "A soul cannot end its own existence" because it will simply be reincarnated. Conversely, TELAH does have the power to "terminate the soul," and "this termination of the soul is the only proper application of the term DEATH." From this perspective, choosing to remove your soul from its body is not really suicide. On the other hand, since TELAH will soon destroy the Earth, choosing not to follow Heaven's Gate means the annihilation of one's soul—death. With this in mind, the Heaven's Gate members were the only people who chose to preserve their souls, while it is everyone else on Earth who chose death.

The second document is a press release that was distributed on March 22, the day the first suicides occurred. Packages containing messages and VHS tapes with "exit interviews" from Heaven's Gate members were mailed to the media as well as to Heaven's Gate affiliates and former members. Disturbingly, the press release states that there is still time to join them in TELAH but that this requires "the ultimate sacrifice and demonstration of faith—that is, the shedding of your human body." This may have been an attempt to reach out to former members of the group, of which there were hundreds.

Some people took Heaven's Gate up on this final offer. Robert Nichols of Marysville, California, had no known connection to Heaven's Gate, but he took his own life on March 27. A suicide note stated, "I'm going on the spaceship *with Hale-Bopp to be with those who have gone before me."[7] He was found with a plastic bag over his head and a purple scarf draped over his torso, emulating the deaths in San Diego.*

On May 6, police found two men who had drifted in and out of Heaven's Gate in a San Diego hotel room. They were wearing black Nikes and covered in purple shrouds. Wayne Cooke was dead with a plastic bag over his head. Charles Humphrey's bag was not secured over his head, and Humphrey was taken to a hospital. Cooke and Humphrey had sent a tape to CNN in which Cooke stated, "I'm not dying, I'm not going to be dead, I'm simply leaving this vehicle."[8] Another former member, James Pirkey Jr. of Atlanta, Georgia, died by self-inflicted gunshot on May 13, 1997.[9]

On February 17, 1998, Humphrey's body was found in a tent near the border of Arizona and California. A plastic bag was sealed around his head with pipes connecting it to his car's exhaust. He wore black clothing and a patch that said "Heaven's Gate Away Team." In the pocket were four quarters and a five-dollar bill. Next to his body was a purple shroud and a note that read "Do not revive."[10]

"USA TODAY" Ad/Statement
"UFO CULT" RESURFACES WITH FINAL OFFER

The following statements could sound very presumptuous. However, these facts do come into focus or "prove" themselves if they are seriously explored a step at a time. They could also sound very "doomsdayish." Though, in truth, they will be the most joyous "sound of music" to the ears and eyes of those who have been waiting for them.

■ The Earth's present "civilization" is about to be recycled—"spaded under." Its inhabitants are refusing to evolve. The "weeds" have taken over the garden and disturbed its usefulness beyond repair.

■ The human kingdom was created as a *stepping stone* between the animal kingdom and the *true* Kingdom of God (the Evolutionary Kingdom Level Above Human).

■ It is the soul that progresses from one kingdom level to another—each kingdom level has its own unique physical containers (bodies) for the souls that reside in that kingdom level.

■ As the human goes out to find servants within the animal kingdom, from beasts of burden to seeing-eye dogs—if that animal grows to find pleasure only in serving its master, no longer identifies as an animal, but sees itself as a family member in that human family, and its behavior is pleasing to that human—the two become *bound* together. The human family then provides the body (a human infant) for that soul to enter, allowing it to move up into the human evolutionary kingdom. (This is not to suggest that all human infants are containers for souls moving up from the animal kingdom, for most human infants are containers for human kingdom returnees still bound to that family unit.)

■ Likewise, when a member of the *true* Kingdom of God receives instruction to incarnate among humans in order to seek out the souls that might want to "separate from the pack" and are desirous of becoming only servants in the Evolutionary Level Above Human, He then offers them the knowledge and behavior that can open that door to them. If that human changes to the degree that he no longer desires any human behavior and he pleases that member of the Kingdom Level Above Human, a *bond* is formed and a body belonging to that new Kingdom is provided for that soul to move up into.

■ Both Kingdom Levels are physical and biological. However, the human kingdom is made up of mammalian—"seed-bearing"—plants or containers, while the Kingdom of God is made up of non-mammalian, non-seed-bearing "containers" for souls, and their young or "children" are those who have risen above—overcome—all human-mammalian character-istics and behavior through the tutorship (midwifing) of a member of the Kingdom of God who has been through that transition and bonded to His Father at a previous time.

■ Just as an animal sees his human tutor as the *one and only* "master," likewise a human, as he becomes aware of a Member of the Kingdom Level Above Human, sees Him as the *one and only* "God." However, the individual that that human related to as God sees Himself as a "child" in that higher, many-membered Kingdom and knows that only through His "Father" (an Older Member in that Kingdom) can He become a better member in that Kingdom.

■ A "student" or prospective "child" of a member of the *true* Kingdom of God can, with the help of an Older Member, overcome or rise out of *all* human mammalian behavior—sexuality and gender consciousness—and all other addic-tions and ties of the human kingdom. He must complete this change to the point of abhorring human behavior before his soul can become a "match" with a biological body of the *true* Kingdom of God—for that new body is genderless and incapable of functioning at a human level.

■ The *true* Kingdom of God, the "Headquarters" of all that is, is a many-membered Kingdom which physically exists in the *highest*, most *distant* Heaven—a *non-temporal* place (*outside of time*, and with *eternal* life). It is the only place from which souls, life, and all ***creating*** originates. Being non-temporal, it *was*, *is*, and *forever will be*—a concept that we, as temporal creatures, are not designed to compre-hend. That Kingdom designed the "temporal" world out-side its "borders" and designed its temporal creatures to have a progression of bodies or "vehicles" (through king-dom levels, such as animal and human) for souls to evolve through. If the soul survives and moves forward through all its tests along the way—it can, with the help of a member of the *true* Kingdom of God, lose its temporal characteristics and become a part of their non-perishable, non-corruptible world. However, *all other souls* who reach a certain degree of corruption (having of their own free will chosen to become totally separate from their Creator) will engage a "self-destruct" mechanism at the Age's end, manifested when opposing camps, be they human or "Luciferian," come together and destroy each other—thus assisting in the plowing under of the "garden" *for* the Creator.

■ The reason the term "TRUE" Kingdom of God is used repeatedly is because there are *many* space alien races that through the centuries of this civilization (and in civilizations prior) have represented themselves to humans as "Gods." We refer to them collectively as "Luciferians," for their ancestors fell away from the keeping of the *true* Kingdom of God many thousands of years ago. They are not genderless—they still need to reproduce. They are nothing more than technically advanced humans who have retained some of what they learned while in the early training of members of the *true* Kingdom of God, e.g., limited space-time travel, telepathic communication, advanced travel hardware (spacecrafts, etc.), increased longevity, advanced genetic engineering, and such things as suspended holograms (as used in some religious "miracles").

■ These "Luciferian" space races are the humans' GREATEST ENEMY. They hold humans in unknown slavery only to fulfill their own needs. They cannot "create," though they develop races and biological containers through genetic manipulation and hybridization. They even try to "make deals" with human governments to permit them (the Luciferians) to engage in biological experimentation (through abductions) in exchange for technically advanced modes of travel—though they seldom follow through, for they don't want the humans of this civilization to grow to be another element of competition. They war among themselves over the spoils of this planet and use religion and increased sexual

behavior to keep humans "drugged" and ignorant (in darkness) while thinking they are in God's keeping. These Luciferians see to it, through the "social norm" (the largest
Luciferian "cult" there is) that man continues to **not** avail
himself of the possibility of advancing *beyond* human.
Many things have become the accepted "norm," but that
doesn't make them right!

■ Just as the biological body is the "container" for the soul,
the soul is the "container" for *Mind* (Spirit). *Mind* trans-
lates into the brain as *information* (knowledge). Information is available to humans from only two sources—the
mind of the Luciferians—or the *Mind* of the Kingdom of
God. The *mind* of the Luciferians yields misinformation
(promoting the behavior and concepts of this world). The
Mind from the *true* Kingdom of God yields *true* information (though the Luciferians and their servants would reverse this interpretation). As we *change*, in the progression
of overcoming humanness—the percentages change—of
which *mind* occupies our soul—Truth *increases* as misinformation *decreases*. If we revert back to humanness, the
process reverses—the Truth is aborted as the soul becomes
more filled with mammalian *mind*. That Truth can even be
taken from us if we abuse it. When our "eye becomes single" or our soul is filled only with *Mind* or Spirit from the
true Kingdom of God, it becomes pure or *Holy Mind*
(Spirit).

■ The *true* Kingdom of God's design permits the presence
of a "Luciferian" element, during a human civilization, as a
catalyst for growth. Without it, we would have no choices—
our **free will** could not be exercised. Our *right* choices find
us in alignment to recognize the Truth when it is offered.

■ Two thousand years ago, the *true* Kingdom of God appointed an Older Member to send His "Son," along with
some of their beginning students, to incarnate on this garden. While on Earth as an "away team" with their "Cap-

tain," they were to work on their overcoming of humanness and tell the civilization they were visiting how the *true* Kingdom of God can be entered. The humans under the control of the Luciferians killed the "Captain" and his crew, because of the "blasphemous" position they held, and quickly turned the teachings of the "Captain"—the Older Member's "Son"— into watered down *Country Club* religion—obscuring the remnants of the Truth.

■ That same "away team" incarnated again in the 1970's in the mature (adult) bodies that had been picked and prepped for this current mission. This time the "Admiral" (the Older Member, or Father, incarnate in a female vehicle) came with the Son—"Captain"—and his crew. As the two Older Members put out a "statement" and held public meetings over about a 9-month period in 1975–76 to bring their crew together, the media tagged them the "UFO cult" because of their expectation of leaving aboard a spacecraft (UFO) at the completion of their "overcoming." The two Older Members then went into seclusion with their crew (students), "lifting them out" of the world for almost 17 years (not accepting any new students), making Earth's surface their classroom. This isolation was absolutely necessary. The *degree* of their *overcoming* of sexuality, addictions, and ties to the human environment had to be taken to the point of *matching* the behavior and consciousness of the Evolutionary Kingdom Above Human. Only then would their *new* "Next Level" bodies be *functional*. They resurfaced briefly for about a 3½-month period in 1992, allowing some of their "dropouts" to rejoin them.

■ *This changeover* (sufficient "overcoming" to inherit Next Level bodies) *has been completed*, and before they return, they are instructed to share this statement with you.

■ The Luciferians are about to be "recycled" (annihilated) at the same time as this human civilization is "spaded." They know that "rumor has it" that their days are numbered.

They refuse to believe it and are desperate to recruit souls from the human kingdom into their "Heavenly Kingdom." There are many "counterfeit" heavens, and each "heaven" is at this time collecting "names in their book," forcing a stand of allegiance, polarizing each individual's commitment to his chosen "God."

■ When members of the Level Above Human are physically present, the opposing forces work the hardest against them in order to support their own position. They do almost anything to keep humans from following the path toward the *true* Kingdom of God. They "turn up the heat" at this time in the area of mammalian behavior, primarily sexuality. This has become such an overwhelming presence in the Earth's atmosphere that even some of the crew that came with us were lost to its temptation. Don't forget that when the Luciferians were expelled, in order to support their own desires, they had to condemn the *true* Kingdom of God and see it simply as another path—inhumane and radically uncompromising.

■ The religious "cults" who have **separated from the world** have "picked up on" one major aspect of what is "in the air" at this time when the information of how to move from one kingdom level to another is available. What they may have failed to recognize is that experienced "clinicians" are necessary to take souls through that "weaning"—that difficult "withdrawal" from human addictions and binding "misinformation" concepts. If it weren't *necessary* to have clinicians present who have *previously been taken through* that transition, we wouldn't need to be here. Some religious "cults" might have children, participate in physical or mental abuse, hold members against their will, have weapons, or break laws in general—while we have long been aware that that type of behavior is inappropriate, especially for a transitional "classroom."

■ When the present "away team" leaves (which will be very soon), the Truth will go with them. You cannot *preserve* the Truth in your religions. It is with you only as long as a *Truth bearer* is with you. Only those from the *Land of Truth* can bear it. It can only be your future if you "reach out and grab it" while it is offered. The Truth can be retained only as one is physically connected with the Next Level, through an Older Member, and that relationship requires that non-mammalian thinking and behavior be sustained.

■ Humans were, from the beginning, given a "prime directive" NOT TO KILL OTHER HUMANS. "In defense" or for "rightness" are no exceptions. Righteousness is what most frequently causes conflict. "I'm right, you're wrong." "You're causing me trouble, I'll wipe you out" (in the best interest of all, of course). The world's systems continue to make laws permitting the breakage of higher laws—God's laws. Weapons designed for killing humans are inexcusable. There are numerous methods of controlling a violent person without the necessity of murder. The *irony* is, each killer sends its victims to *exactly* where they want to go (to their chosen heaven). Humans *fight* for their *desires*—what they choose to *not overcome*—what they cling to. Our *desires* and *attachments* (or lack of them) *determine* which heaven we're going to.

■ A soul cannot end its own existence. Though it may incarnate many times and the body or vehicle it is wearing may be terminated, only the *true* Kingdom of God—the Evolutionary Level Above Human can terminate the soul. This termination of the soul is the only proper application of the term *DEATH*.

■ When a soul "awakens" in a particular "season" or incarnation (usually sometime between college age and midlife), it is *picking up* where it *left off* at the end of its previous incarnation. What an individual participates in prior to that "awakening" is of no real significance. If a soul had previously

overcome such human characteristics as family ties and relationships, at his "awakening" he is seen by those around
him as suddenly becoming unstable, for he is compelled to
once again separate from those imposing ties and seek to
connect with what he had previously sought or connected
with. What he primarily *learns* is what *is not* for him as he
seeks for the Highest *Truth* or *Reality*.

■ The media seems *devoted* to "saving" the public from
radical ideologies or "cults," particularly of seeming "religious" types. Also a news "scoop" requires haste. These
two elements together predetermine that they search for any
and all negative quotes that will discredit the groups' leaders and the groups' behavior. The fact still remains that negative reporting far outsells positive reporting—and after all,
positive reporting of radical material can end or ruin a
reporter's career. Well, it won't be hard to discredit this
group from its leaders down, for prior to and during their
"awakening" and subsequent coming together, they all
made many mistakes and learned from them. Plus—you
don't give up the ways of the world without the condemnation of those who still advocate what you have overcome.

■ When we came before (2000 years ago) the world
"cleansed" or "saved" *their* world from our "blasphemy"
and merely got us our boarding passes back to the *true*
Kingdom of God on the *true* "Enterprise" (spaceship or
"cloud of light"). If you seek to cleanse the world of our
"blasphemy" this time, you would simply be the instrument
of *our* "days being shortened" while destroying *your* "last
chance" in this civilization to *advance*.

■ Now at the close of an Age—every significant soul of this
civilization has returned (and is in or attached to a physical
body) to reap their reward. Most who *think* they are *for* the
Kingdom of God are in fact working for the opposing
side—the counterfeit "Gods"—and will want to condemn
us. Your actions, even your thoughts of condemnation to-

ward us, out of allegiance to your "God," will cause *our* part of the Heavens to look upon *your* "god" with the same rejection.

■ Many say they live only for the "Harvest Time"—the "Last Days"—the "Second Coming." Those are all finally here!—Will you accept *us as them*? You cannot *bypass* us even in your prayers—you cannot *insult* your Creator by refusing to go through the ones He has sent to you. There are souls here now for the express purpose of connecting— and eventually bonding—with the Next Level through us. Those souls will be protected—out of harm's way—and "saved" from the approaching sorting out, recycling, and "spading under" of the Luciferians and their human servants. If you can get your name in our "book," on our spacecraft's computer (and only there), making your actions reflect that desire—then you will go with us.

SUMMARY: Our surfacing is in reality a test of the public's "civility." Can a society that is still dealing with bigotry and prejudices against races, religions, and sexual preference extend the *right of existence* to some who see *humanity* as a *stepping stone* toward the Kingdom of God, and desire to take that step and briefly offer it to others? Or is Earth's present civilization still as primitive as it was 2000 years ago? We'll see!

CAUTION: If the above information is *consumed* or *assimilated,* you may experience such side effects as loss of marriage, family, friends, career, respectability, and credibility. Continued use could even result in the loss of your membership in the human kingdom.

To be issued to the News Media 3/22/97

By the time you read this, we suspect that the *human bodies we were wearing have been found* and that a flurry of fragmented reports have begun to hit the wire services. For those who want to know the facts, the following statement has been issued.

HEAVEN'S GATE "Away Team" Returns to Level Above Human in Distant Space

RANCHO SANTO FE, CA—By the time you receive this, we'll be gone—several dozen of us. We came from the Level Above Human in distant space and we have now exited the bodies that we were wearing for our earthly task, to return to the world from whence we came—task completed. The distant space we refer to is what your religious literature would call the Kingdom of Heaven or the Kingdom of God.

We came for the purpose of offering a doorway to the Kingdom of God at the end of this civilization, the end of this millenium [*sic*]. We came from that Level, that time, that space, and entered this one. And in so doing, we had to enter human bodies—which we did, for the most part, in the mid-seventies. Now it was time for us to leave those bodies (vehicles)—bodies that we borrowed for the time we were here (by previous arrangement) for this specific task. The task was not only to bring in information about that Evolutionary Kingdom Level Above Human, but to give us the experience of working against the forces of what the human evolutionary level, at this time, has become. And while it was a good learning experience for us, it also gave all who ever received knowledge from that Kingdom an opportunity to recognize us and this information, and to even move out of the human level and into the Next Level or the Next Evolutionary Level, the "Kingdom of Heaven," the Kingdom of God.

The Kingdom of God, the Level Above Human, is a physical world, where they inhabit physical bodies. However, those bodies are merely containers, suits of clothes—the *true identity* (of the individual) is the soul or mind/spirit residing in that "vehicle." The body is merely a tool for that individual's use—when it wears out, he is issued a new one.

No one can enter the Kingdom of Heaven by trying to live a good life in this world, and then, thinking that when this world's life takes your body, you get to "go to heaven." The *only* time that Next Kingdom can be entered is when there is a Member or Members of that Kingdom who have come into the human kingdom, incarnated as we have, offering clarification of that information. To get into a discarnate condition just by disconnecting from your body doesn't mean that you are going to go anywhere, whether that loss of body is "premature" or not. When we step out of our "vehicle," we have to know where and who our "tour guide" (our Shepherd) is—for what's next. We have to know we can connect with a Shepherd whom we trust, and that we have decided, "If that Shepherd will have me, I want to continue to be a sheep—and I will do everything I can to please that Shepherd."

Periodically, that Next Level sends in a Representative—a Shepherd—and offers a graduation class, offers life, out of this evolutionary level into that Next Evolutionary Level, and we are at the end of one of those times. TI and DO were the names used by the Representatives of that Next Level, the Kingdom of God, sent to the "surface" of this planet to serve as our Teachers/"Midwives" at this time.

During a brief window of time, some may wish to follow us. If they do, it will not be easy. The requirement is to not only believe who the Representatives are, but, to do as they and we did. You must leave *everything* of your humanness behind. This includes the ultimate sacrifice and demonstration of faith—that is, the shedding of your human body. If you should choose to do this, logistically it is preferred that you make this exit somewhere in the area of the West or Southwest of the United States—but if this is not possible—it is not required. You must call on the name of TI and DO to assist you. In so doing, you will engage a communication of sorts, alerting a spacecraft to your location where you will be picked up after shedding your vehicle, and taken to another world—by members of the Kingdom of Heaven.

Only a Member of the Next Level can give you Life—can take you out of "Death"—but it requires that you disconnect, separate, from the last element holding you to the human kingdom.

We know what we're saying—we know it requires a "leap of faith." But it's deliberate—designed for those who would rather take that leap than stay in this world.

We suggest that anyone serious about considering this go into their most quiet place and ask, scream, with all of their being, directing their asking to the Highest Source they can imagine (beyond Earth's atmosphere), to give them guidance. Only those "chosen" by that Next Kingdom will *know* that this is right for them, and will be given the courage required to act.

Some Relevant Scriptures

- Therefore doth my Father love me, because I lay down my life, that I might take it again. No man taketh it from me, but I lay it down of myself. I have power to lay it down, and I have power to take it again. This commandment have I received of my Father. JOHN 10:15–18
- He that believeth on me, the works that I do shall he do also. JOHN 14:12
- And except that the Lord shorten those days, none shall be saved: but for the elect's sake, whom He has chosen, He hath shortened the days. MARK 13:20
- He who loves his life will lose it, and he who hates his life in this world will keep it for eternal life. JOHN 12:25
- Blessed are the dead who die in the Lord. REVELATION 14:13

Notes

THE BACCHANALIAN AFFAIR

1. Livy, *The History of Rome*, vol. 5, trans. William Masfen Roberts (E. P. Dutton, 1912), 318.
2. Sarolta A. Takács, "Politics and Religion in the Bacchanalian Affair of 186 B.C.E.," *Harvard Studies in Classical Philology* 100 (2000): 301–10.
3. Livy, *History of Rome*, 316–26.
4. An aedile was an elected official in charge of maintaining public buildings and regulating public festivals. The Republic had two classes: the patricians (ruling class) and the plebeians (commoners). The office of curule aedile was open to either class, but the office of plebeian aedile was open only to plebeians.
5. Roman citizens who are not currently serving in the military.

LEGENDS OF THE WICKER MAN

1. *Caesar's Commentaries on the Gallic War*, trans. Edward Brooks Jr. (Penn Publishing, 1895).
2. *The Geography of Strabo*, trans. Horace Leonard Jones (G. P. Putnam's Sons, 1923).

THE ORGIES OF THE CHRISTIANS

1. M. Minucius Felix, *Octavius*, trans. David Dalrymple (G. Bell, 1854).
2. Protagoros was a sophist philosopher born around 480 BCE. His book on the gods begins with "Respecting the gods, I am

unable to know whether they exist or do not exist." He was expelled, and his book was burned.

3. M. Cornelius Fronto, from Numidian Cirta, was a teacher to Emperor Marcus Aurelius. He gave an oration against Christians that has been lost to history.

4. Tertullian, *The Apology of Tertullian for the Christians*, trans. T. Herbert Bindley (Parker, 1890).

THE *NARRATIONS* OF PSEUDO-NILUS

1. Excerpted from Daniel F. Caner, *History and Hagiography from the Late Antique Sinai* (Liverpool University Press, 2009).

2. David Frankfurter, *Evil Incarnate: Rumors of Demonic Evil and Satanic Abuse in History* (Princeton University Press, 2006), 122.

3. Dawn Perlmutter, "The Sacrificial Aesthetic: Blood Rituals from Art to Murder," *Anthropoetics: The Journal of Generative Anthropology* 2, no. 2 (1999/2000), https://anthropoetics.ucla.edu /apo502/blood.

THE ORLÉANS HERESY

1. Paul of St. Père-de-Chartres, *The Synod of Orléans,* 1022, trans. Jacob Doss.

2. Michael Frassetto, "The Heresy at Orleans in 1022 in the Writings of Contemporary Churchmen," *Nottingham Medieval Studies* 49 (2005): 11.

3. Frassetto, "Heresy at Orleans," 5.

4. Charybdis is a sea monster from Greek mythology. Three times a day, the monster would suck in seawater, creating whirlpools that dragged down ships.

WILLIAM DORRELL,
THE INVINCIBLE VEGETARIAN MESSIAH

1. Lucy Cutler Kellog, *History of the Town of Bernardston, Franklin County, Massachusetts 1736–1900* (E. A. Hall, 1902).

2. William Adams, *Fewell: A Series of Essays of Opinion for Churchmen* (Joseph Robinson, 1846), 197–98.

3. Robert W. Balch, "Looking Behind the Scenes in a Religious Cult: Implications for the Study of Conversion," *Sociological Analysis* 41, no. 2 (1980): 137–43, esp. 141–42.

4. The Pocumtuck Valley Memorial Association in Deerfield, Massachusetts, was founded in 1880. Today it runs one of New England's oldest museums.

THE AWFUL DISCLOSURES OF MARIA MONK

1. *Awful Disclosures of Maria Monk: As Exhibited in a Narrative of Her Sufferings During Residence of Five Years as a Novice and Two Years as a Black Nun in the Hotel Dieu Nunnery, at Montreal, Ont.*, rev. ed. (D. M. Bennett, 1878).

2. Jeanne Hamilton, "The Nunnery as Menace: The Burning of the Charlestown Convent, 1834," *Catholic Historian* (1996), www.ewtn.com/catholicism/library/nunnery-as-menace-the-burning-of-the-charlestown-convent-1834-10894.

3. Ray Allen Billington, "Maria Monk and Her Influence," *Catholic Historical Review* 22, no. 3 (1936): 283–96.

4. Dennis Castillo, "The Enduring Legacy of Maria Monk," *American Catholic Studies* 112, no. 1 (2001): 49–59.

5. Karen Hanrahan, "'They Just Ignored My Tears, They Ignored My Unhappiness': Former Irish Nuns Reveal Accounts of Brainwashing and Abuse," *The Conversation*, May 26, 2023, https://theconversation.com/they-just-ignored-my-tears-they-ignored-my-unhappiness-former-irish-nuns-reveal-accounts-of-brainwashing-and-abuse-197569.

6. Philip Jenkins, *The New Anti-Catholicism: The Last Acceptable Prejudice* (Oxford University Press, 2003).

7. The French verb *drageur* means "drag" but can also convey making a sexual advance to someone.

"THE PATHOLOGY AND TREATMENT OF MEDIOMANIA"

1. Frederic R. Marvin, *Philosophy of Spiritualism and the Pathology and Treatment of Mediomania: Two Lectures* (Asa K. Butts, 1874).

A VAMPIRE CULT IN KANSAS CITY

1. "A Band of Fanatics: Horrible Practices of a New Religious Sect in Missouri," *Daily Boomerang* (Laramie, WY), January 27, 1890.
2. Mark Silk, "Journalists with Attitude: A Response to Richardson and van Driel," *Review of Religious Research* 39, no. 2 (1997): 137–43, esp. 141.

CYRUS R. TEED, THE ELECTRO-ALCHEMICAL MESSIAH

1. J. Philip Arnold, "Research Note: Did David Koresh Plagiarize Cyrus R. Teed," *Nova Religio* 26, no. 3 (2022): 111–12.
2. Lynn Millner, *The Allure of Immortality: An American Cult, a Florida Swamp, and a Renegade Prophet* (University of Florida Press, 2015).
3. Cyrus R. Teed, *The Illumination of Koresh* (Guiding Star, 1899).
4. "The Site of the New Jerusalem," *The Times*, April 12, 1896, Sunday Special, p. 32.
5. It is unclear what movement this is referencing. In 1890s Georgia there was a series of Black men, as well as some Black women, claiming to be the second coming of Jesus and prophesying the imminent end of the world. One paper describes a man named "Bell" who declared that the world would end on August 16, 1889. On this date, all white people would become Black, and all Black people would become white. Bell was taken to a mental asylum. He was replaced by another Black man named Edward James, who said that he was the messiah and that the world would end on August 16. James was arrested and also sent to a mental asylum. Three subsequent Black prophets are described. See "Plenty of False Christs," *Advent Review and Sabbath Herald*, February 3, 1891, p. 71. Emerging religious movements in the Black community were less likely to have access to publishing and other resources, and their leaders were more likely to be arrested and confined to prisons or asylums. Because of this, historians know far less about Black religious movements during this period than about their white counterparts.
6. See the entry on George J. Schweinfurth in this volume (p. 107).
7. John Cowan was a physician and phrenologist who wrote on sexual health and women's health. In 1869 he published a book

for married couples called *The Science of a New Life*, which was endorsed by suffragist Elizabeth Cady Stanton.

8. Edward Bellamy (1850–1898) was a journalist and author. His novel *Looking Backward* (1888) describes a future where the United States has become a socialist utopia where private property has been abolished.

GEORGE J. SCHWEINFURTH, THE FAILED MESSIAH OF WINNEBAGO COUNTY

1. Workers of the Writers' Program of the Work Projects Administration in the State of Illinois, comp., *Rockford* (Graphic Arts, 1941), 77.
2. "A Fanatic's Power," *Pittsburgh Dispatch*, May 13, 1889, pp. 1, 6.
3. This article may have been a republication of an article published in *The Herald*.
4. Peddlers of books and literature, especially Bibles.
5. "RANK BLASPHEMY: Theological Drivel Uttered by a Schweinfurthite," *Sterling Gazette* (Sterling, IL), August 22, 1890.
6. "George Jacob Leaves Heaven," *Sterling Gazette* (Sterling, IL), November 25, 1902, p. 2.

INVASION OF THE YOGA CULTS

1. Mabel Potter Daggett, "The Heathen Invasion," *Hampton Columbian Magazine* 27, no. 4 (1911).
2. Hugh B. Urban, *New Age, Neopagan, and New Religious Movements: Alternative Spirituality in Contemporary America* (University of California Press, 2015), 215.
3. J. Gordon Melton, "Perspective: Toward a Definition of 'New Religion,'" *Nova Religio* 8, no. 1 (2004): 73–97.
4. Joseph P. Laycock, "Yoga for the New Woman and the New Man: The Role of Pierre Bernard and Blanche DeVries in the Creation of Modern Postural Yoga," *Journal of Religion and American Culture* 23, no. 1 (2013): 101–36.
5. Quoted in Stephen Prothero, "Hinduphobia and Hinduphilia in U.S. Culture," in *The Stranger's Religion: Fascination and Fear*, ed. Anna Lännström (Notre Dame University Press, 2004), 14.

6. Tameshnie Deane, "The Devadasi System: An Exploitation of Women and Children in the Name of God and Culture," *Journal of International Women's Studies* 24, no. 1 (2022), article 8.

7. Prothero, "Hinduphobia and Hinduphilia in U.S. Culture."

8. Robert Browning (1812–1889) was an English poet and playwright. In 1877, the first group was established to discuss his work, and by 1900 hundreds of such groups existed throughout North America and the British Isles.

9. In the Indian subcontinent a *zenana* was a part of a Muslim household reserved for women. Some Hindu families also constructed *zenanas*.

10. Also called a chador, this is a type of shawl worn by women in the Indian subcontinent.

THE TRIAL OF ALEISTER CROWLEY

1. Milton Bronner, "Astounding Revelations of Wickedness When 'Beast 666' Went to Court," *Lima Sunday News* (Lima, OH), June 24, 1934.

2. Betty May, *Tiger Woman* (Gerald Duckworth, 1929), 178.

3. Quoted in Lawrence Sutin, *Do As Thou Wilt: A Life of Aleister Crowley* (St. Martin's, 2000), 367–68.

4. Nina Hamnett, *The Laughing Torso* (Ray Long and Richard R. Smith, 1932), 173.

5. Quoted in Sutin, *Do As Thou Wilt*, 369.

6. Quoted in Sutin, *Do As Thou Wilt*, 372.

THE BIRTH OF BRAINWASHING

1. Edward Hunter, "'Brain-Washing' Tactics Force Chinese into Ranks of Communist Party," *Miami Sunday News*, September 24, 1950.

2. Edward Hunter, *Brainwashing: From Pavlov to Powers* (Bookmailer, 1960), 309.

3. Allen Welsh Dulles, "Brain Warfare—Russia's Secret Weapon," *U.S. News and World Report*, May 8, 1953, 54–58.

4. The Kuomintang (KMT) is a Chinese political party that ruled mainland China from 1927 to 1949, prior to the party's relocation to Taiwan as a result of the Chinese Civil War.

THE COMING OF THE SAUCER RELIGIONS

1. Quoted in Alex Wigglesworth, "Giant Rock: A Century of Stories in the Mojave Desert," *Los Angeles Times*, June 23, 2024, www.latimes.com/environment/story/2024-06-23/giant-rock-a-century-of-stories-in-the-mojave-desert.
2. Dana Howard, "Convention Report," *Flying Saucer News*, April 1955.
3. "Aetherius Speaks," *Flying Saucer News*, August 1955.

THE JONESTOWN "DEATH TAPE"

1. Q042, aka "The Death Tape," transcribed by Fielding M. McGee III of the Jonestown Institute.
2. Michael Bellefountaine, "Christine Miller: A Voice of Independence," *Alternative Considerations of Jonestown & Peoples Temple*, March 12, 2014, jonestown.sdsu.edu/?page_id=32381.
3. Jack Beam was a member of the Peoples Temple. He was a fifty-four-year-old white male born in Louisville, Kentucky. He was involved in the planning and finance committees.
4. Al and Jeannie Mills were aliases used by Elmer and Deanna Mertle after they defected from Peoples Temple. They founded a group called Concerned Relatives, which ultimately persuaded Leo Ryan to visit Jonestown. The Mills and their daughter were murdered in their home in Berkeley, California, in February 1980. The crime was never solved.
5. Debbie Blakey was one of Jones's most trusted aides before she defected in May 1978. She wrote an affidavit stating that Jones had described plans of mass suicide, and this helped motivate Leo Ryan to visit Jonestown. Handwritten notes recovered at Jonestown detail violent fantasies of killing Blakey.
6. Jonestown researcher Michael Bellefountaine listened to the tape and heard Miller say, "It's not that I am afraid to die."
7. Other transcriptions record Miller stating, "I'll handle that."
8. Richard Dwyer worked for the US embassy in Guyana and accompanied Leo Ryan on his inspection of Jonestown. He returned to the airstrip with Ryan and was wounded when gunmen attacked. On the tape, Jones calls to "Take Dwyer," but Dwyer was not present—he was at the airstrip. It seems that Jones meant Don Sly (aka Ujara) but repeatedly misidentified him as Dwyer.
9. A producer for the National Geographic documentary *The Final*

Report: Jonestown Tragedy insisted that he heard the tape as saying, "Now. Shoot 'em now!" However, this seems implausible because only two people were shot.

10. Maria Katsaris was a twenty-five-year-old white female born in Pittsburgh, Pennsylvania. She was one of Jones's mistresses.

INTERNAL DOCUMENTS FROM THE BRANCH DAVIDIAN SIEGE

1. Catherine Wessinger, "Branch Davidians (1981–2006)," *World Religions and Spirituality Project*, October 10, 2016, wrldrels.org/2016/02/25/branch-davidians-2; Michael A. Graham, MD, "Forensic Pathology Evaluation of the 1993 Branch Davidian Deaths and Other Pertinent Issues," Appendix J to Final Report to the Deputy Attorney General Concerning the 1993 Confrontation at the Mt. Carmel Complex, Waco, Texas, November 8, 2000, by John C. Danforth, Special Counsel.

2. Eugene V. Gallagher, "Davidians and Branch Davidians (1929–1981)," *World Religions and Spirituality Project*, August 3, 2013, wrldrels.org/2016/10/08/davidians-and-branch-davidians/.

3. Joseph P. Laycock, "Field Notes: The Branch Davidian Press Conference and Thirtieth Anniversary Memorial, 19 April 2023," *Nova Religio* 27, no. 1 (2023): 99–108.

4. Wessinger, "Branch Davidians (1981–2006)."

5. Wessinger, "Branch Davidians (1981–2006)."

6. Robert Bryce, "Lethal Weapon: FBI's Use of Tear Gas Questioned at Davidian Trial," *Austin Chronicle*, July 7, 2000, www.austinchronicle.com/news/2000-07-07/77866.

7. Dick Reavis, "What Really Happened at Waco?," *Texas Monthly*, July 1995, www.texasmonthly.com/arts-entertainment/what-really-happened-at-waco.

8. Lee Hancock, "Waco: FBI to Acknowledge Use of Pyrotechnic Devices—New Account on Branch Davidian Fire Expected," *Dallas Morning News*, August 25, 1999, www.cesnur.org/testi/waco.htm.

9. Stephan Talty, *Koresh: The True Story of David Koresh and the Tragedy at Waco* (Mariner, 2023), 379.

10. Catherine Wessinger, *How the Millennium Comes Violently: From Jonestown to Heaven's Gate* (Seven Bridges, 1999), 4.

11. Quoted in Stuart A. Wright, "Explaining Militarization at Waco: The Construction and Convergence of the Warfare Nar-

rative," in *Controversial New Religions*, ed. James R. Lewis and Jesper Aagaard Petersen (Oxford University Press, 2004), 90.

12. Wright, "Explaining Militarization at Waco," 89.

13. Adam Nossiter, "Warning of Violence Was Unheeded After Cult Leader's Gun Battle in '87," *New York Times*, March 10, 1993, A14.

14. Wright, "Explaining Militarization at Waco," 87.

15. Davy Aguilera, affidavit sworn before Dennis G. Green, United States Magistrate Judge, Western District of Texas—Waco, February 25, 1992, constitution.org/1-Corruption/waco/affidavt .htm.

16. Dan Gifford, William Gazecki, and Michael McNulty, producers, *Waco: The Rules of Engagement* (Fifth Estate Productions, 1997).

17. Susan E. DeBusk, "Interview of SSA Peter A. Smerick," August 24, 1993, courtesy of the Lee Hancock Collection at Texas State University.

18. Catherine Wessinger, "'Deaths in the Fire at the Branch Davidians' Mount Carmel': Who Bears Responsibility?," *Nova Religio* 13, no. 2 (2009): 31.

19. Catherine Wessinger, "The FBI's 'Cult War' Against the Branch Davidians," in *The FBI and Religion: Faith and National Security Before and After 9/11*, ed. Sylvester A. Johnson and Steven Weitzman (University of California Press, 2017), 233.

20. David Hardy, "Waco: Carlos Ghigliotti's Report," *Of Arms & the Law*, April 26, 2016, armsandthelaw.com/archives/2016/04 /waco_carlos_ghi.php.

21. Catherine Wessinger, "FLIR Video of Tank Driving Inside Building to Gas Branch Davidian Mothers and Children," April 1, 2023, YouTube, www.youtube.com/watch?v=ddXU2FHdkXk.

22. Bryce, "Lethal Weapon."

23. Nine o'clock a.m. Central Standard Time was probably the time for the "Daily," which was held twice a day. See Wessinger, "Branch Davidians (1981–2006)."

24. No telephone was thrown out the front door. When he went outside, Craddock reeled in the telephone line and held it up to show the agents in the Command Post/undercover house that it was severed. See Oral and Videotaped Deposition of Graeme Craddock, October 28, 1999, vol. 1: 192–96, in Isabel G. Andrade, et al. v. Phillip J. Chojnacki, et al., United States District Court for the Western District of Texas, Waco Division, No. W-96-CA-139.

25. This was likely Marjorie Thomas and Misty Ferguson, who were both badly burned and either fell or jumped from second- or third-story windows. Ferguson was a teenager, and her burns were so severe that her fingers had to be amputated.

26. This was Marjorie Thomas, age thirty, from England, who was severely burned in the fire. She was probably unconscious and could not give her identifying information to the agents.

27. There were no "bunkers." On the west side of the building, there was a tunnel that led to a partially buried school bus and an unfinished storm shelter that was created in case of tornadoes.

THE SENTENCING OF SHOKO ASAHARA FOR THE AUM SHINRIKYO ATTACK

1. Excerpt from a sentencing statement, Case Number: Heisei 7-141, February, 27, 2004, Tokyo District Court, Criminal Division 7, trans. Drew K. Richardson.

2. The Japanese term rendered here as a "cult" is *kyoudan*. Although this word technically means "religious organization," in practice it is similar to the word "cult" because it is vague and functions as a catchall term for marginal groups. More established religious groups, including Buddhist temples, Christian churches, and even shrines, are generally not referred to as *kyoudan*. After the 1995 Aum attacks, Japan increasingly began to use the word *karuto* as a Japanese rendering of the English word "cult."

THE DEPARTURE OF THE HEAVEN'S GATE GROUP

1. "Texan UFO 'Tour Leaders' Formerly Promoted Occult," *Lubbock-Avalanche Journal*, October 18, 1975, p. 1.

2. Evan Thomas, "'The Next Level,'" *Newsweek*, April 7, 1997, 28–35. The article implies that the source of this information was Houston radio-show host and gay-rights advocate Ray Hill, who knew Applewhite. However, when Applewhite met Nettles in 1972, Hill was in prison for burglary.

3. Benjamin E. Zeller, *Heaven's Gate: America's UFO Religion* (New York University Press, 2014), 36–37.

4. Quoted in Barry Bearak, "Death in a Cult: The Victims: Time of

Puzzled Heartbreak Binds Relatives," *New York Times*, March 30, 1997, A1.

5. Zeller, *Heaven's Gate*, 38.

6. Ray LaFontaine, "Talk Radio's Comet Caper," *Washington Post*, February 23, 1997, C5.

7. Don Stanziano, "Cult Inspires First Copycat Suicide," *North County Times* (Escondido, CA), April 2, 1997, p. 4.

8. Todd S. Purdam, "Ex-Cultist Dies in Suicide Pact: 2d Is 'Critical,'" *New York Times*, May 7, 1997, A1.

9. Deb Simpson, *Closing the Gate: A Heaven's Gate Cult Biography* (Piney D, 2013).

10. "Do Not Revive," CBSnews.com, February 20, 1998, www.cbsnews.com/news/do-not-revive.

Index